MW01493409

IMPLEMENTING THE WEALTH MANAGEMENT INDEX

Since 1996, Bloomberg Press has published books for financial professionals on investing, economics, and policy affecting investors. Titles are written by leading practitioners and authorities, and have been translated into more than 20 languages.

The Bloomberg Financial Series provides both core reference knowledge and actionable information for financial professionals. The books are written by experts familiar with the work flows, challenges, and demands of investment professionals who trade the markets, manage money, and analyze investments in their capacity of growing and protecting wealth, hedging risk, and generating revenue.

For a list of available titles, please visit our web site at www.wiley.com/go/bloombergpress.

IMPLEMENTING THE WEALTH MANAGEMENT INDEX

Tools to Build Your Practice and
Measure Client Success

Ross Levin

BLOOMBERG PRESS
An Imprint of
WILEY

Published by John Wiley & Sons, Inc., Hoboken, New Jersey.

Published simultaneously in Canada.

The first edition of this book was titled *The Wealth Management Index: The Financial Advisor's System for Assessing & Managing Your Client's Plans & Goals*, Published by McGraw-Hill, Inc. © 1996.

For general information on our other products and services or for technical support, please contact our Customer Care Department within the United States at (800) 762–2974, outside the United States at (317) 572–3993, or fax (317) 572–4002.

Wiley also publishes its books in a variety of electronic formats. Some content that appears in print may not be available in electronic books. For more information about Wiley products, visit our web site at www.wiley.com.

Library of Congress Cataloging-in-Publication Data:

Levin, Ross.
   Implementing the wealth management index: tools to build your practice and measure client success / Ross Levin.
      p.   cm.
      The first edition of this book was titled: The wealth management index. Published by McGraw-Hill, Inc. 1996.
      Includes bibliographical references and index.
      ISBN 978-1-118-02764-6 (cloth); ISBN 978-1-118-15978-1 (ebk);
      ISBN 978-1-118-15979-8 (ebk); ISBN 978-1-118-16022-0 (ebk)
         1. Financial planners—United States.   2. Financial services industry—United States.
   I. Levin, Ross. Wealth management index.   II. Title.
   HG179.5.L48   2011
   332.6—dc23
                                                                                         2011029929

Printed in the United States of America

10 9 8 7 6 5 4 3 2

MIX
Paper from
responsible sources
FSC® C005928

To Mimi, Vera, And Bridget, Who Continue
To Give Me Riches Far More Vast
Than I Could Have Imagined.

Contents

Introduction   xi

CHAPTER 1

Turning a Concept into a Practice   01

The Format   02

The Wealth Management Index Overview   03

The Wealth Management Index   04

Conclusion   11

CHAPTER 2

Building and Operating a Practice   13

What Do You Want to Be When You Grow Up?   13

Partners   21

Broader Ownership   23

Conclusion   32

CHAPTER 3

Growing Your Business   33

Quantitative Prospect Metrics   33

Behavioral Types of Prospects   35

The Prospect Meeting   39

Questions   42

Other Questions   46

Next Steps   47

Conclusion   49

CHAPTER 4

Developing Staff   51

The Client Team   51

Leadership Pipeline   52

Conclusion   52

CHAPTER 5
Training Staff in Using the Wealth Management Index   **65**
The New Hire Process   65
Conclusion   83

CHAPTER 6
The Work Plan   **85**
Pre-meeting   85
Post-meeting   87
Agenda   92
Conclusion   92

CHAPTER 7
Objective Setting   **95**
Asset Protection   95
Disability and Income Protection   98
Debt Management   103
Investment Planning   105
Estate Planning   107
Conclusion   112

CHAPTER 8
Scoring the Wealth Management Index   **113**
Spreadsheet   114

CHAPTER 9
Asset Protection (Preservation)   **117**
Components   119
Have You Articulated a Life Insurance Philosophy?   119
What Are Your Concerns Regarding Risks of Large Losses from   128
     Medical, Long-Term Care, Property/Casualty, and Personal
     or Professional Liability Issues?
Have You Defined and Protected Your Business Interests?   138
Conclusion   142

CHAPTER 10
Disability and Income Protection (Protection)   **145**
What Are the Income and Lifestyle Needs and Wants of Your Family   147
     Currently and Prospectively?
Have You Evaluated All Current Sources of Income and Potential   159
     Changes to These Sources?
Are You Fully Utilizing All Benefits Available to You?   168
Conclusion   189

CHAPTER 11
Debt Management 191
Have You Established Your Philosophy Regarding 192
    Using Savings or Credit?
Is Your Type of Debt Appropriate Given Your Wealth-Management 196
    Objectives?
Conclusion 201

CHAPTER 12
Investment Planning (Accumulation) 203
Have You Developed an Investment Philosophy? 205
Have You Determined the Mechanics for Managing Your Portfolio 222
    and the Evaluation of What Success Looks Like?
Conclusion 228

CHAPTER 13
Estate Planning (Distribution) 231
Have You a Philosophy on Wealth Transfer? 232
Have You Articulated Your Charitable Philosophy or Mission Statement? 244
Have You Planned For Incapacitation, Elder Care Issues, 248
    and Final Planning Needs?
Conclusion 251

Epilogue 253
About the Author 255
Index 257

Introduction

I wrote *The Wealth Management Index* when our daughters were two, our business was tiny, and life was fun, but complicated. Now it is 16 years later, our daughters are heading off to college, our business is bigger, and life is fun, but complicated. So while things have changed or shifted in ways that I may not have expected, they are merely different, not better or worse.

I bring this up because I have a few operating principles that have helped guide me over most of my life:

- I feel incredibly grateful for all the people I have met who have shared hours or moments with me because they make my life rich
- I believe that while it is really important to think about what we want, I think it is more important to want what we already have.
- I believe that impermanence is part of life
- I believe in the Serenity Prayer—Grant me the serenity to accept the things I cannot change, the courage to change the things that I can, and the wisdom to know the difference

These precepts are the groundwork from which the index was created, our business was built, and hopefully, how I live my life. I hope that this book is a gift to the profession, only in the sense of sharing the ideas on which Accredited Investors was developed, while acknowledging that many of you do certain aspects of wealth management differently than we do. Our business has been transformed through the sharing of ideas at conferences, study groups, and friendly interactions with people one would think could be competitors. But we really don't compete with each other; each of our fundamental objective is to serve the right clients for our practices.

I have a long list of thank-yous which is guaranteed to be incomplete.

I want to thank my business partner of a quarter of a century, Wil Heupel, for walking this path with me from the beginning. His skills offset my weaknesses.

Kathy Longo came into Accredited Investors a dozen years ago and became an owner shortly after. She has done an amazing job of being a partner, when Wil and I had such a storied history, and has effected change in the firm that we never would have been able to see or do without her.

The staff at Accredited, many of whom are mentioned in the book, have been a tribute with which to partner. They continue to help me grow as they grow. While I can't mention all of the staff, a few in particular helped with this draft of the book. Jacob Wolkowitz and Sean P. Smith helped develop and test many of our investment planning concepts. Steve Gilbertson and Chris MacBean have done extensive work on our spending policies. Joan Kurlander used her law background to insure that I didn't embarrass myself with estate planning, and W. Alan Williams put his CPA to use with regard to my tax planning work. Brandon Jones and Lori Dierke gave me the approved Accredited Investors documents and spreadsheets (many of which they developed) to be included in the book, and Suzy Ridenour helped make sure that everything was where it should be.

Our clients have come to us believing in how we deliver wealth management and have shared their lives and stories with us.

The biggest outside professional influences in my life have come from my two study groups—The Alpha Group and Group 2020. The Alpha Group—my first study group currently consisting of Mark Balasa, Jim Budros, John Cammack, Chris Dardaman, Harold Evensky, Charlie Haines, Tucker Hewes, Mark Hurley, Deena Katz, Ram Kolluri, Don Phillips, Peggy Ruhlin, Lou Stanasolovich, Mark Tibergien, Greg Sullivan, and John Ueleke—has openly shared practices and friendship with me that has made a huge difference in my approach to business. I met most of these friends through my involvement on the boards of International Association for Financial Planning (IAFP), the Financial Planning Association (FPA), and the Certified Financial Planner Board of Standards (CFP)—the payoff for my volunteer experience far exceeded my contribution.

I was invited to join Group 2020 a few years ago, and it consisted of many people whom I knew of but did not know. Janet Briaud, Tim Chase, Cheryl Hollins, Michael Joyce, Richie Lee, Kathy Lintz, Ron and Suzette Rutherford, and yes, Charlie Haines again, opened their firms and hearts to me and have continued to help me grow and see things differently.

There are far too many others in the profession to name, for example, all the people with whom I served on the boards of the IAFP and CFP Board of Standards, the number of writers who have asked for my opinion and sometimes even used it, and the various people who have e-mailed me, called, or written to me because something in a column I wrote for the *Journal of Financial Planning* caught their interest.

My editorial team at Wiley/Bloomberg was incredible: Judy Howarth edited my chapters almost before I wrote them and put up with my missing of deadlines (okay, I am a Myers/Briggs ENFP); my acquisitions editor, Laura Walsh, believed in the book and sold it to the publisher; and Vincent Nordhaus, who was responsible for the editorial production.

My biggest thank you goes to my wife Bridget, and our daughters, Mimi and Vera, who continue to show me unconditional love, even when I have bitten off more than I can chew.

IMPLEMENTING THE WEALTH MANAGEMENT INDEX

CHAPTER 1

Turning a Concept into a Practice

When I wrote *The Wealth Management Index* in 1996, it was at a time when we were experiencing a bull market of epic proportions. As clients were making money hand over fist, we were trying to temper their enthusiasm with an approach to wealth management that would measure their personal success based on all the things that they had expressed as important to us—and many things which they had not considered. We were implementing a tool that consolidated all the various aspects of financial planning into a process by which the client could begin to understand the many components of their financial life on which decisions needed to be made.

Much has changed since 1996 and nothing has changed. We still need to help clients understand the importance of all areas of wealth management and they still often place too much importance or attention on asset management. The most important change for our firm is that we have a much bigger practice—more than 35 employees, around a billion dollars of managed assets, and an approach to building a business and delivering comprehensive wealth management in a way that has been true to our values.

My intention with this book is to open up our practice to you as a way for you to incorporate those things which you find beneficial and let go of those ideas that may not resonate with you. This is not a book on how to run a practice; my belief is that each wealth management practice has to discover its own unique role in the vast space of helping clients achieve their objectives. But regardless of what your business currently looks like, I know that you will benefit from me sharing the stops and starts that we have experienced in trying to do what is right for our clients and our business. We certainly don't have all the answers, but I think we have some. The difference between building a wealth-management practice and a long car ride with young kids is that with a practice, you are never there yet. Circumstances change, staff changes, the clients change, the environment changes. The only guarantee is impermanence. Yet it is important to draw a line in the sand as to what your firm stands for and who you wish to serve.

A few years ago, I invited 20 practitioners from around the country to make a donation to the Foundation for Financial Planning and in return spend a day with us to meet our staff and go through all the aspects of how we do business. We labeled this program Be Our Guest, and since then other firms, in concert with the Foundation, have also done this. When we first chose to offer the glimpse into our firm, we discussed whether we should exclude firms from our community from participating. Was there a risk that our openness could be used against us in competition for clients? Only if we believed that there were a finite subset of clients and it was in the best interest of them to work only with us. That is not our belief. There are a number of great firms doing great work for a wide variety of clients. In fact, just subscribe to Bob Veres's newsletter, *Inside Information* or regularly read *Financial Planning, Investment Advisor, FA,* or *Investment News* and you'll see how many different ways there are to succeed in this business. I know that our firm will continue to grow because our offering resonates with a certain subset of the client population. Certain prospects are better suited to our comprehensive practice than others. It is always in the prospect's best interest to work with a firm who can not only deliver sound advice, but do so in a way that reaches that prospect.

As I write this book is there a risk that firms may try to capture our intellectual property and become more like us? I could not think of a greater compliment. But what I really hope is that firms take some of our ideas and make them their own. And I hope that they improve upon some of the things that we are doing and continue to share them with others so that clients can be served in ways that improve the quality of their lives.[1]

The Format

This book is both a practice management guide as well as a tool introducing, explaining, and implementing the Wealth Management Index (WMI). In the area dedicated to practice management, I will go through how we run our practice. I will be covering our technology, processes, communication, and client interaction. I will go through what we do when the prospect first walks in the door to how we manage the client relationship over the course of our years together. I will also discuss how we try to engage our staff. Chapter 9 through the end of the book covers the index's distinct components. This will break down all the areas of the WMI and how we discuss each area in the client meetings. It will also include some of the tools that we developed or purchased to help in our analysis.

While I am writing this book, it is based on all the efforts put forth by my partners, our staff, meetings that I have attended, and my two key study groups—the Alpha Group and Group 2020. My coworkers will be the first to tell you that I am not a detail guy, so it may seem somewhat ironic that I developed a concept around detail. But it was really a way to protect me from my weaknesses and emphasize my strengths. Talking with the clients and understanding their motivations was more fulfilling for me than going step by step through tax returns and documents. The index made sure that I didn't miss anything when forced to do the necessary work that was less engaging for me. Each of us has areas that resonate with us and we would be far happier spending most of our time doing these things. But as we grow a business, we may find ourselves working doing the things that don't represent our callings, but are necessary to help our client's reach theirs. Even if you only use the index for its checklist component, you will be certain that you haven't missed some key area of your client's plan. And you won't be facing the unmitigated dread we have all felt at some time in the past when a client asks "why haven't we discussed this." Our practice has become large enough where I am spending the majority of time doing the things to which I can add the most value. I describe myself as someone who knows better what is happening 10 years from now than 10 minutes from now, and now I spend most of my time reading, writing, thinking, and working with clients. A dream job.

Fortunately, my partners are the opposite of me. This started with me creating the initial concept of the WMI, but Wil Heupel, my co-founding partner of Accredited Investors, Inc., making it possible to use this in our practice. From there, people within the company have taken the role to great lengths with an ardent fervor of how to communicate what we are doing in a way that clients can receive the information.

The Wealth Management Index Overview

The index itself has changed from when I first wrote the book. We have modified categories and included new ones. The wealth management landscape is dynamic and it has been important for the index to keep up with the changing environment. It has become more detailed than the first version, but not so detailed that it becomes an impediment to planning—where looking up and out is often more valuable than looking down.

Another discovery that we made was that many clients are not interested in a score; they are interested in the progress that they are making toward their objectives. This means that the scoring portion of the index has been changed within our practice to a progress component. We communicate to the client where we stand with the various areas as we are going through them. There is no set point when a client is done with planning, so progress is forever monitored. But I have heard from many of you that scoring was something that you valued about the index. For those of you who are interested in this, the scoring component still exists. There are more categories and more decision points than in the first version, yet not too many to make scoring impractical.

We use the index by creating main categories with subcategories underneath them. The subcategories are how we outline the goals for the client and report progress back to them through our agendas, meetings, and follow-up letters. Each subcategory has a number attached that flows through our WMI database.[2] The key advantage to this system versus the original WMI is that as new areas begin to develop, we can add them more easily. For example, long-term care insurance was a relatively nascent industry when I first wrote *The Wealth Management Index*. Today it is an area that we review with every client, regardless of whether or not we recommend the purchase of a policy.

For this chapter, I simply will lay out the index, without providing a detailed explanation as to its use. The fundamental premise of the index is a blend of the right and left brains. We need to combine the thinking and feeling aspects of the client in order to best serve them. Therefore, the index does not simply give technical solutions. In addition, it creates a framework for opening up discussions in the areas to be analyzed. But f you are the type who wants to know who wins the reality TV show without watching the episode, then by all means, jump to Chapter Nine and get right into the guts of the index.

The Wealth Management Index

There are five key components to the index:

1. Asset Protection (Preservation)
2. Disability and Income Protection (Protection)
3. Debt Management (Leverage)
4. Investment Planning (Accumulation)
5. Estate Planning (Distribution)

Under each of these components there are a series of broad questions that are then addressed through their subcomponents.

Asset Protection (Preservation)—25 Percent

Have you articulated a life insurance philosophy?—34 percent[3]

111 Assess the living and liquidity needs of survivors and dependants—60 percent (5.1 percent)

112 Assess the possibilities of living benefits from existing insurance—10 percent (0.85 percent)

113 Analyze the strategy of maximizing pension income through life insurance—10 percent (0.85 percent)

114 Assess estate tax wealth-replacement needs and wishes—20 percent (1.7 percent)

What are your concerns regarding risks of large losses from medical, long-term care, property/casualty, and personal or professional liability issues?—33 percent

121 Review medical insurance including liability limits, co-pays, Medicare, and COBRA—20 percent (1.65 percent)

122 Understand feelings regarding long-term care and evaluate needs—20 percent (1.65 percent)

123 Determine amount of self-funding on property/casualty deductibles and limits—10 percent (0.825 percent)

124 Understand personal liability needs—10 percent (0.825 percent)

125 Review professional liability limits and appropriate tail insurance—20 percent (1.65 percent)

126 Review benefits and drawbacks of asset transference and retitling for long-term care or liability considerations—20 percent (1.65 percent)

Have you defined and protected your business interests?—33 percent

131 Evaluate business structure—10 percent (0.825 percent)

132 Determine business valuation and develop succession plan—30 percent (2.475 percent)

133 Establish/review buy/sell and business continuation agreements—20 percent (1.65 percent)

134 Determine needs due to disability—20 percent (1.65 percent)

135 Establish appropriate funding mechanisms for buy-out upon death—20 percent (1.65 percent)

Disability and Income Protection (Protection)—20 Percent

What are the income and lifestyle needs and wants of your family currently and prospectively?—35 percent

211 Review current cash flow and budget needs—30 percent (2.1 percent)

212 Determine the amount of income that you wish to replace if you were to become disabled—20 percent (1.4 percent)

213 Determine purpose and costs of one-time large expenditures including education, vacation homes, or assistance for family members—10 percent (0.7 percent)

214 Establish your financial independence goals and the price to be paid to achieve them—30 percent (2.1 percent)

215 Review your annual charitable giving objectives and how they should be funded—10 percent (0.7 percent)

Have you evaluated all current sources of income and potential changes to these sources?—25 percent

221 Understand current and projected earned income for your family—20 percent (1 percent)

222 Review all pass-through income from S-corporations, Limited Liability Corporations, or Partnerships—20 percent (1 percent)

223 Review the cost/benefits of various pension pay-out options—15 percent (0.75 percent)

224 Analyze social security income options including those for children under 18—15 percent (0.75 percent)

225 Understand required minimum distributions from retirement—10 percent (0.5 percent)

226 Determine the amount of portfolio withdrawals to fund expected three-year cash-flow shortages—10 percent (0.5 percent)

227 Objectively consider any expected gifts or inheritances—10 percent (0.5 percent)

Are you fully utilizing all benefits available to you?—15 percent

231 Review participation in pre-tax reimbursement and cafeteria plans—25 percent (0.75 percent)

232 Determine levels of participation and type of company retirement plans (qualified and non-qualified)—25 percent (0.75 percent)

233 Review all available stock purchase and stock option plans including any necessary filings—25 percent (0.75 percent)

234 Evaluate whether any forms of IRA contributions, rollovers, or supplemental retirement plans on self-employment income are appropriate—25 percent (0.75 percent)

Are you proactively engaged in tax planning for you and your dependants?—25 percent

241 Determine appropriate levels of withholding and estimated tax payments—15 percent (0.75 percent)

242 Determine whether tax-loss harvesting is possible and appropriate—15 percent (0.75 percent)

243 Review gifting opportunities and strategies—20 percent (1 percent)

244 Determine whether to accelerate or defer income and/or deductions for tax bracket or AMT reasons—30 percent (1.5 percent)

245 Evaluate the recharacterization or conversions of IRAs to/from Roth IRAs—20 percent (1 percent)

Debt Management (Leverage)—10 Percent

Have you established your philosophy regarding using savings or credit?—30 percent

311 Determine desired level of emergency fund and credit lines—35 percent (1.05 percent)

312 Evaluate appropriate credit cards for limits and benefits—25 percent (0.75 percent)

313 Develop a strategy for when you wish to be debt-free—40 percent (1.2 percent)

Is your type of debt appropriate given your wealth-management objectives?—70 percent

331 Review the best financing terms on all properties considering time horizons, interest rates, and deductibility—34 percent (2.38 percent)

332 Review the best financing terms and deductibility terms on lines of credit and alternative debt—33 percent (2.31 percent)

334 Determine your current ratio as well as credit ratings—33 percent (2.31 percent)

Investment Planning—25 Percent

Have you developed an investment philosophy?—60 percent

411 Define your attitude toward investment risk—10 percent (1.5 percent)

412 Determine whether the portfolio return objectives are consistent with these attitudes—10 percent (1.5 percent)

413 Define the various time horizons for which you are saving—10 percent (1.5 percent)

414 Determine legal, investment, regulatory restrictions or unique circumstances impacting your portfolio—10 percent (1.5 percent)

415 Determine a suitable asset allocation—60 percent (9 percent)

Have you determined the mechanics for managing your portfolio and the evaluation of what success looks like?—40 percent

421 Decide accounts to consolidate, transfer, or maintain separately and how they will be handled for policy and advice—55 percent (5.5 percent)

422 Determine asset location—15 percent (1.5 percent)

423 Review portfolio performance relative to appropriate benchmarks—30 percent (3 percent)

Estate Planning—20 Percent

Have you a philosophy on wealth transfer?—70 percent

511 Determine the amount of after-tax inheritance and how it is to be received—40 percent (5.6 percent)

512 Determine survivor liquidity needs outside of trustee control and to pay estate taxes—10 percent (1.4 percent)

513 Direct proper ownership (including revocable trusts), beneficiary designations, and determine guardians and trustees—10 percent (1.4 percent)

514 Determine where estate discounting techniques and wealth-transfer entities—Family Limited Partnerships, Qualified Personal Residence Trusts, Grantor Retained Annuity Trusts, defective trusts, Irrevocable Life Insurance Trusts, and others—are appropriate—10 percent (1.4 percent)

515 Finalize documents and Crummey notices—10 percent (1.4 percent)

516 Determine whether a family meeting should be facilitated and appropriate family governance prepared—15 percent (2.1 percent)

Have you articulated your charitable philosophy or mission statement?—10 percent

531 Develop and share your charitable mission statement and money values—50 percent (1 percent)

532 Evaluate lifetime giving and/or giving at death—25 percent (0.5 percent)

533 Evaluate charitable lead trusts, remainder trusts, gift annuities, donor-advised funds, and private foundations—25 percent (0.5 percent)

Have you planned for incapacitation, elder care issues, and final planning needs?—20 percent

541 Discuss writing an ethical will as well as creating a DVD through a personal historian to communicate your values—30 percent (1.2 percent)

542 Implement power of attorney documents for financial and health care purposes—40 percent (1.6 percent)

543 Establish pre-need written procedures for family to execute final wishes—30 percent (1.2 percent)

Tracking Progress

Overwhelmed? Actually, this process makes it easier to keep track of the areas on which we are working. No longer do we fear that something is not being covered, because it is all laid out in a manner that is relatively easy to follow.

It's clear, though, that no practice can work on everything at once. Later in the book, I will spend considerable space going through the analysis of the component pieces of the index. There is a significant amount of advice being delivered to the client. We have found it most effective for meetings to break down the five main categories of the WMI and tackle only one or two of them in the client meeting. Each meeting uncovers further work to be done and new objectives to be established. Therefore, updates on the previous meeting's assignments are provided as new analysis on the current area is being introduced. Essentially, the wealth-management plan is rolling.

This is central to the theme of what we do. You cannot deliver a financial plan once and be done. Any decision closes the door on certain possibilities and opens it on others. Some prospects will think that the plan would be delivered and after that it is mostly housekeeping and investment management. I have said that wealth management is like running a marathon—just because you have trained for and completed one doesn't mean that you will be in shape for the rest of your life. In any given year, certain components may take priority over other areas, but each area needs to be addressed as a way to insure that issues are constantly being uncovered.

This points out another truth about what we do—over the life of a client relationship, there will surface one or two things that inevitably will make the relationship incredibly valuable to the client. In our practice, we have handled deaths, disabilities, chemical-dependency issues, sales and purchases of businesses, marriages, divorce, and everything else that can happen in life. Invariably, after any of these startling events occur, clients will become more grounded in the relationship and fully understand the value of comprehensive wealth management.

Since there are so many things that must go on at once, we have established a tracking system that measures the progress we are making on each objective. The system involves 10 components:

WMI—status updates for goals

Not Discussed/Not Defined	0
Opened Discussion	2
Redefine or Revisit Goal	3
Goal Established	4
Research and Modeling Completed	5
Analysis and Recommendation Completed	6
Presentation and Approval	7
Implementation in Progress	8
Goal Strategy Implemented	10
Archived (Goal no longer applies)	1

As we go through each of the areas of the index, we are monitoring our progress in all of our communications to the client in the following way:

Objective is established and categorized using the numbering system.

For example, a client letter or agenda item would state:

241: You wish to insure that you are withholding enough from your regular earnings to avoid having to pay estimated taxes on your outside earnings.

We then discuss how this objective was decided.

Since you feel that last year's outside income was unusually high, you would rather, if necessary, adjust withholding later in the year to avoid penalties.

We assign the staff person (or client if it is their responsibility), establish a due date, and put a number as to where we are in the process. When we first establish the goal, we assign 4 to it. As we make progress through the analysis and implementation, the corresponding number will change. These numbers serve as the tool for scoring the index.

If a strategy was implemented, the client would get a 10 in that particular area under which the goal was stored and therefore get full index credit. If we only presented the analysis, the client would receive a seven and therefore get 70 percent of that particular component. If there are multiple objectives under the same component, then each objective is scored separately to create a combined score for the component.

Conclusion

The practice of comprehensive wealth management is complex. There are constantly moving targets, various assignments and follow-up, shifting priorities, and personalities. A disciplined, accountable approach increases the likelihood of success in the client relationship and client outcomes. This book will share with you the things that we have done to build a thriving practice that combines systems to create consistency coupled with the approach that ensures each client a unique and personal experience.

Notes

1. I think Roy Diliberto from RTD Financial Advisors based in Philadelphia was the first one I heard describe our purpose as wealth managers "to improve the lives of our clients." This has always resonated with me because it speaks to the depths to which our relationships are formed and the importance of the work that we do.
2. Our database was developed internally by Lorenz Oliver-King, who spends his days improving it and upgrading it. The advantage of this is that we have a database for customer-relationship management that is centered completely on how we do business. The disadvantage is that we have a full-time employee updating it and modifying it. If we were starting over, we would probably purchase a system like Junxure (www.junxure.com) or ProTracker (www.protracker.com) which can incorporate some of our principles but by which we could offload the programming to a company established to do it.
3. The formula for the value of each component of the index is determined by first taking the value of the particular category (Asset Protection, Disability and Income Protection, Debt Management, Investment Planning, and Estate

Planning), multiplying this by the value of the broad, value-based question within the category (i.e., Have you articulated a life insurance philosophy—34 percent) multiplied by the value of the technical question underneath the value-based question (i.e. Assess the living and liquidity needs of survivors and dependants—50 percent). The value of the example above would be $0.25 \times 0.34 \times 0.50 = 4.3$ percent of the total index.

CHAPTER 2

Building and Operating a Practice

This chapter covers the various questions to consider as well as the steps needed to take as you build or operate your practice. I will be sharing many of the tools which we have incorporated into growing our own business. I will also discuss some of our successes and mistakes.

What Do You Want to Be When You Grow Up?

When I started in wealth management in 1982, I had no clue as to what the field would become or how my future would be shaped. And as we grew from a solo shop to a partnership to a business with three owners and more than 35 employees, I was struck by several things that influenced us over the years. This list makes sense for us; I know that other firms may have a different (and even contrasting) viewpoint.

1. *Avoiding big mistakes may be more important than getting big decisions right.* Over the course of several years, we have survived problematic hires, working with the wrong types of clients for our offering, administrative snafus, regrettable investments, and even a misadventure into a whole new business—becoming a sports agent. The key for us, though, was honestly reviewing the situations into which we got ourselves, and quickly trying to extricate ourselves from the problems. For example, after I just finished negotiating with the Green Bay Packers on a contract for our only client, the General Manager at the time asked if I would be

interested in representing a friend of his family's. I paused, took a breath, and told him "No thanks." I said that I hated doing this and it distracted me from what I was good at doing. This leads to point number two.

2. *Incremental growth works better than giant leaps.* There are some who have built their businesses through acquisitions. This is something that we have never really attempted. One of the strengths of a firm like ours is a very clear culture. We work well with a certain type of client, in a particular way. We look for staff that has certain characteristics which are consistent with this culture. Many of our hiring mistakes came from bringing in senior people from places with a radically different approach to business. We were enamored with credentials or background, but lost sight of the fact that the very act of success in these other environments could preclude the same thing from happening in our environment. This is one reason why we get concerned about purchasing other practices. We are not only buying the clients, but their shared history with the wealth manager. While growing through referrals and other marketing approaches is slower, it has some distinct advantages. Clients who come from other clients have a better sense of what they are getting and often share some personality traits with their referrers—with whom we have a successful relationship. Also, gradual growth puts less of a strain on cash flow and enables you to invest resources on your strengths. As Marcus Buckingham writes in his book *Now Discover Your Strengths*, "Each person's greatest room for growth is in areas of his or her greatest strength."[1] I believe that this is true of practices as well. By focusing on the areas where we have been successful, rather than entirely new areas that would come from the integration of another practice, we have built a sustainable and enduring business model.

3. *Don't let your reach exceed your grasp.* The big decisions that we have made, such as buying our office building, were really not that big. When we bought our building, we were faced with a leasing decision for 8,000 square feet with no opportunities for more contiguous space if we grew versus, for virtually the same payment, purchasing a 16,500 square foot building that we could renovate. This building will allow us to grow to around 55 people. While there was certainly a resource commitment to the renovation project, we don't find ourselves in lease negotiations with the possibility of moving every five years. In the February 2011 edition of *Investment Advisor* magazine, Mark Tibergien writes that "a study on operating performance conducted three years ago {2008} revealed that 25% of all independent firms with assets over $100 million had at least a second location."[2] We believe that we have such a small market

share in the Twin Cities that we are better off building market share here rather than venturing into new markets—even if our clients lead us there. While I think it is critical to keep thinking about what you wish to become, I think one should do this very thoughtfully and carefully. Just an aside, we try to make sure that we have the staff in place to bring in new clients before we develop marketing initiatives. If we are successful with the campaign, we don't want to end up compromising our service because of the new business.

4. *You control far less than you think.* I keep a copy of Reinhold Niebuhr's Serenity Prayer on my desk: "God, grant me the serenity to accept the things I cannot change, Courage to change the things I can, And wisdom to know the difference." These words have had a tremendous impact on me as things swirl around me. I remember being quoted in an article several years ago that my partner and I wanted to keep our practice small. Guess what—we couldn't. Happy clients referred us to their friends and family. Great staff needed opportunities to grow and be challenged. Success often begets success. Economists Brian Arthur and Kenneth Arrow describe path dependence and increasing returns. Returns can expand when you find a niche in which you can excel or dominate. Positive feedback loops are created where success leads to more success.

5. *Good fortune plays a pretty significant role.* If you do everything that I suggest in this book, you will still have a vastly different practice than what we have. It may be better, it may be worse, but it assuredly will be different. For example, not all of our clients refer people to us. We have been fortunate that some of our bigger clients also happen to be good referrers. While there may be programs we could institute to increase the chances of obtaining referrals, it is still a little bit of a crapshoot as to who will refer you to whom. Great business or great fortune? I think good business practices enable you to jump on good fortune as it's presented, but if it never shows up, there is nothing on which to jump. Most of us should take a step back and pay attention to the fact that our success has come from not simply our own choices, but from the pioneers of the industry before us as well as a sizable dose of good fortune.

6. *None of us really know what anyone else is doing or why.* It is easy in this business to get discouraged. You may look at someone who appears to have great success and wonder how the heck they could have done it. The truth is you don't know if they really have done it nor do you know what they have done. When I give talks on practice management, I try to be as open as possible. But my talks still are my interpretations of

looking back from where I am today. I am not completely sure that the stories I tell accurately reflect what happened, I know that they simply reflect my view of what happened. More important, we have no real way of knowing what could have happened with alternative histories. Which decisions could we have made that would have enhanced or impeded our growth? In the complex adaptive systems in which we operate, there are an infinite number of choices and results from those choices.

7. *Resilience and forgiveness are essential.* There are inevitably going to be things that go wrong, but how you recover from them, and how you both ask for and give forgiveness will have a huge influence on your fate. Forgiveness is forever giving up hope of changing the past. At times we need to forgive others for things that they have done and at other times we need to forgive ourselves for things that have happened. During the dark days of '08, it was very difficult to look clients in the eye and say that our diversified portfolios were down less than the market's but way more than we had hoped. We were genuinely sorry that clients were feeling anxious. But unless we forgave ourselves, we would never have been able to stay engaged with clients during these tumultuous times—which were thankfully very short-lived.

Integrating some of the concepts listed previously, the real question becomes what is the type of practice that you wish to have. I have been a firm believer in crafting your personal plan before developing your business plan. I have seen far too many people with successful practices and bankrupt personal lives. I believe that the great thing about our field is that we can have great flexibility as well as great opportunity.

One of the reasons that we began to grow the practice was because my wife (Bridget) and I had young twins. Bridget and I knew that we wanted to be able to create experiences for our family. Since our practice at the time was quite small, vacations never really were vacations—it felt like I had to be on call to handle client situations. This was especially true because my partner, Wil Heupel, and I had discrete areas of expertise; I ran the investment planning area and Wil handled the estate planning. Both of us were involved in general financial planning. By beginning to build the firm, we could have people who could handle questions and issues when either of us was gone. This may seem obvious, but it is amazing how little time you get to reflect on the practice when you are steeped in the middle of it. As the firm grew, I was able to create pockets to spend more time with my family. We were able to take three to five weeks off at a time to visit various places in the world. Now that our daughters are heading off to college, we have few regrets about the time we spent together. This would not have been the case if we didn't make a decision to build the business around our life goals.

I think the areas that you want to get right in your business plan are relatively easy:

1. Who do you want to serve? You can slice this objectively and subjectively in many ways—size of client, profession, personalities, and so on. Currently, we serve clients with $2,000,000 or more of investment assets. We also have developed specialty practices with physicians, business owners, and intergenerational wealth. We also want to work with clients who value the comprehensive and integrative nature of our work. This we screen by how forthcoming they are in the prospect interview. While you may change your target client over time, you will have to deal with those legacy clients who no longer meet your profile. This is a tough thing to do. One of the ways we have tried to deal with this is by establishing criteria for other firms to whom we can send either prospects who don't qualify or clients who are too costly for us to continue working with (but who may be very profitable for a smaller firm).

2. How do you want to serve them? Obviously, our stake in the ground is the Wealth Management Index whose essence is comprehensive and personal wealth management. This decision means that we need more time with clients and more staff to execute our vision. Because of the time commitment and necessary staff resources, we also have to have higher minimum retainers or fees.

3. Who do you want on the bus? This is right out of Jim Collins's *Good to Great*. In describing great companies, he says "they first got the right people on the bus (and the wrong people off the bus) and *then* figured out where to drive it."[3] Traditionally, we have been lousy at this. We originally hired people that we liked rather than people who could do the job. We were slow to let people go who were not able to do the job. When they eventually were transitioned out or quit (because they could not handle the position) they would leave frustrated with the organization and negatively communicate things about us that we may have felt were unjustified but, as professionals, did not feel it appropriate to try and refute. We have learned a lot over the years. I think the best advice is to hire slowly (but by all means hire), put new hires on a probationary period, manage hard during that period, and give honest assessments as to their likelihood of making it. This is not only right for the business, but it is the humane thing to do. Deena Katz likes to call this "freeing up their future."[4]

4. If you were successful, what would it look like? We use this with clients as it relates to our relationship, but it is also a great question to ask of yourself when you are trying to figure out your practice. One of the things that I had to learn to do was build in time to think about the practice. This is different than managing it. Setting strategic directions needs to be done in a climate of possibility. I believe that this can best be handled through quiet time.

These decisions are equivalent to Lorenz's butterfly effect for chaos theory—initial conditions have a huge impact on the future that you are going to craft for yourself. If you start by taking any client who walks in the door even though they are not with whom you really want to be working, you will be unhappy. If you do a great job, you will continue to get referred to more clients of the same type. Eventually, your practice is a mess.

Accredited Investors, Inc. Guiding Principles

We have some guiding principles for our firm that have helped us to define who we are and who we want to be. We share these principles with our clients.

We believe that our purpose as an organization is *improving the individual and collective lives of all that we serve.* This statement is meant to include clients, staff, community, and others with whom we are involved. Our fundamental premise is that we believe in the value of comprehensive professional wealth management. We see this value every day at work with our clients. Our purpose is to help the client determine what is important to them and bring congruity between their actions and their values. Our aspiration is to build a committed relationship with our clients and sustain this relationship over their lifetime. In order to do this, we have core beliefs that we tell our clients:

- Wealth management involves maximizing your wealth. At Accredited Investors, Inc., we define this as integrating all of your resources—financial, emotional, physical, and spiritual.
- Our planning expertise will help you strike a healthy balance between these resources.
- The in-depth level of communication between us will determine our level of success. Wealth management is personal, so we often ask that you share with us some of the many things that you don't share with anyone but your family.
- We believe in integrating the five key areas of wealth management—Asset Protection, Disability and Income Planning, Debt Management,

Investment Planning, and Estate Planning. We believe all of these areas are integral for achieving your personal financial success.

- We also believe in spending your life wisely. We believe that life decisions cannot be made solely based on their financial impact.
- We believe that a competent and fulfilled staff is critical to develop and execute the goals of our clients. We treat our staff with respect and ask that our clients do as well.
- We believe that we should enjoy this process and trust each other. If that stops happening, we believe our relationship needs to be reevaluated.
- We believe in the value of synergy. A healthy communication and exchange of ideas between all related advisors is essential to achieving your desired success.

Our Commitment to Clients

In addition to the guiding principles on which our firm was built, we have commitments that we make to clients.

- We are committed to independence as a fee-only wealth-management firm. Accredited Investors does not accept compensation from third parties for product recommendations, nor does it accept or give fees to other professionals for referrals. We will seek to remove any and all conflicts of interest from our relationship.
- We are committed to acting as your fiduciary. We will treat your assets, personal information, and values with the same care we would demand for ourselves.
- We are committed to protecting your privacy. Your personal information will be held in strict confidence and will never be shared with third parties without your prior consent.
- We are committed to integrity. With that, we are committed to our company values, which will never be compromised.
- We are committed to being non-judgmental. We will respect your dreams and values as you declare them and share them with us and will tailor our advice and services to reflect these dreams and values.
- We are committed to providing you with supreme service. Our staff will respond to your emails and phone calls as soon as possible. In addition, we will assist you by any means necessary to provide requested information or follow through on the implementation of any recommendations.
- We are committed to earning your complete trust in us.

Client Commitment to Us

But this relationship is not a one-way street. We also have expectations from clients that we share with them.

- We expect you, our clients, to be honest about your goals, personal information, and financial history.
- We expect you to be open to the challenge of exploring deeper meaning in money and your lives.
- We expect you to notify us if you do not completely understand or feel discomfort with any recommendation, strategy, or direction.
- We expect you, our clients, to treat our staff with respect. Should a conflict arise, however, we would like to know. Please express and discuss your concerns with principals.

We have been in situations where very successful clients did not treat our staff in a way with which we were comfortable. We have met with clients and explained what we observed, asked clients for their perspective, and discussed what we felt needed to be changed. One particularly aggressive client told us that he had never been approached about this before and was very appreciative of our candor. He has since modified his behavior. If he slips into old patterns, we talk with him about it.

Our Commitment to the Community and Our Employees

Again, we believe that we have a role in the world and want to represent ourselves in a manner consistent with our values.

- We strive to provide a fun and fulfilling work environment for our employees.
- We are committed to supporting the professional development of all of our staff members.
- We believe in giving back to the communities that have provided so much for us. As part of this commitment, our office closes once or twice a year for a day of service. Our staff is also given five paid personal days each year with which to volunteer for any non-profit organization.
- We are committed to giving back to our profession through the sharing of ideas and resources. Many of our staff members are active in industry organizations.

We try to invest a lot of resources in our staff. We close the office three or four times a year for two-day sessions with an industrial psychologist who helps us work on issues like active listening, assertiveness, making proper apologies, and other areas that will improve how we relate to each other and our clients.[5]

We pay for our staff's credentials, annual professional-licensing fees, organizational fees, and create a budget for them to attend local meetings or national conferences. The budgeted amount is based on their position within the organization. We choose to pay our own way for due diligence meetings and seminars rather than have the fund companies pay our way. Again, we are trying to maintain our independence.

Partners

My founding partner, Wil Heupel, and I have very different personalities. I am more strategic and future oriented. Wil is more concrete. He can take my ideas and make them work. When we added Kathy Longo as a partner, her personality was somewhere between ours.

We have worked very hard on our relationships. We have used several outside consultants—business and industrial psychologists—to help us develop communication skills, assertiveness, and openness among us that have made the partnership work. We went into the partnership with the attitude that when it gets hard, we were going to do whatever we could to get through it. Our business took a very long time to build, so the initial years were difficult. I think we survived because of our trust in each other and the belief that we would be there for each other, as well as our shared vision of what we were going to try to accomplish. We didn't have clients, but we had ideas on how we could serve them if we ever did!

The other factor that helped was that initially both of our wives had good jobs. While Wil and his wife, Julie, had two kids, Bridget and I had no children. The fact that our wives were bringing home enough money to handle our day-to-day living costs allowed us to indulge in our fantasy of building a business. Had we not had this, it is difficult to know whether we could have stuck things out.

Partnering is one of the most difficult things that you can do. I often get people calling me to ask questions about forming partnerships. Let me share with you some of the things to think about:

- In a 50/50 partnership, who has the power to make decisions when you don't agree? In Wil's and my relationship, I tended to be able to make the big directional decisions while Wil was able to make the running-the-business choices. We almost always agreed, but when we didn't and a decision needed to be made, we would defer to me for the strategic decisions and Wil for the operational ones. This has continued as we have broadened our ownership. Kathy is treated as an equal partner with regard to decision making, even if she isn't one through ownership.

- What are the things that you share? Wil and I have always had shared values and beliefs regarding what we wanted our clients to experience. When Kathy joined us, she had similar views. If you are not aligned here, the partnership will almost certainly fracture at some point.

- What are the skills that you bring to the table and how are they valued? Wil and I had very different strengths and weaknesses. Since I was the external business developer, I initially valued my contribution to the firm as more valuable than Wil's—even though we split everything 50/50. It was only after I recognized that I could not do this on my own that the partnership really began to work. I think it is better when partners have different capabilities and when they recognize that there are certain things that each individual simply may not be good at. I think partnerships thrive through admissions of weakness rather than exaggerations of strengths.

- Talk directly to the person rather than create triangles. With three partners, when one of us has an issue with someone else, we talk directly to each other. If we can't resolve it, we bring in the other partner. It is very easy for two partners to gang up on the third one. I think that we have done a good job of avoiding this. Honest feedback is crucial to a successful relationship. When we have been unable to deliver it to each other, we bring in someone from the outside.

- Use testing to determine compatibility and to anticipate problem areas. We use a variety of tests for people coming in at different levels of the firm. These tests are administered by an outside consultant. The primary tests are: a) the Myers-Briggs Type Indicator® which was created by Katherine Briggs and her daughter, Isabel Briggs Myers to sort personalities using four Jungian dichotomies—Introversion/Extroversion, Sensing/Intuition, Thinking/Feeling, Judging/Perceiving; b) The Fundamental Interpersonal Relations Orientation-Behavior™ instrument used to measure how people interact with each other; and c) The CPI 260® which describes individuals the way others see them.

- Work on a buy/sell which describes the agreements to which you adhere regarding who can own the business, how valuations are determined, what should happen if the business dissolves, how a payout can occur, how disability is treated. This is useful to start even before you partner. This is an expense that will save you in the long run. If things fall apart during the buy/sell process, consider it money well spent and move on. We have had a few buy/sells in our years together. They provide remarkable insight as to what each of the partners is thinking and how they view the partnership.

- Don't push too hard to make something happen. Sometimes the idea of having a partner is far better than the reality of one. When things are difficult on the front end, there is a good chance that they won't get better on the back end. We were bringing in a career-changing attorney and spent several months trying to answer every imaginable question and address all his concerns. If you want certainty, a wealth-management practice is not the best place to find it. Needless to say, after we addressed all the issues, he quit two weeks into it. The change was too dramatic. In retrospect, we wanted the credentials more than the individual—a dumb, costly mistake.
- Make sure you really want a partner. A partner is not a lackey. Some of us who have been around for a while think we want a partner because we have this valuable asset that we need to monetize. If you are not willing to relinquish control, do not have a partner.

The best part of having partners is that you do not feel as isolated in your practice. There are a lot of decisions and responsibilities in running a successful practice. Having others to bounce ideas off of and help execute is a tremendous benefit. Ironically, as the organization grows, it can be quite lonely running it.

I used to believe that I could have a flat organization where everyone is treated equally. I learned, though, that there is no such thing. An owner of a business simply has more power because they have the ultimate say in the future of those they employ. As a result, creating appropriate boundaries and using power effectively are essential. I like to engage individuals in deep conversation. People tell me that I live in subtext—I am looking for the meaning behind the words rather than just the words. This is uncomfortable for some employees who don't wish to share so much with their employer. It took me a long time to realize that it may not be appropriate to engage in deeper conversations with all employees.

Broader Ownership

As firms grow in size, the concept of partners has changed dramatically. Many of us who have been practicing for a number of years have a next generation of employees to whom we want to sell pieces of our practice. In Mark Hurley's comprehensive white paper he talks about a number of reasons why internal sales to employees can be a good idea—especially for a fee-only wealth-management firm. Following are some of the benefits that resonated the most with me.

1. Recruit and retain a next generation of professionals who are capable of and are interested in continuing the business after the founders have departed.
2. Broadening ownership reallocates not only the upside economics of a firm, but also the downside risk by having employees exchange a portion of their current compensation for a portion of a firm's future earnings.
3. It helps institutionalize the firm's client relationships.
4. It helps to institutionalize the firm's marketing capabilities and brand by granting tangible and leverageable incentives in growing the firm since the firms' stock is worth more.[6]

   Several firms distinguish clearly between ownership and management. Even though someone may be an owner of stock, they do not necessarily have influence over how the firm is being managed.

The hard thing for most of us to get our arms around is the concept of ownership as compensation, rather than as giving up a piece of our soul. A public company issuing stock options has no such feelings attached to this act. As our industry grows up, we probably need to view this subject differently.

In talking with some other firms who have expanded ownership, the biggest issues that they faced were the lack of entrepreneurism in the next generation and the concern that when their practices were eventually sold, the minority shareholders did not get enough money to be able to walk away from the business and, therefore, made the deal drag out longer than it otherwise would have.

With our own practice, it is interesting to note the difference between those who think like a business owner and those who think like employees. During the market meltdown of 2008 and early 2009, we called our staff together and let them know that we were not laying off anyone and that we were going to hold salaries constant. We let them know that we would not be giving salary increases until our revenues recovered. We also said that if things stayed bad (which we did not expect), we would evaluate looking at suspending our 401(k) match. One of the staff members asked whether they could take a salary cut and then have a disproportionate increase when our revenues recovered. He was willing to share our pain for a potential to participate in the rebound. Most employees don't think like that.

The twenty-first century wealth manager may have been trained in college to enter the field, circumventing the need to acquire clients. They have the technical knowledge necessary to deliver a quality product. This background, coupled with business owners who hold things close to their vest, make it very difficult for these employees to get a real sense of what it is like to own a business. They will most likely come up through a management track. Some of the more successful, larger firms are creating expectations and rewards around business development that will help these younger employees understand the grease for the wheel of the business. Lou Stanasolovich of Legend Financial Advisors, among others, has practiced open-book management with his staff. While we have not been comfortable with this level of openness, for Legend's firm it has helped put everyone on the same page with regard to what they are trying to accomplish and how they are progressing toward their goals.

The most important misconception to overcome is that you have worked hard over the years and when the time is right you will sell the business. The White Knight approach to business continuation will leave you hanging on long after your armor has rusted. From our own practice, our business continuation planning has taken years, with several missteps along the way. If you are serious about serving your clients after you no longer are active in the field, then dealing with this issue needs to be on the front burner.

Another misconception is that you will find a slow deer to sell your business to. We are the hunted, not the hunter, so the likelihood of a buyer knowing less than we do is silly. If you think about strategic or financial buyers interested in your practice, they have far more acquisition experience than you do. You may do this once (unless you are like my friend, Ram Kolluri, who has successfully sold his business a few times), but your buyer has done this several times. Don't be fooled; these buyers are usually smarter in this area than we are.

Staffing

Our approach to building a staff has also been very incremental. When Wil and I first started, we hired a secretary/assistant who was making more than we were. Over time, we continued to build our staff based on allowing each of us to focus on our core competencies. We knew that Wil and I were better in front of clients working at the strategic level than we were entering data into spreadsheets.

Hiring good staff obviously has risks and rewards and problems and opportunities. We continued to improve our hiring over time—both people and processes. The biggest mistake that we made in hiring was having budget dominate our decisions. Generally you get what you pay for. Once we began hiring the best people for the tasks at hand, relatively quickly they paid for themselves. But this was a giant leap of faith.

We also found that we did not do as well with people who came from a very corporate background. This may change as the company becomes less entrepreneurial, but I don't think so. Hiring out of the larger accounting firms worked fine; hiring from the larger wealth-management firms did not. I attribute it to the difference between really viewing ourselves as fiduciaries putting the client's interests first rather than making decisions that are suitable for the client. This is not a minor distinction, although it is often downplayed. People who have come from places with a real fiduciary standard should be asking "Is this the right thing to do and the best thing to do?" This is a different question than "Is this appropriate for the client given the circumstances?" In fact, an important distinction is recognition of from where we came. Our background may help us see how we address a problem or a prospect. If someone came from a background where acquiring clients was more important than acquiring the right clients, it may be difficult for them to discern the difference.

We prefer to hire people with experience rather than right out of school, although we have had success with those coming out of the excellent college financial-planning programs. The advantage in hiring people with more experience is not about knowledge as much as it is about them seeing the difference between how we operate as compared with other organizations. They can see quickly whether we are a good fit and are less likely to fall victim to the grass-is-always-greener thinking.

One of the most important books that impacted our hiring was *Topgrading* by Bradford D. Smart. He discusses the value of human capital and says, "The single most important driver of organizational performance and individual managerial success is talent."[7] His premise is that organizations have A, B, and C players. The most successful organizations are filled with A players, manage their B players, and do not hire or keep C players. Smart defines topgrading as: "To fill every position in the organization with an A player, at the appropriate compensation level."[8] Someone may be an A player in one role and get promoted to a position in which they are no better than a C (think about the sales person who ends up becoming sales manager). It can also work the other way.

In our company, we hired an extremely bright person to work on the comprehensive wealth management side. He was a nightmare there. His style did not work well with his managers, he was disinterested in many aspects of the comprehensive plan, and he questioned everything. His profile was perfect for our investment-management team, though. This was a great hire, but for the wrong area. He has since earned his Chartered Financial Analyst and is managing our investment area.

It is difficult for most organizations to hire people who are better than the person doing the hiring. If you want A players, then it is important to get the training and experience to be an A player yourself, or hire people in the areas in which you will never be an A player, so you don't feel threatened.

I have never been an A player manager, so we had to build around me a system that incorporated better people in those areas. As someone who started and grew a business, it was at times difficult to recognize that I had to begin to follow sets of rules that I had previously rejected. My role within the organization was changing; I was still spending most of my time in areas in which I was an A player, but to exist within the company, I had to modify the behavior that was now problematic, but worked when we were smaller.

All new hires come into our company on a probationary three-month period. They are managed during this timeframe to be certain that they are suitable for the job for which they were hired. It is best to be honest early in the relationship so the employee can find a place where they have a better chance of success. An employee who may be a B or C in one place could be an A in another place or in a different role. Again, we found this with our corporate hires. They were great at the place from which they were coming, but not very good with us.

When we are having problems with an employee's work effort, we put them on a performance-review plan. This is a 90-day program during which we set clear expectations and meet weekly to manage back to him or her. If the employee is still not meeting standards, then we need to help him or her find a new place to work. It seems roughly a quarter of the people who have been put on performance review raise their game to a level by which they become A or solid B players. If someone does succeed after a performance improvement plan, it is a signal to us that we were not clear enough in our expectations for the employee. If someone does not succeed after this type of program, they were probably simply a bad hire for us.

If I were to stereotype from the talks to planners that I have given around the country, I think most wealth-management businesses wait too long to make a hire and then don't hire the level of person that they need to perform the job. The employees that you are hiring should create operating leverage for you, but only if you train them to perform. If you are skimping on the level of employee, you will inevitably have to be more involved in their training. Higher paid, higher caliber employees may require less input and actually be more cost effective.

"There is a physical limit to the number of active client relationships an adviser can manage well. . . . For your firm to grow, you'll need to add capacity—more people—and leverage your business better. From a value standpoint, the most valuable financial-advisory firms are those that are not substantially or solely dependent on the owner for success. Such dependence marks the difference between a business and a book of business."[9]

It is important to decide whether you wish to go this route, because if you start on it and are successful at it, you no longer have control over it. I used to think that we would stay a small, boutique shop. As we hired better people and did more for our clients, we acquired more clients who needed to be served by better people. These better people need an opportunity to grow within the organization so structure needed to be created. The whole thing becomes like the song about the little old lady who swallowed a fly, then a spider to eat the fly, a bird to catch the spider, and on and on.

I mentioned earlier some of the testing tools that we use for partner level. We use some of those tools for those applying for entry-level positions. We also use the Kolbe Index to test interviewee strengths in areas such as fact finding, quick start, and others. **Most important, though, is that we don't interview people prior to testing them**. This has made a major difference in our hiring practices. We receive the resume to see whether we wish to go further. From there, we then administer the tests. If they test well, we then call them in for an interview. While this concept costs a bit more, it really helps us avoid falling in love with candidates without the skill set to do the job and then creating excuses as to why they tested the way they did.

Organizational Chart

We have had various organizational charts over the years, but as our business has grown, we have had to distinguish between doing the work *of* the organization—comprehensive wealth management—and doing the work *on* the organization—managing the business. When we were smaller, the principals were responsible for both areas. This is no longer the case.

Of the Organization

Each new client has a team put together just for them. This team consists of a principal, a lead, a support, and an investment analyst. In addition, some administrative positions work with all clients on paperwork, scheduling, and so on. Generally, the principal would be considered strategic (integrating the big-picture issues with the day-to-day nuts and bolts), the lead more tactical (performing analysis and making recommendations), and the support more administrative (setting up the work that needs to be analyzed).

The investment analyst executes the investment plan and reports on investment performance. One thing that I have noticed that is different about our organization than about many others is that we view investment management as discreet from the wealth-management role. Some of our wealth managers may know almost nothing about investing. We have found the investment planning area to be scalable; the wealth management area is not.

Virtually everyone we hire on the wealth management side comes in as a 100 percent supporting role. This is because it takes several months to become familiar with how we operate the wealth-management relationship. Over time, supports can take on lead responsibilities. There is not a ceremony where they graduate into the lead role; rather, it is more of a seesaw. They keep taking on more clients as a lead and relinquish support on other clients until they fully become leads. Their compensation changes based on the percentage of their time they serve as leads when compared to the time spent as a support. We try to have between 40 and 60 relationships for each lead and support—depending on the complexity of those relationships.

We also do not build teams for the organization where you are always working with the same people (silos). This is for three reasons:

1. We want best practices to move freely within the company. Communication is unfettered when you spread out the interaction.
2. We want to create opportunities more quickly for employees. Under a team approach, for a promotion to occur, we would have to build a whole new team—this means two new hires plus the promotion.
3. We really want our clients to be clients of the firm, not of any individual within the firm. If someone leaves the organization, it is easier to replace them with this model. One of my friends in this business used the silo approach. They had a whole silo leave, which caused major issues for their business.

While you can see the advantages of operating this way, there are some disadvantages.

1. There automatically becomes matrix management. Since supports may be working with different leads, each lead needs to clearly communicate performance issues to the performance manager, in addition to talking with the supports themselves. Our organizational structure has one person on the leadership team managing the leads and another managing the supports.

2. Different leads may have different styles. This can create some confusion for what the support people are expected to do. We believe firmly in Daniel Pink's arguments for what motivates employees: autonomy, mastery, and purpose.[10] We want our leads to put some twists on things, but they can't do so much that they disrupt the system.
3. As people within the organization advance, clients see a transition in who works with them. This is usually not an issue, but it needs to be carefully explained to the client.

Our investment-management analysts are assigned to clients as well. While we make investment decisions using a process that I will describe later in the book, the analyst is responsible for communicating investment changes and results in client meetings. They typically spend around 15 minutes in a client meeting, so have a much larger client load than the leads and supports. All of our investment decisions are made by our investment committee, so regardless of the analyst on the account, the client is typically receiving similar advice. The exceptions occur with unmanaged assets that the client wishes to continue holding or low-basis assets that make little sense to sell.

In addition to regular client meetings and firm correspondence, with so many people on the account, clients receive many touches by their team.

On the Organization

In smaller firms, the owners tend to make all the decisions and do the majority of the managing. That is too bad, because we are often awful at it and hate it. But until the organization reaches a certain size, it is too expensive to hire people for some of those tasks.

There are many things that can be outsourced more efficiently than hiring people to do them. Bob Veres, Joel Bruckenstein, David Drucker, and Andy Gluck are tremendous sources for this area.

Generally, I don't think it works very well to hire an outside president for an organization. Most of us are not willing to cede control to someone in that role and it can end in a deflating power struggle. On the other hand, the firm growth will ultimately be dependent on your ability to hire, train, and promote good people. If you cannot do this, than you may need to find resources that can.

We have two leadership teams in place: the owners of the business and the managers of the different areas within the business. We originally had the owners doing all the work, but as the firm has grown, we expanded responsibilities. We also have performance managers who may not be on the leadership team, but still have management responsibility.

We have developed a leadership pipeline. This pipeline describes skill levels needed to advance within the organization and tools available to help staff get there. In addition to our mentoring, we provide professional coaching for those we place into leadership roles because almost all of us need this type of help in order to succeed.

Spending the money on organizational development has been one of the most critical aspects to our growth. Our quarterly two-day meetings with the industrial psychologists have helped us uncover issues within the firm that could have caused significant problems. These meetings helped us better understand communication gaps and workflow issues. Developing discipline around our decision making—a very painful thing for an entrepreneur like me—has dramatically decreased the uncertainty of where the firm is heading. Years ago, I used to say that Wil and I would change directions extremely quickly. Now, I compare us (and Kathy) to a drum major in a marching band. If we make a quick turn, the people closest to us may be fine, but in the back of the line, the tuba players crash into the trombonists.

We also discovered when it makes sense to include everyone in our decision-making process. In the spirit of openness, we used to tell the staff everything we were considering as we were considering it. We didn't realize that incomplete information was causing uncertainty. Dr. Jim Grubman helped us understand a key thing—the difference between privacy and secrecy. Something is private and does not need to be shared until it reaches a point where someone is affected by it. Once someone is impacted, if we don't talk about it, it becomes a secret. For example, as we were developing our organizational chart, we were deciding who should be in what role. As we worked on this, we began to realize that some of the people who we considered to be high-potential managers may not have been with the company as long as others who could eventually be reporting to them. Until the decision was made, though, we did not need to disclose this. In the past, I might have said something like "We are working on an organizational chart which will involve new reporting relationships. These will be based on skills, not experience." My desire to disclose would have created uncertainty in everyone; no one would have known where he or she fell. This still caused a disruption for those employees who felt that they may have been passed over, but if I had shared that we were thinking about this before we actually were ready to execute on it, the uncertainty would have caused much more havoc.

One of the most important aspects of working on the business is that strategic decisions are made by those who are strategic thinkers. While this may seem obvious, it is not the case. For example, as a firm becomes more seasoned and the original owner is looking to cash out, they may be making decisions that impact what they believe their sale price will be rather than decisions that will help the business grow. There may be times when you are comfortable with continuing operations as they currently are, without looking out on the horizon to see what may be changing and how the grounds are shifting. Not everyone needs to be involved in all aspects of the business. Make sure that those who are considering the future of the firm are those who are looking forward, not backward.

Conclusion

The foundation of the practice is built on hiring the right people and having them spend as much time as possible on the things at which they are the best. The next chapter will go through how to train those people once you have identified them.

Notes

1. Buckingham, Marcus, and Donald O. Clifton. *Now Discover Your Strengths.* New York: The Free Press. 2001.
2. Tibergien, Mark. February, 2011. "Location Dislocation." *Investment Advisor.* p. 58.
3. Collins, Jim. *Good to Great.* New York: HarperCollins. 2001.
4. Deena is now a professor at Texas Tech University, but her sage counsel and many quips can be found in any number of practice management books she has authored.
5. We have used several different people over the years and have found that some are better suited for particular things on which we are working. The key is consistency in their deployment.
6. Hurley, Mark. June, 2010, "Creating, Measuring and Unlocking Enterprise Value in a Wealth Manager." *Fiduciary Network.* p. 36–48.
7. Smart, Bradford D. *Topgrading—How Leading Companies Win by Hiring, Coaching, and Keeping the Best People.* New York: Penguin Books. 2005.
8. Ibid.
9. Tibergien, Mark, and Owen Dahl. *How to Value, Buy, or Sell a Financial Advisory Practice.* New York: Bloomberg Press. 2006.
10. Pink, Daniel. *Drive—The Surprising Truth About What Motivates Us.* New York: Riverhead Books. 2009.

CHAPTER 3

Growing Your Business

Everything that we do starts with clients. If you want to create opportunities for the great people in your firm that you have hired, you will need to grow the business through new clients. We know that we can count on a certain amount of business from existing clients' liquidity events or their savings, but turning the right prospects into clients is essential for long-term success.

Quantitative Prospect Metrics

A mutually beneficial, long-term client relationship is something for which we all strive. A practice like ours, with very high staff-to-client ratios and therefore high client direct costs, requires a certain financial expectation to make the relationship work for us and the prospect. We have a minimum fee that we need to receive annually, with an expectation that this fee will increase over time. In order to support this fee, we need to create enough value for the client. If our fees are too low, it doesn't work for us; if they are too high for the value that we can deliver, it doesn't work for the client.

The challenge in any practice is that your costs change over time. If you are taking on prospects as clients who are not in the sweet spot of your practice, you will be creating long-term issues for the practice. While it is hard to walk away from business, it is necessary to be able to do this to grow into the type of practice that you wish to build.

The present value of a client relationship is a function of four factors:

1. The initial fee that you charge
2. The growth or reduction of this fee from contributions or withdrawals over time
3. The duration of the relationship
4. A suitable discount factor

If you set the discount factor aside (because it should be the same for all clients unless you want to get cute and modify it based on client phenotype or career), then the first three categories interact closely with each other. For example, we will work with a corporate executive with a stock option program at a lower initial fee because of the expectation that this fee will grow over time. Sometimes we get this wrong.

Some of our corporate executives are using their stock options as current lifestyle enhancers rather than as sources to build and retain their wealth. This causes a miscalculation in the value of the relationship. We may have started with a lower initial fee and had a compromised growth rate because much of the option income was spent. If these clients lose their jobs before their options have become more valuable, or if they work for a company whose stock is dead money, we may never be fairly compensated for the work that we are doing.

Because of this, if you take on lower-level corporate executives, you may want to work really hard to diversify among companies. In our state, we have headquarters for technology, food, banking, manufacturing, and health care companies. We manage our risk of lower-fee executives by trying to limit the work in particular companies. Once executives have more significant positions, this is not an issue. The advantage of working with high-level executives is that they are often interesting clients and the work is complex, challenging, and, if all goes well, financially rewarding. But if you don't develop a strategy in this market, you could be radically underpaid.

This calculus is helpful as you work with those who are accumulating in their portfolios as compared with those who are spending down their portfolios. From a practice perspective, you want to have breadth within these categories. We categorize prospects as to the phase they are in: accumulation—those who are building their portfolios, preservation—those who may not be adding much to their portfolios but are also not yet living off of them, and spend down—those who are regularly taking money from their investments. The term spend down is a misnomer in the sense that many clients who are living off their portfolios will still have those accounts grow with inflation.

We also look at our current client list by their ages and their lifestyle phase. Some of our older clients may not be spending their portfolios, but their age matters because we will have to decide whether it will make sense for us to work with their children after the client passes away. Since the children could have a different set of values than their parents, they may not be a good fit. I am not trying to be clever when I make a distinction between a relationship with a client (which I view as interpersonal and subjective) as compared to a client relationship (which is objective).

Often a good indicator of the duration of the relationship is an understanding of how long the prospect has been with previous advisors. I once heard Mark Balasa of Balasa, Dinverno, Folz say, "If I have a prospect say that this idiot did this and this idiot did that, pretty soon I know that I am going to be the next idiot."

In our firm, we have strategically developed special offerings for doctors and for executives—both of whom with which we have considerable experience, and who often grow their portfolios over time. As we work within a physician practice or for corporate executives, we can develop scale because we understand their benefits, their other shared advisors, and have a relationship with human resources or their practice manager. But we do this recognizing the caveats I mentioned above.

Behavioral Types of Prospects

Once you have established the type of firm you want to be, you can then establish the types of people with whom you wish to work. Because our minimums are relatively high ($2,000,000 at the time of this writing), our typical client is in their late 50s, unless they are business executives or come from inherited wealth. For many of our professional clients, we are managing their self-directed retirement plans. We also have intergenerational client relationships—what is now often referred to as multi-family office work. A financial screen is a way to understand what your revenues will be from a relationship, but it doesn't help you in establishing who is the type of person with whom you wish to work.

Our prospect meetings are typically filled with questions by which we ultimately gather the facts of the case, but more importantly, through which we are trying to understand the critical issues that the client feels they are facing, how they feel about their money, what a successful relationship would look like, and how they view the resources available to them.

At a simple level, it seems that the working relationship with their wealth manager comes from one of four client/prospect phenotypes:

1. Relationship
2. Fear
3. Curiosity
4. Greed

Relationship Clients

These clients are those interested in working closely with their advisor and forming a bond with them. They tend to be conversational. The initial meeting flows smoothly and they relate well. These clients want to be comfortable with you and want to *feel* that they are in good hands. These clients are often great long-term clients and very good to work with. They need to stay engaged in the process, even though they may defer many of the decisions to you.

It is very important to establish boundaries and expectations with these clients. You need to be clear as to how much and what type of communication you will be providing. Because you will probably really like these clients, you may unwittingly create unreasonable expectations by the length and frequency of your original phone calls and meetings. It is also important to be very direct when something does not go as planned rather than, because of shame, avoiding the issues.

Since many of your meetings with these types of clients may be about feelings and items only indirectly related to wealth management, summary letters moving the process forward are critical.

The most important ingredient for a long-term, mutually beneficial relationship with this type of client is trust. During the market meltdown in 2008 and 2009, we were often reaching out twice a week to clients, letting them know that we were engaged in their situations. The feedback after this crisis from many of them was that they knew that they were being taken care of.

Losing a relationship client is very painful. When we went to a new fee structure, we had to contact our existing clients and let them know how and why we were implementing it. One of our relationship clients did not like their fee going up and, it seemed, felt that our relationship should have allowed an exception for them. The problem with exceptions is that you can't rightfully justify it for one client and not others. The client ended up leaving us and we both felt hurt and betrayed. As I look back, I probably violated a personal boundary by changing the nature of the relationship.

We do not negotiate fees up to $10,000,000, because we feel that if we give someone a deal, then we would be obligated to go back to other clients and provide them the same deal. We don't think that this is good business.

Fear-Based Clients

These people have had either bad experiences with their other advisors or have little financial experience. These clients also typically do not isolate their fear to their finances; many of the things that they avoid come from their fear. Jungian psychoanalyst James Hollis writes, "The meaning of our life will be found precisely *in our capacity to achieve as much of it as is possible beyond those bounds fear would set for us.*"[1] These clients can be frustrated by their fears, even though they are ruled by them. Often these clients are the recent benefactors of an inheritance, the financially uninvolved spouse in a divorce, or the successful business owner who has sold the business and now needs to live off the assets.

While these clients are also reliant on you, they need education. You want to work with them, not take care of them. You want to help them gain confidence around money issues. Even though these clients may defer to you (as a tool for avoidance), make sure that they are not retreating from you. If things get too overwhelming, they literally check out of the meeting. You may be talking, but not be heard. These clients need to be involved in the process so that they can overcome their inherent desire to procrastinate. They are so afraid of making a wrong choice that they make no choice, until they suddenly, and often inexplicably, move forward with a decision.

Again, follow-up letters that emphasize decisions made and areas of agreement are very important. If handled well, the fear-based client will often turn into a relationship one.

We had one prospect come in with her second husband. She came to us as a referral from a money coach, who understood how she was being handcuffed by her fears. Neither she nor her husband had blended their finances and both were spending far less than their portfolios would allow. We met with them and told them that we didn't think the timing was right to work together and, since they were spending so little of their portfolio, they didn't need to make a change to achieve their desired outcomes. They called six months later and wanted to come in again. During this meeting, they indicated that they were ready to do something different and we enlisted them as clients. Before the assets transferred, she had her husband call and say that she couldn't go through with the change. One of the things they said was that they didn't understand that the mutual funds we use charge internal fees in addition to our fee (even though their total costs were higher where they currently were).

While we initially carefully went over the fees that clients pay, it was clear that the broker with whom she was working was playing off her fears by sabotaging how we do things. This was a very vulnerable type of prospect, so rather than try to convince them that their broker seemed disingenuous, we encouraged them to continue to stay doing what they were doing.

Curious Clients

German philosopher Walter Bennett said, "All knowledge takes the form of interpretation." Knowledgeable or curious clients are working with you because of their perceived time constraints. This means that they really believe that they can do what we do if they only had the time to do it. They are big readers and often come to meetings with newspaper or magazine clippings. And they usually are looking for advice that validates what they already believe.

The challenge with this type of client is to gain their trust through your own expertise. With the first two types of clients, your knowledge is a given and the relationship is more critical. With this type of client, you need to prove that you are technically competent. These clients require great detail work. It is also important to not simply give in to their predilections, but provide support for your contrary positions. A truly curious client can be persuaded by a well-researched argument.

Even if these clients appear to convert to relationship clients, don't underestimate their need for information, and ostensibly, control. After you have made joint decisions, continue to support those with articles or books that you can send their way. Be prepared to readdress issues.

One of our clients is a very detail-oriented doctor. She subscribes to several investment newsletters and services. As we began to reposition her portfolio, she had several concerns over various investments (using Morningstar reports to support her positions) or allocation choices. Once we took a step backward and spent more time on regression to the mean, asset allocation, and our process for making decisions, she was temporarily more comfortable. We sold out of a mutual fund that was very highly rated by Morningstar but had increased their assets by 600 percent. This particular manager had been a Manager of the Year by Morningstar. She interpreted this as an endorsement by them; obviously something it was not. We felt that because of its size, this concentrated fund would eventually no longer be able to perform as consistently as it had in the past. But it was only, in some ways by coincidence, after the fund went from the top one percent to the bottom one percent did she see the why behind our hows. Since she somewhat reluctantly sold out of the successful mutual fund, we would have needed to continue to support our thesis to her until the fund underperformed. If it never did so, we would have continued to have our work cut out for us with other recommendations.

Greedy Clients

I don't think that it is possible to have a long-term relationship with this type of client. The question to ask yourself is whether you want a short-term one. These clients are interested in ever-changing objectives, only some of which are articulated. They are prisoners to short-term results. They are initially attractive because they have high energy, but they are often capricious. You start off on a pedestal with them and eventually get knocked off of it. While the client may say they want comprehensive wealth management, they really only want returns. This chasing means that they eventually blow themselves up.

These clients hate to lose and obsess about their failures if something goes wrong. They believe in the incompatible theories of market timing and stock selection and perfect information. They are a practice train wreck that create havoc with your staff and have you continually performing tasks that are one-offs. They will inevitably leave you.

The best thing to do with these types of prospects is not convert them into clients. They simply suck the oxygen out of a practice.

The Prospect Meeting

When someone calls into the office to ask about our services, either Kathy or I talk with them prior to setting up a meeting. During this brief call, we want to get a sense of whether we are the right firm for them. Invariably, people will describe their situation and we can get a sense as to whether they will meet our minimums. We also encourage people to go to our web site to read about the firm and its processes. On the first page of our web site, there is a sentence that states: *Accredited Investors' services are best suited for those with $2 million or more to invest.*

This language is not subtle, but it is also not a firm line. If someone is not a good fit for the firm, we direct them to other fee-only planners with lower minimums that may be more appropriate. We vet these firms based on minimums, size of the firm (we like to have a firm with at least five people), an understanding of their processes, and an interview with their principals. Over time, some of the firms to which we have sent prospects have had their minimums grow to a place where we have had to enlarge our pool in order to meet the needs of those whom we cannot serve.

Most people are coming to us either because something has made them uncomfortable or their situation has changed. What I find most interesting is that the types of clients we attract differ depending on the environment. While not all clients come for the following reasons, the themes were relatively consistent.

In the 1980s the people who came were those who were just beginning to learn about financial planning. Many were coming to see if we could create ways to save on their taxes for them. In the 1990s it was people who felt like they were late to the party for equities and wanted to become more heavily invested. In the 2000s we saw people who were blown up by a lack of diversification. And now in the 2010s it is the "do-it-yourselfers" who come to us because they feel that the environment is precarious and they no longer trust themselves. I am sure that in the next decade our prospects will be those people who are inheriting money and are inexperienced with it as well as those retirees who are concerned about outliving their resources.

If someone does seem to be a good fit, we then forward them to an assistant to set up the meeting and to e-mail or write a letter including what documents it would be helpful for them to bring. We allocate an hour for the meeting. Figure 3.1 is an example of the e-mail and the needed documents form.

FIGURE 3.1   Sample Letter and Needed Documents.

Dear _____,

Thank you for your interest in our firm. We look forward to meeting you on _____. Attached is a list of documents that can be helpful, but not essential, to have at this meeting. If it makes sense for us to work together, bringing these documents will allow us to hit the ground running.

Here are directions to our office:

Best regards,
Suzy

Financial Information

We are committed to a holistic planning relationship with a focus on you and your life. We will continually review and integrate your goals and financial data in the following areas:

Please provide us with copies of the following documents (if applicable)

➢ **Asset Protection**
- Life Insurance Policies
- Property & Casualty Insurance Policies (Home, Auto, Umbrella, etc.)

- Health Insurance Policies
- Long-Term Care Insurance Policies
- ➤ **Disability & Income Protection**
  - Tax Returns (Previous 2 Years—Federal and State)
  - Current Pay Stubs
  - Expense Summary (Quicken Reports, etc.)
  - Social Security Benefit Statements
  - Stock Option Statements
  - Pension Plan Statements
  - Disability Policies
  - Employee Benefits Summary
- ➤ **Debt Management**
  - Mortgages
  - Home Equity Loans
  - Other Outstanding Debts
- ➤ **Investment Planning**
  - Brokerage Statements
  - Retirement Plan Statements (401k, 403b, etc.)
  - IRA Statements
  - Children's Account Statements (529, Uniform Transfers to Minors Act, etc.)
  - Other Investments (Home, Personal Property, Business Interests, etc.)
- ➤ **Estate Planning**
  - Wills
  - Trusts
  - Power of Attorneys (Financial and Health Care)
  - Health Care Directives
  - Beneficiary Designations (Retirement Plans, IRAs, Life Insurance, etc.)
  - Other Legal Documents (Prenuptials, Divorce Decrees, etc.)

The initial meeting is not only a time for the prospect to see whether they want to work with us, but a chance for us to see whether we feel that they would be a good fit for our business. This is important because if the prospect is not a good fit, we want them to end up in a place where they can have a successful wealth-management relationship. We need to listen hard to what the prospect is *and* isn't saying. The only way to do this is through effective questioning.

The prospect is a person, not an object. I mean that in the sense that it is not our objective to convert a prospect into a client, but rather to build a long-term relationship with people who share our values, appreciate how we do business, and are willing to pay for our services. As philosopher Martin Buber describes relationships, "As experience, the world belongs to the primary word I-It. The primary word I-Thou establishes the world of relation."[2] When we look at the prospect as anything other than a person (a revenue source, a CEO, etc.) we are viewing them as an object. Other than the kids from Jersey Shore, who wants to be objectified? When we look at the prospect as a person we germinate the seeds of a lasting relationship. In an I-Thou relationship, we work with the client collaboratively and act as a fiduciary.

While the prospect comes into our initial meeting with a bunch of folders holding all their material, we don't start our meeting with the material. The information generally serves a technical need, but we want to focus first on the relational need. For those prospects less comfortable talking about goals, the information provides a crutch. For most others, though, reviewing it too early gets in the way of holding a rich discussion. Some prospects won't bring in any material and expect the meeting to be about us selling our services. This may serve their purpose, but it doesn't serve ours. Again, we are striving for relationship. We also don't want to be the "it" in Buber's terms.

The first few minutes of the initial meeting sometimes go quite smoothly and at other times may feel like what I suspect an awkward blind date would feel like. We try to do everything we can to put the prospect at ease. This starts with our pre-meeting communication and continues with how they are greeted and seated when they first come into the office. Our office looks more like an advertising agency than a staid, financial company. We try to subconsciously impress upon prospects and clients our creativity.

During the initial minutes of the prospect meeting, there is small talk by which we try to form a connection through areas of common purpose or common people. This is generally driven by us, but can be driven by them.

Questions

We have found that the best way to engage in crucial conversations with prospects and clients is through open-ended questions. The other thing that we have found is that it helps to listen to the answers to these questions.

There is nothing worse than trying to engage a prospect in conversation and thinking about the next thing you want to ask while the prospect is revealing potentially critical information about themselves. If you are doing this, then you are not really present for the process. "Our right to be heard is violated in countless ways that we don't always remember, by others who don't always realize,"[3] writes Michael Nichols. A prospect knows that you are listening when their answers lead to further related questions and probing.

What Brought You Here?

The initial question we ask is "What brought you here?". This is the question by which we find the itch that needs to be scratched. But it usually isn't as clear as you may think. It is important to get to the subtext of what is being said, not simply the words. For example, if the prospect says "So and so can't stop saying enough nice things about you so we wanted to see what you were about", it is important to get a feeling for which of the things being said made them make the appointment. A follow-up may be, "I am happy to hear that. What were some of the things that they said we did for them that resonated with you and your situation?" Sometimes the most important things are those that are not initially said.

We had a prospect in the advisory business that subsequently became a client. He responded to the "What brought you here" question with the explanation that he felt like he no longer had the time to take care of his own portfolio. This seems like a normal response when taken at face value, but think about it. If someone was happy with how his or her portfolio was performing, then generally time is not an issue. It is only when someone feels overwhelmed by the decisions that need to be made, or feels regret about past decisions, that time is a concern. We talked about a variety of things, but did not get into what the portfolio was. When he called to say that he was dropping everything off, he was apologetic as to how he was invested. He was also embarrassed. I don't believe that if we had immediately tried to go through the information that we had asked him for in this meeting that he would have become a client. He needed to know that we were going to work with him and not judge him.

As some questions get answered, the answers lead to more and different questions being asked. You need to let the discussion lead you into places that you may not expect rather than quickly get back to your list. Intensive listening is the most important thing that you can offer.

If We Were to Do a Really Good Job for You, What Would You Have Experienced? What Would You Be Saying about Us Three Years from Now?

This question provides insights into what the client is expecting from the relationship, but it also indirectly tells us what the clients have not received from their existing relationships. If you can't deliver on what the prospect wants, then you may not want them for a client. For example, if the prospect is talking about unrealistic rates of return, you need to let them know that you don't think you can achieve them. In the book *The Power of a Positive No*, William Ury explains "Your first challenge is to facilitate an agreement that addresses not just your interests but theirs as well. . . . Negotiation is not just about getting to Yes but about getting to the *right* Yes. You can get to a satisfying agreement only by saying No to other possible agreements that do *not* satisfy your interests."[4] Remember, your objective is not to land a client, but to engage in an I-Thou relationship.

One prospect had not really paid for advice before, so was interested in establishing a relationship with us at the minimum level, but wanted us to review and comment on their outside accounts. We let them know that we can talk to them in broad terms, but we can't really manage portfolios that we are not managing. We have been burned in the past by trying to reduce fees through treating stocks that clients wanted to keep as non-managed, but not being clear enough with them regarding the fact that we won't be looking at them at all. When the stock drops, the client wanted to know why we didn't sell it. As a prospect is trying to evaluate our value to them, we need to be careful about being realistic regarding what we can and can't do.

What Do You See as Your Most Pressing Issues?

This simple question is a treasure trove of information. Once a prospect begins to tell us the areas with which they are most concerned, we continue to ask what else is important. We continue to ask until there are no more answers. We also ask why each issue is important to them. Go beyond simply being a scribe; listen more than you talk, but be sure to keep probing.

This question also is useful in establishing priorities and setting expectations for the relationship. For example, when prospects are most interested in investments, we try to start off working on the cash-flow areas so that we can be clear regarding for what purpose we are investing.

Who Are Your Other Advisors? What Are the Things That You Have Liked and Disliked the Most in Working with Them?

We have no interest or intention in dislodging our prospects' advisors, be they certified public accountants (CPAs), attorneys, insurance agents, or others. We can hopefully work with these advisors to create a plan that is coherent among all the areas of the client's wealth-management needs. We also would like to gather insight as to what has worked in other relationships to better understand how the prospect best receives information.

What Are the Financial Choices You Have Made about Which You Feel Really Good? What Was Your Process for Making Those Decisions?

Initially, prospects are generally more comfortable talking about things that they have done right. Everyone has made some good decisions, be they things that they have bought or not bought, experiences for which they have paid, or discussions that they have had. Helping them think about the process involved in making those decisions expands the conversation.

Axiomatically, poor decisions are often the result of poor processes. As prospects talk about things that they have done well, they inevitably become more comfortable in discussing areas in which they have fallen down.

What Has Stood in The Way of Your Planning?

The fact that the prospect is in your office indicates that there are things about which they are uncomfortable. Many times people will simply say time, but that is a straw man for other issues—lack of confidence, incongruence between partners, fear. Trying to get a handle on the prospect's self-defined obstacles is an invitation to a better understanding of what may surface in the future.

What Were the Money Messages That You Received Growing Up?

I first heard this question many years ago from Richard (Dick) Wagner and often use it to help prospects safely describe their money profiles. It is amazing how when they are asked this, they will say, "I'm just like my . . . .".

Will You Be Interviewing Anyone Else?

We like to know with whom we are competing. We don't say anything bad about the other firms (if we know something about them), and in fact, usually will say something positive. We will point out things that we may do differently than them.

Other Questions

There are additional questions that wealth managers ask in their interviews which we don't use directly, but may incorporate. Maybe the most well known are the three questions posed by George Kinder. He uses these to help prospects or clients imagine scenarios for themselves. He asks the questions and then has them write down the answers. Here are the questions.[5]

Scenario 1: Plenty of Money

You may not be as rich as Bill Gates or the Sultan of Brunei, but you do have all the money you need, now and in the future. *What will you do with it? From this moment forward, how will you live your life?*

Scenario 2: Just a Few Years Left

You've just come back from a visit to a doctor who has discovered from your lab reports that you only have five to 10 years to live. In a way, you are lucky. This particular disease has no manifestations, so you won't feel sick. The bad part is that you will have no warning about the moment of your death. It will simply come upon you in an unpredictable instant, sudden and final. *Knowing death is waiting for you sooner than expected, how will you change your life? And what will you do in the uncertain but substantial period you have remaining?*

Scenario 3: Twenty-Four Hours to Go

Again you have gone to the doctor, but this time you learn you'll be dead within 24 hours. The question isn't what would you do with the little time you have. Instead, ask yourself, *"What feelings am I experiencing? What regrets, what longings, what deep and now unfulfilled dreams? What do I wish I had completed, been, had, done, in this life that is just about to end?"*

Next Steps

The questioning aspect of the meeting may take up to 45 minutes. After that, we ask whether they are comfortable in sharing with us some of the information that they brought. As we go through the information, we continue to ask questions specific to the documents that are spurred by what they give us.

Toward the end of the meeting, we ask whether they have any questions for us. They usually want to know how we work, with whom will they be working, and what are our fees.

Figures 3.2 and 3.3 are samples of what we give the prospects related to the depth of our services as well as our organizational chart. When the prospect asks what is the next step, we let them know that we will gather and scan all of their information and put together our proposal. After this meeting, we mail a letter to them that includes our contract. When we get our agreement back, we set up a meeting for three weeks out and begin the necessary steps to work with the client.

FIGURE 3.2 Wealth-Management Services at Accredited Investors Inc.

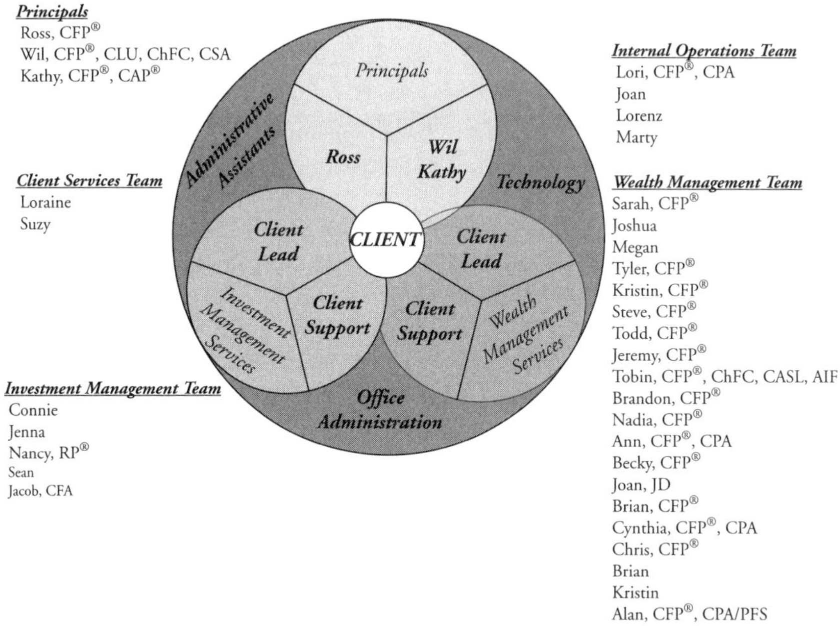
Principals
Ross, CFP®
Wil, CFP®, CLU, ChFC, CSA
Kathy, CFP®, CAP®
Client Services Team
Loraine
Suzy
Investment Management Team
Connie
Jenna
Nancy, RP®
Sean
Jacob, CFA
Internal Operations Team
Lori, CFP®, CPA
Joan
Lorenz
Marty
Wealth Management Team
Sarah, CFP®
Joshua
Megan
Tyler, CFP®
Kristin, CFP®
Steve, CFP®
Todd, CFP®
Jeremy, CFP®
Tobin, CFP®, ChFC, CASL, AIF
Brandon, CFP®
Nadia, CFP®
Ann, CFP®, CPA
Becky, CFP®
Joan, JD
Brian, CFP®
Cynthia, CFP®, CPA
Chris, CFP®
Brian
Kristin
Alan, CFP®, CPA/PFS
Principals
Ross
Wil
Kathy
Administrative Assistants
Technology
CLIENT
Client Lead
Client Lead
Investment Management Services
Client Support
Client Support
Wealth Management Services
Office Administration

FIGURE 3.3 Accredited Investors Inc. Wealth-Management Program.

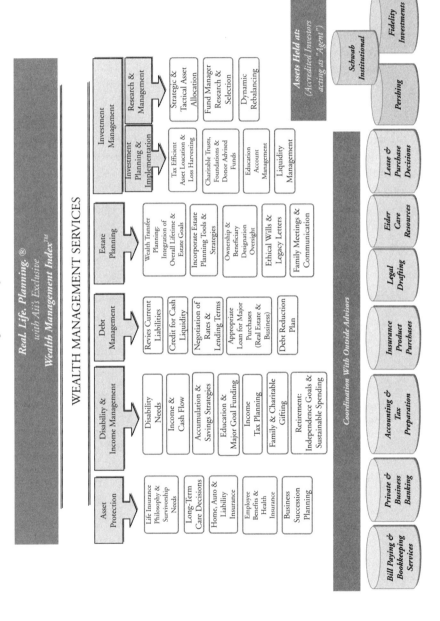

Conclusion

The prospect meeting may start off as a form of minuet, where the slow dance of building trust and a relationship evolves into a decision about whether a mutually beneficial relationship is possible. While the essential ingredient to any wealth-management relationship is trust, it can only be truly gained if you desire to work with the right clients and in the right way. The best way to determine this is through great questions and even better listening.

Notes

1. Hollis, James. *What Matters Most*. New York: Gotham Books. 2009.
2. Buber, Martin. *I and Thou*. New York: Touchstone. 1970.
3. Nichols, Michael P., PhD. *The Lost Art of Listening*. New York: Guilford Press. 2009.
4. Ury, William. *The Power of a Positive No*. New York: Bantam Books. 2007.
5. Kinder, George. *Seven Stages of Money Maturity*. New York: Dell Publishing. 1999.

CHAPTER 4

Developing Staff
The Client Team

When a prospect becomes a client, we establish a team. On the wealth-management side, the team consists of a principal, a lead, and a support. In the investment-management area, an analyst is assigned. Additionally, administrative staff is responsible for the paperwork and trading. Interns scan and categorize all the client information.

The team is created with a fit in mind for the client with whom they will be working. It is likely that everyone on the team will be interacting with the client, so it is important to match both skill set and personality.

When building a team, keep in mind each person's highest and best use. For a typical practice with an owner and an administrative person, the owner wants to spend as much time as possible in strategy, tactical, and client-facing work. The administrative person should be handling all areas for which they have the skills to perform—typically beginning with paperwork and trading, but eventually moving into data management and modeling.

Building a practice is like raising a child—it is a constant act of letting go. In order for the practice to grow, the owner needs to continue to have others do the things that he or she had always done in the past. Even if we charge by assets under management, we are in the business of selling our time. Not all the work that we do is equally valuable, yet we charge the same price for it. Therefore, you are limited by the hours that you are willing to work and the work that you are willing to delegate.

How people move through the organization determines who is available in what role for each team. I want to share with you how we have created a leadership pipeline[1] for these different roles. As I described in an earlier chapter, each client has a principal, lead, support, and analyst working on their account. We would expect each of these people to be in a different phase relative to our Leadership Pipeline.

Leadership Pipeline

Everyone in the organization has certain skill levels, and advancement in the organization occurs when you master the skills required for each level. We have broken down our pipeline into different stages (phases) as opposed to positions. Within each phase, there are expectations and skills regarding:

- Organizational culture
- Leadership
- Relationships
- Communication
  - Methods
  - Feedback/Conflict Resolution
  - Professionalism
- Business Acumen
- Education

Our Leadership Pipeline chart, which we are continuing to develop within the firm, is outlined at the end of the chapter.

Conclusion

Currently, our owners are our principals. Our principals are strategic in their approach to wealth management, looking at client situations from 50,000 feet and bringing it down to the things that are most relevant to them.

No principal will be equally proficient in each area of wealth management, but the experience requirement is an essential separator between knowledge and wisdom. We expect the people that we hire to be smart, but wisdom often comes through the experience of seeing various clients and client situations. This distinction can certainly be frustrating for bright, ambitious employees, but one of the things that we have learned throughout the years is that the longer you are in business, the less you know. Certainty is not a term to be used in almost any client interaction. Behavioral finance has taught us how overconfident we can be in our investment decisions, but we often see really smart young employees overconfident in their belief systems regarding how to do wealth management.

As you can see, the team that is established for the client will have a diverse range of experience and expertise. This type of approach allows continuity in relationships as supports move into lead roles. In a high functioning environment, the support can eventually push the lead up the client relationship as the lead eventually moves the principal out.

When this takes place, a conversation with the client must occur. We ask permission of the client for the change of leads. Often, the new lead for the client was someone with whom they were comfortable in the support role. The change occurs to provide opportunity for both the lead and the support, so the clients are usually comfortable with it. If a client is not comfortable, we will not make the change. How the staff is hired and developed is critical to establishing a practice that can grow over time. We were very slow to create a formal pipeline for leadership and were basically fortunate that our staff was content enough to stay with us while we crafted it. Once the pipeline was created, though, it made some staff uncomfortable with their skill set. While some felt like this created opportunity for them, others felt that they could not develop the needed skills to grow in the organization. Once the pipeline is established, hiring decisions work through it. But initially, clarity creates chaos because the new structure does not work for everyone.

Continuity of staff relieves a tremendous burden on the founders and owners of a business. When there is high staff turnover, clients wonder what is happening with the business and whether it has a sustainable model. They may not use those terms, but it definitely is in the back of their minds.

Notes

1. We have used some of the principals in Ram Charan, Stephen Drotter, and James Noel's book, *The Leadership Pipeline*, published by Jossey-Bass, in San Francisco, in 2001. We have created our version with the help of James Grubman, PhD, and Kathy Bollerud, EdD, two independent consultants through whom we have had great success in establishing business protocols.
2. Leadership Agility comes from the book written by Bill Joiner and Stephen Josephs, and published in 2007 by Jossey-Bass, a division of Wiley out of San Francisco. According to the book there are five levels of leadership agility – Expert (solving key problems), Achiever (accomplish desired outcomes), Catalyst (mobilizing breakout endeavors), Co-Creator (realize shared purpose), and Synergist (evoke unexpected possibilities).

Accredited Investors Inc.
Leadership Pipeline

Phase 1	Phase 2

Culture

1) Contribute general lightness and fun to a high energy, fast paced atmosphere.

2) Embrace the dynamic work environment and value change.

3) Own mistakes and successes.

4) Reflect on experiences and make changes, as necessary.

5) Understand the importance of work life balance and strive to improve own experience within the structure and systems.

6) Embrace a service mentality (with others and through company charity initiatives —Personal Volunteer Time Off/service days)

7) Understand and follow all compliance procedures.

8) Embrace and appropriately manage your autonomy.

1) Focus on developing others in a team environment, encouraging creativity and an atmosphere of fun.

2) Help to focus on continuous learning.

3) Respect work life balance and the impact on self and others.

4) Openly celebrate successes of others and provide recognition through appreciation opportunities.

Leadership

1) Produce accurate, high quality, & timely work.

2) Engage and participate in group discussions.

3) Able to prioritize workflow.

4) Aware of personal workflow and impact to team.

5) Work primarily in the "expert" capacity of leadership agility.[2]

6) Follow standard operating procedures and best practices.

1) Able to appropriately delegate workflow; define rather than do the work.

2) Make valuable contributions to group discussions on a regular basis.

3) Aware of and ability to anticipate and manage work flow for self and for all team members.

4) Understand context and use it to improve experiences.

5) Develop leadership agility and the ability to move easily between "expert", "achiever", and "catalyst."

6) Demonstrate respect for firm processes and procedures as an example to others.

Phase 3	Phase 4
1) Develop initiatives that support firm culture and values.	1) Emphasize quality of life throughout the entire organization.
2) Drive continuous improvements in the firm (processes, quality standards, client service, best practices, and culture)	2) Operate through and embody encouragement, trust and support.
3) Respect work life balance and the impact on the firm as a whole.	3) Synthesize the value of the individual with the value of the firm.
4) Aware of and tend to the culture within each department and the impact to the overall culture of the firm.	4) Dedicated to personal and professional education and growth for all members of the organization.
5) Ensure that firm projects include a compliance overview.	5) Focused on overall firm satisfaction (morale).
	6) Aware and tend to the culture of the firm as a whole.
1) Delegate "through others" as opposed to direct delegation.	1) Accept ultimate responsibility for the quality of the firm's output.
2) Think across departments and firm wide.	2) Set strategic direction, manage change, and lead teams.
3) Act upon and implement strategic initiatives	3) Shift from assertive style to receptive style.
4) Attract and retain new team members to the firm.	4) Have leadership agility; can move easily between "expert", "achiever", and "catalyst" levels.
5) Able to influence, empower, inspire, and engage others.	5) Attract, grow, and retain key leaders to the firm.
6) Provide mentoring and coaching to develop others.	6) Convey trust in people's competence to do their jobs.

(continued)

Accredited Investors Inc.
Leadership Pipeline

Phase 1	Phase 2
Leadership *(continued)*	
	7) Provide challenging assignments and coaching to facilitate individual development.
	8) Take action quickly when performance is not meeting expectations.
Relationships	
1) General attitude and actions are reflective of a team orientation (volunteering, active participation, collaboration, etc)	1) Build the "team" image in order to highlight the depth and breadth of the firm.
2) Respond in an appropriate timeframe.	2) Develop and manage well functioning and efficient teams.
3) Develop & maintain good working relationships.	3) Committed to the success of others and the team as a whole.
4) Build strong respect, confidence, and rapport with others.	4) Create a collaborative team environment and value input from others.
5) Maintain confidentiality.	5) Provide growth opportunities.
6) Ability to engage in basic small talk and finding some common ground to establish a beginning connection.	6) Engage in deeper and more meaningful conversations.
7) Display a high level of integrity.	7) Encourage an open atmosphere for communication to occur.
8) Available as a resource.	8) Ensure the team provides top quality service.
9) Keep others up to date with relevant & timely information utilizing appropriate systems and processes.	9) Demonstrate empathy to concerns expressed by others.
	10) Viewed as a trusted advisor and a solid sounding board.
	11) Begin to encourage referrals from existing client & vendor networks.

Phase 3	Phase 4
	7) Able to influence, empower, inspire, and engage firm leaders and the company as a whole.
	8) Provide mentoring and coaching to develop firm leaders.
1) Build and develop well functioning and efficient department teams (e.g. Technology, Admin, Strategic Planning Areas, Education, Lead Advisory Services, Support Advisory Services, Operations, etc).	1) Maintain lasting relationships.
2) Develop trusting and honest relationships with direct reports.	2) Actively engaged in and able to bring in new clients & vendors outside of existing network.
3) Maintain appropriate confidentiality with direct reports.	
4) Able to read and stay tuned into the state or overall mood of the firm.	
5) Integrate client & staff needs with firm development and initiatives.	
6) Think from the client's and staff's perspective when developing processes & procedures.	
7) Actively encourage and engage in referrals from within the existing client & vendor network.	
8) Begin to develop a client & vendor network outside of existing connections.	

(continued)

Accredited Investors Inc.
Leadership Pipeline

Phase 1	Phase 2

Communication

Methods (written, verbal, non-verbal, & visual)

1) Communication is clear, concise, professional, and in accordance with Accredited Investors standards.

2) Have a basic understanding and use of good verbal & non-verbal communication skills.

3) Organized and easy to follow (e.g. what's the message, use of headlines, etc).

4) Able to fully communicate thoughts and ideas.

5) Show assertiveness.

6) Begin to develop "language fluency" (i.e. proper use of jargon).

7) Convey complex topics in a simple and easy to follow way.

8) Utilize visual techniques to communicate ideas and concepts when appropriate.

1) Utilize & recognize good verbal & non-verbal communication skills on a regular basis.

2) Able to communicate thoroughly and effectively in larger group settings.

3) Approach encourages active participation from the group.

4) Able to tailor message to the audience.

5) Utilize & recognize "language fluency" (i.e. proper use of jargon) on a regular basis.

6) Adjust "tone" depending on the message content and person receiving the message.

7) Distinguish the appropriate method of communication to utilize (e.g. phone call vs. email).

8) Provide direction on when to present ideas visually and utilize appropriate resources to do so.

Feedback/Conflict Resolution

1) Aware of appropriate situations in which feedback is needed.

2) Provide feedback in a timely manner (72 hour rule).

3) Aware of the 6W of feedback and makes efforts to appropriately utilize these steps.

4) Adhere to 5 to 1 ratio (positive to constructive).

5) Receptive to feedback and implement appropriate change.

6) Display authenticity when giving feedback and receiving feedback.

1) Fluently utilize the 6W of feedback when appropriate.

2) Hold an "appreciative stance." Assume positive intentions...

3) Relate feedback to the individual goals (why it matters).

4) Provide upward feedback.

5) Provide day to day coaching & feedback for growth opportunities.

6) Open the communication lines for honest and direct feedback.

7) Mine for conflict.

Phase 3	Phase 4
1) Able to communicate thoroughly and effectively through various outlets (media, internal and external professional groups, etc).	
1) Coach others on providing appropriate feedback utilizing the 6W of feedback. 2) Begin to utilize conflict management/resolution skills amongst multiple parties.	1) Coach/mentor in conflict & feedback situations. 2) Regularly utilize conflict management/resolution skills.

(continued)

Accredited Investors Inc.
Leadership Pipeline

Phase 1	Phase 2

Professionalism

1) Dress professionally and appropriately for the Accredited Investors culture & general business environment.

1) Seen as a strong professional role model & example for others.

2) Create a positive first impression.

2) Execute appropriate "thanks" through written notes, lunch, coffee, etc when engaging with other professionals (speaking events for education, etc).

3) Adaptable and maintain a positive and constructive attitude.

3) Execute professional referrals to advisors & vendors in network.

4) Exhibit self-awareness.

4) Fill a leader role in existing advisor & vendor relationships where appropriate.

5) Have a professionalpresence (poise, calm, respectful, etc).

5) Actively build broader professional networks.

6) Maintain professional conduct at all times.

6) Awareness of major economic, political, and social forces affecting clients, staff, and community.

7) Consistently punctual and have high attendance for all company meetings.

8) Utilize existing advisor & vendor network.

9) Begin to build broader professional networks.

10) Aware of opportunities within the firm to expand the existing network.

Business Acumen

1) Willing to learn from anyone or anything anywhere at any time.

1) Mindful of the implications of decisions for all affected parties including the business.

2) Self aware of own work and mindful of the impact to resources.

2) Seek out intradepartmental conflicts and work to mitigate or resolve.

3) Demonstrate flexibility by moving tasks to the correct level in terms of costs and importance.

Phase 3	Phase 4
1) Forward thinking in thought and action.	1) Exhibit strong social & professional presence.
2) Actively encourage referrals from existing network.	2) Show comfort in a variety of social settings.
3) Identify opportunities to expand and/or deepen current advisor network.	3) Engage with the media and at a higher level in professional organizations/ publications (books, papers, news broadcasts, Financial Planning Association, National Association of Personal Financial Advisors, etc).
4) Evaluate current advisors for "in network" appropriateness.	4) Active in the community and/or industry leadership (board participation).
	5) Build brand awareness and firm recognition.
1) Conscious of financial and opportunity costs to business.	1) Have a long-term focus on business development & firm growth (e.g. appropriate client relationships, hiring staff, etc).
2) Agile in responding to changing financial needs of the business by inspiring others to take command.	2) Define cost structure for the firm (salaries, budgets, overall cash flow, etc)
3) Articulate a clear and collective vision for the firm that unites owners, employees, clients, and community.	

(continued)

Accredited Investors Inc.
Leadership Pipeline

Phase 1	Phase 2

Business Acumen *(continued)*

	4) Identify gaps in the firm and work to solve the issue.
	5) Accomplished at good meeting management.
	6) Mindful of resource usage of the overall team.

Education

1) Achieve relevant certifications.	1) Become a subject matter expert.
2) Adopt and master relevant software suites.	2) Focus less on knowledge and expertise and more on the interpretations, presentation, and meaning of the output.
3) Identify specific subareas of interest.	3) Identify and implement more complex strategies utilizing the appropriate resources.
4) Develop a strong and comprehensive base of knowledge applicable to area of expertise (e.g. investments, wealth management, technology, etc)	4) Seek out contradictory information and continually challenge own biases and assumptions.
5) Provide comprehensive and accurate recommendations.	
6) Participate in training others.	
7) Create and implement goals for personal development while utilizing appropriate resources.	
8) Seek new experiences to develop capabilities.	
9) Participate in educating others within the firm (meetings, routing relevant articles, etc).	

Phase 3	Phase 4

4) Seek out and consider appropriate data, intuition, ideas, and experience to make decisions and solve problems.

5) Generate new ideas that add value, nurture fresh approaches and appropriate risk taking.

6) Think strategically about improving and streamlining client service.

7) Mindful of resource usage for departments and for the firm as a whole.

Phase 3	Phase 4
1) Have awareness of the skills of everyone at the firm and ability to effectively leverage those skills.	1) Work through others to obtain the information necessary to implement a wide variety of strategies.
2) Coordinate and use the knowledge of all the various parts of the firm.	2) Identify outside consultants to further overall firm educational initiatives and goals.
3) Relate your area of expertise to broader firm concerns.	
4) Informed of secular trends, regulations, and other issues affecting the business and community environment.	
5) Expand firm educational resources beyond specific content areas (e.g. new ideas/resources for practice management for the firm as a whole).	

CHAPTER 5

Training Staff in Using the Wealth Management Index

This chapter will give a sense of how we inculcate the Wealth Management Index (WMI) for our new hires and discusses the various methods we use to bring people into the particular culture of Accredited Investors, Inc.

The New Hire Process

When someone becomes an employee of Accredited Investors, Inc., they go through a training process that includes learning how to use the WMI. Before they begin this process, though, they conduct a formal meet and greet with everyone in the company. They meet in 30-minute sessions with one or two people at a time so they can become familiar with their coworkers and understand the various roles that each person has within the firm. This also creates a chance for the informal network to begin. We value collaboration as a principle and these meet and greets foster this. They also help new hires to understand who they should go to for what needs.

We also have a mentor assigned to new hires. This person is someone who has responsibility for bringing the new employee into the practice. The mentor is different than the employee's performance manager.

Within the firm, we use a system called SharePoint as our intranet. On this system, employees can find everything from our standard operating procedures to our organizational charts to staff member responsibility for expertise in discreet aspects of the planning process—for example, mortgages, Social Security, long term-care, and so on. It also serves as an informal communication tool where people can post things that they want to share with everyone yet not fill up already crowded e-mail in-boxes. For new hires, spending time on SharePoint can give them an in depth understanding of how the firm works. Figure 5.1 is our new hire schedule.

FIGURE 5.1   Tentative New Hire Schedule.

Tentative New Hire Schedule

Week 1
  Phase 1

> Human Resources Time Needed—3 hours
> Meet and Greets—1 day
> Welcome to Accredited—1 hour
> Aii Day to Day—3 hours
> Basic WMI Training (binder)—2/3 days
> Technology—2 hours
> Client Meeting Overview—2 hours
> Goals and Journals—2 hours
> Common Deliverables—1 hour
> Strategic Planning Areas (SPA) Overview—1 hour

Week 2 and Week 3
  Phase 2

> High Level Shadow (2–3 days)
> Preparing for a Meeting (4–6 days)

Week 4

> Other Position Specific Tasks (2–3 days)

  Phase 3

> SPA Overview—4.5 hours (1 hour with SPA Area Leads and
>   0.5 hour with KG)
> Advanced WMI Training—3 hours
> Advanced Interpersonal and Communication Skills
>   Training—1 hour (Kristin G)
> Naviplan—3 hours
> CS Planner—3 hours
> Planning Assumptions and Deliverables Overview—1 hour
>   (PAD Member)

Wealth Management Index Fundamentals

The WMI is a complex system. There are so many areas that are covered, that without a system in place to manage it, it is overwhelming. But new employees don't need to know all the nuances of the index, they simply need to understand the various components of wealth management. Once they familiarize themselves with data from all the areas we cover in the wealth-management agreement, they can then move on to integrating the index into planning (see sample content from this document in Figure 5.2).

FIGURE 5.2　Introduction for new staff to WMI Document.

INTRODUCTION TO WMI

INTRODUCTION

WMI is Accredited Investors Inc.'s homegrown software system designed to help track client data, goals, and analysis. The system is based on the structure of Ross Levin's financial planning guide *The Wealth Management Index.*

The Wealth Management Index divides comprehensive wealth management into five interconnected disciplines: Asset Protection (AP), Disability/Income Protection (DI), Debt Management (DM), Investment Planning (IP), and Estate Planning (EP).

Asset Protection (AP) covers wealth-management strategies that intend to preserve an individual's wealth and protect it from potential risks. This consists primarily of various types of insurance: life insurance, long-term care insurance, property and casualty insurance, and medical insurance.

Disability and Income Protection (DI) focuses on planning for income and taxes. This consists of protecting future income needs with disability insurance, budgeting current income with cash flow studies, and, primarily, income tax planning.

Debt Management (DM) is focused on tracking and analysis of personal debt and net worth. Personal debt is typically divided into home loans, such as mortgages and home equity lines of credit, and personal loans.

Investment Planning (IP) is concerned with the ownership and maintenance of any assets reflected on an individual's balance sheet as well as the appropriate investment management for the individual's portfolio of assets. This includes individual savings, managed investment accounts, qualified retirement plans, business ownership, home ownership, and non-traditional assets.

Estate Planning (EP) consists of strategic planning for asset transfer at death as well as the tracking of any documents that may be relevant to an individual's estate. This includes beneficiary designations, legal documents such as trusts and wills, and the assignment of legal representatives.

WMI integrates the *Wealth Management Index* disciplines into a client-management system that includes both data storage and goals-based progress tracking, as well as many other tools to assist in client service.

Table of Contents (TOC)

WMI's data storage system, called TOC, uses the five Wealth Management Index disciplines, as well as three additional categories, to file any pertinent client data or account information. The TOC section is located by opening WMI and clicking the TOC icon on the main tool bar.

The TOC categories are:

<u>INFO</u>: Client correspondence such as contracts, billing, discussion letters, and meeting notes. This area also holds the "temp bin" which is a graveyard for bad scans

<u>AP</u>: Any type of insurance coverage

<u>DI</u>: Disability policies, cash-flow planning analysis (client and Aii prepared), pension information, Social Security statements, and any tax-related documents or information

<u>DM</u>: Client balance sheet, home loans, personal loans, credit reports

<u>IP</u>: Any asset-related documents, including savings accounts, managed investment accounts, retirement accounts, home ownership, and business ownership

EP: Estate information including legal documents and asset-flow analysis

MDL: Any financial models such as financial independence, life insurance needs, or education-funding analysis

APX: Miscellaneous items such as company benefit information and divorce decrees

Each TOC category contains items that contain information about specific accounts, plans, or planning areas. Here, users can update account values, ownership designations, beneficiary information, and any other account-specific information. Using the view-expander button in the top left corner of each TOC category allows users to access all of this information.

Goals

Goal-focused planning is an essential element of what makes Accredited Investors Inc.'s wealth management culture unique. The goals-based tracking system in WMI uses the five *Wealth Management Index* disciplines to categorize and track various wealth-management goals established for a client. Each entry has an explanation of the client's goal, a current numerical status, a field to provide progress updates and any appropriate next step, and the staff member assigned responsibility for that next step.

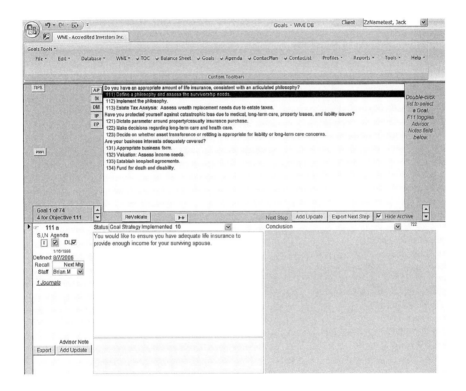

The foundation for the WMI is the goals section. This area describes what the clients want to accomplish and guides what work needs to be created to achieve these objectives. We also use this as the reference point for tracking progress toward these outstanding goals. History for each action relative to the goals is stored within this section, giving background for someone being newly assigned to a client. We derive a Goal Report and Meeting Agenda specifically from this section. The goals menu is organized by the different series described earlier—100 Series: Asset Protection, 200 Series—Disability and Income, 300 Series—Debt Management, 400 Series—Investment Planning, 500 Series—Estate Planning.

We use a table of contents (TOC) structure for our electronic filing system for client information. Everything we receive from a client (tax returns, insurance policies, loan statements, wills and trusts, etc.) is scanned and stored under their appropriate category. Paid interns—typically college students interested in wealth management—are responsible for scanning and storing information. Here is an example of some of their procedures for doing this:

Daily Tasks

> SCANNING
> General

- Stamp document with scan stamp
- Sign into the scanner. If using the old scanner use your name and the first 4 letters of your password. On the new scanner a pop-up box will prompt you to choose your name.
- Choose Tools/Incoming Scans/Client/Appropriate TOC item
  - If the scan is for a prospective client or lead, erase the client name, and hit "I" under Client
- Old Scanner:
  - If one sided, put document in face up and hit the green button
  - If two sided, choose two sided and put document in face up, then flip document and scan back side
  - To log out, hit red button twice
  - To cancel scan hit red button once
- New Scanner:
  - Choose appropriate setting (1-single sided black and white (B&W); 2-double sided B&W; 3-single sided color; 4-double sided color; 5-jpg.)
  - Insert documents face down and press Send to
- Choose appropriate category on WMI, refer to steps below if there is not a TOC item
- Update account balances if necessary
- Move cursor over client's name to see support name (third listed name), write this person's name on the document
  - If client is an Investment Management client (only first and fourth names) write Investment Management Administrator's name

Update Account Balances

- Typically only on Investment Planning (IP) items
- Before updating make sure the value already inputted isn't newer than value on statement

Create New Items

- Hit Create above TOC Items
- Choose appropriate category
- Add as much information to Title as appropriate
- If the new TOC has an account number:
  - Hit Basic to switch to Full View
  - Save scan, afterward a screen will appear
  - In the screen type the account number, value, and value date

Investment Management (IM) Folder

- All items in IM folder go to IP items
- Most items are clearly marked, but if you have trouble figuring out who the client is under, use Portfolio Center to search for client
- Never update the date or account value
- Documents must be scanned to all highlighted accounts
- Checks should be scanned to both the account and to Accredited Investors/ Correspondence/Compliance-Checks
- These scans don't go back to the supports, but are placed back in the folder and returned to investment administrative support

PDFs/Electronic Scans

- Electronic scans have first priority
- If file is not in .pdf format choose Print/PDF995/C Drive/Img/Bin
- If it is in .pdf save to C Drive/Img/Bin
- Follow normal scanning instructions listed previously

Multi-Client Mode

- Used to streamline scanning several similar scans at a time (ex: trade tickets, billing, quarterlies)
- Under the first client, choose the appropriate place for scanning
- Name and date the document

- Choose Multi-Client Mode
- Simply change client name to save several scans in same TOC

Disperse Documents to Supports

- Use key to open cabinet labeled Support Folders
- Disperse documents to appropriate supports
- Lock the cabinet when done
- On Fridays, put the supports' documents in their mailboxes' manila folders

Locking Documents

- Any documents that have not been scanned at the end of the day should be locked in the mailbox in the Scan Pile folder

Other

- If PDFs are password protected, put password in document title
- Often planners will ask that you return the original documents to them after scanning
- Client copies should not be stamped
- Large documents (tax returns, estate documents) can be returned immediately
- When people are listed on documents that are not clients, they may be co-clients. To search for them, you can use Portfolio Center:
  - Log in
  - Use Ctrl + F to search for the name
  - If the name is found right click/Go to Details/Member Of
  - Try searching the names listed here in WMI
  - The above can also be done to search for names to match account numbers if only the account number is provided.
- To recatalog a scan: find image and right click/recatalog image/correct location/save/Go
- For multiple one-page scans (trade tickets, billing, investment administrative support folder) scan the document as one scan, choose Browse Image Bin on toolbar/right click scan/Open with/Adobe Acrobat/ Edit/Extract Pages/all pages/Choose extract as separate pages/C Drive/ Img/Bin
  - You can delete the original document and save all images in WMI

Received Assets Pricing

- Log onto Portfolio Center
- Choose Interfaces/Schwab/Transactions/the last business day (Do the same for Fidelity by substituting Fidelity for Schwab)
- Sort by activity
- Check for Receipt of Securities
- If there are receipts, check each of them individually:
  - Return to the main Portfolio Center page
  - Choose Securities, search for the security (Can be under different tab on left)
  - Choose History
  - Scroll to the bottom, make sure price before receipt has an Interface Entry or Manual Entry price
  - If price is copied, go to Yahoo Finance and get the price
    - Go to www.yahoo.com/finance
    - Type in the security's symbol
    - Choose Historical Prices
    - Find **closing** price for appropriate date
    - Return to security's history page
    - Choose New/type appropriate info/OK/Save
    - Exit Security History
    - Refer to download to see which account received the security
    - Choose that account/Transactions
    - Double click transaction
    - Hit $ next to Total Market Value
    - Save transaction
  - If a security can't be found save it on the Update (W Drive/Intern/ Update 1/Occasional Tasks tab/Needed Pricing)
- For any received assets or credited securities check the account type it was received in. If taxable, basis will need to be updated.
  - Add any needed basis to the basis list in the aforementioned Intern spreadsheet
- Prices are also available on bigcharts.com
- Ask for pricing clarification if desired price is the same day as a dividend
- If assets are transferred on a day following a closed market (Good Friday, etc.), make sure the last day the market was open is copied to the day of closure

We have established procedures like this for everything that we do. This allows people to step into roles more quickly and with less personal training.

These procedures have been established over time and typically written by the people who have been performing the tasks.[1] Unfortunately, sometimes we have to modify procedures when we discover mistakes being made. Our firm philosophy is that we want to be the first to know when a mistake is made so that, regardless of cost, we can fix it and decide whether procedures need to be changed accordingly. We try not to punish for mistakes because we don't want to discourage employees from confessing them. In fact, this is such a part of our culture that we removed the hold harmless language whereby firms claim to not be responsible for mistakes that they have made, typically a part of most wealth management client contracts.

The Table of Contents menu is broken up into the following areas:

- INFO: Information—This area is where we scan our agreements and fee statements, authorization letters (permission to contact a client's other advisors), correspondence, and a temporary bin.
- AP: Asset Protection—Here we scan their various insurances by category including term life, cash value life, property casualty, long-term care, medical, and Health Savings Accounts.
- DI: Disability and Income—In this area we scan the various components that we will be analyzing for disability and cash-flow work. Things like their actual disability policies, cash-flow statements that client's furnish or ones that we develop, tax-planning work, our separately run Schedules B and D, stock options grants and our analysis surrounding them, deferred compensation agreements, pension information and our analysis, social security statements as well as our analysis regarding when to begin receiving the benefits, education profiles, retirement plan elections, and any business employment agreements.
- DM: Debt Management—Here we store their balance sheet, home loans, other loans, and credit bureau reports.
- IP: Investment Planning—This area holds a lot of information. We break things down and include our investment policy statements, the reports that we send out, tax deferred accounts, tax free accounts, children's accounts, parent's accounts, charitable gift accounts, homes and other personal property, other investments, already exercised options or company stock, business ownership, investment approvals (for those clients with whom we don't have discretion), and transferred accounts.
- EP: Estate Planning—This area holds all of our work as well as the attorney's work on things like asset and liabilities ownership, beneficiary designations, wills/trusts/powers of attorney, pending trusts, a document summary, Crummey notices, ethical wills, and our estate tax analysis.

- MDL: Models—We store many of the models that we do for clients ranging from educational needs analysis, death capital needs analysis, financial independence modeling, and so on.
- APX: Appendix—Here is a stopgap for things like company benefits, divorce decrees, and other things that may not easily fall into the preceding categories.

The ability to refer to any of these things in client meetings has been a tremendous benefit for all of us. For example, if a client has a question about the beneficiaries on their will, it is readily available. The time it takes to get these things entered is nothing compared with the time saved and credibility gained when clients see that all of their complex financial information is readily accessible to us. We can also upload any of these documents to a secure client vault which they can give permission for other advisors to access. One piece of feedback that we continuously receive, though, is that we ask for a lot of information. For some clients, this is a huge frustration. We are moving to a custody relationship with clients where we will be able to take passwords. This, coupled with a program like By All Accounts, will enable us to reduce our informational requests. Also, when we do request information, we need to be careful that the request is not loaded with jargon. For example, clients who don't know what an estate planning document is understand what a will or trust is.

It is important for us to get the information correct on balances within our system because we use this to create profiles for clients. For example, as we enter account values in our table of contents area, they move to the balance sheet. Each area interacts with each other area. Data only needs to be inputted once.

We have our own database that we developed for our practice. This has advantages and drawbacks. The biggest advantage is that we can make it do whatever we want it to. The drawback is that we have a full-time programmer dedicated to making changes. Our switching cost to a new database system is huge. All in all, I think practices are far better off buying an existing database with open architecture than crafting their own.

Database management has changed tremendously since we internally developed ours. Your database decision is one that you need to make carefully, because once you have chosen it, for better or worse, you are stuck. Migrating to new databases is a real pain; choosing a good one up-front can help you leverage your practice. Joel Bruckenstein and David Drucker publish a newsletter and have a conference related to wealth-management technology. They have also been leaders in the virtual office movement. Andrew Gluck of Advisor Products is also recognized as an expert in this area. Lastly, subscribing to industry gadfly

Bob Veres'[2] *Inside Information* is a must for anyone wanting to learn about trends in the industry, including, but not limited to, technology.

Database Scavenger Hunt

We have created a scavenger hunt for people to comb through the database. We have a list of random questions regarding certain clients that we pose through which employees can become familiar with where to find answers within our system. For example, "Who are the guardians for the children should something happen to John and Jane Doe?," or "What has been the wealth created after fees for the Smiths?." We want staff to know where to look and to become comfortable that almost everything that they need is at their fingertips.

Client Deliverables

Deliverables are the standardized templates and profiles used to analyze and present client data. Generally, these are presented to clients in meetings, but some are used internally.

Deliverables for client meetings are typically set on the Deliverables List that comes with a client meeting agenda. This list is established by the client lead and is approved by the principal during agenda setting.[3] It is usually up to the client support to complete any appropriate deliverables for the lead's review prior to the meeting (for more information, see the Preparing for a Meeting section).

Most deliverables that are used by wealth managers (WMs) come from one of two sources. The first source is the WMI Profiles or TOC Tools menus (see Figures 5.3 and 5.4). The profiles and reports found here present client data that is collected within the WMI tracking system and are generally produced with little additional input.

The rest of the deliverables come from a more fluid bank of approved templates. These templates are regularly updated and must go through the Planning Assumptions and Deliverables (PAD) group[4] for approval to become a client deliverable (see Figure 5.5).

Common Deliverables

   a. Investment Manager–Wealth Manager Meeting
     i. Found in Approved Templates folder
     ii. IM-WM is a standard (internal use only) deliverable that is used for all client meetings
     iii. It contains relevant information to facilitate communication between the IM and WM teams

FIGURE 5.3 WMI Screen Shot—1.

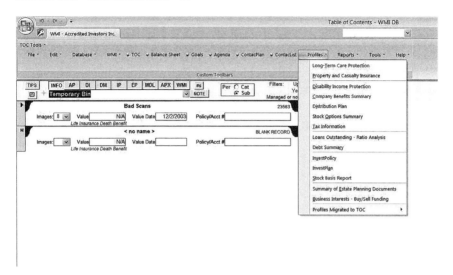

FIGURE 5.4 WMI Screen Shot—2.

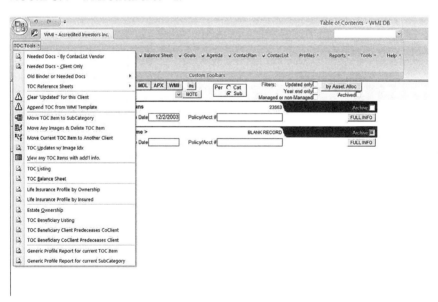

FIGURE 5.5   WMI Approved Templates.

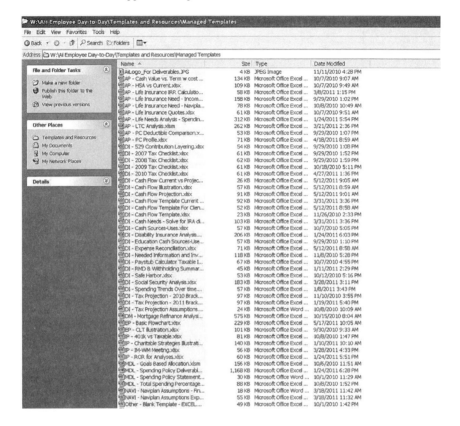

     iv. Used to help make decisions regarding portfolio rebalancing, cash reserves, and tax management of the portfolio

     v. Relevance will eventually be limited by iRebal (more to come on this later)

  b. Balance Sheet

     i. Auto output from WMI (use Balance Sheet button on main tool bar)

     ii. Another standard (external-use) deliverable that is used for all client meetings

    iii. Tracks balances of both managed accounts and unmanaged accounts, other client assets, and any appropriate liabilities

   iv. Guidelines for how often to update various items can be found in the client-meeting standard operating procedures (SOPs) (more to come in the Preparing for a Meeting section)

  c. Profiles (Stock Options, Life Insurance, Beneficiary, Estate Ownership, etc.)

   i. Output functions from WMI

   ii. Most do not require new input when producing for a meeting

   iii. Info should be recorded as accounts are created or updated—verify information before presenting for a meeting

  d. Cash Sources—Uses

   i. Found in the Approved Templates folder

   ii. Used for most client meetings as a way to facilitate discussion on an appropriate amount of cash to hold within the client portfolio. We typically try to hold at least two years of cash within a client portfolio.

   iii. Tracks cash within managed accounts, outside savings accounts, fixed income sources, as well as income from business, employment, and social security

   iv. Analysis conclusions on CSU may influence recommendation

  e. Tax Return Checklist

   i. Found in the Approved Templates folder

   ii. Annual review of each client's tax returns

   iii. Not necessarily presented to clients every year (unless errors are found)

   iv. Goal 242 is updated whenever this deliverable is completed

  f. Estate Flowchart

   i. Found in Approved Templates folder

   ii. Used as a way to analyze the impact of a client's estate documents or their legacy goals and potential tax liabilities upon passing away

   iii. Also provides a visual for clients to understand the structure of their estate documents

   iv. Tracks the flow of all assets to various beneficiaries

   v. Typically prepared when asset level changes significantly or when new estate documents are drafted

   vi. Includes a review of agents and representatives appointed by the client in various estate documents

  g. Life Needs Analysis

   i. Found in Approved Templates folder

   ii. Uses income replacement as a method to calculate a clients' needed level of insurance coverage

   iii. Compares projected need to current coverage

   iv. Often includes quotes for term insurance to replace or supplement current coverage

h. Spending Policy
   i. Found in Approved Templates folder
   ii. Developed over several years to replace generic 5 percent Spending model for clients
   iii. Calculates a sustainable spending level, for clients in the portfolio spending phase, based on the client's age, asset level, supplemental income sources, future needs, and projected tax liabilities
   iv. Designed to minimize needs to reduce spending in down years, given that the client adheres to required adjustments and alarms
   v. Does not replace these use of Financial Independence Models for clients in the accumulation phase
   vi. A more in-depth look at the Spending Policy will be covered later in the book

Figure 5.6 shows our structure for client meetings.

FIGURE 5.6 Client Meetings.

CLIENT MEETINGS

i. Accredited Investors Meeting Philosophy
ii. Different Types of Clients
   a. Prospects
   b. First-year clients
   c. IM clients
   d. WM clients
   e. Dependents
iii. Client Meeting Type
   a. IM
   b. Anniversary Meeting

Conclusion of Meeting:
   - How are we doing?
   - What have we done particularly well?
   - Where can we improve?

Anniversary Items
   - Clint Info Screen update
   - ContactList review and update (indudes referred to)
   - Delete T drive Meeting folders from 2yrs ago (i.e. in 2011, delete 2009)

- iRebal Clint profile review
- Resource Units calculation

iv. Structure of a Meeting

Meeting Agenda

April 21, 2011

1:00 pm Central

<u>Investment Related</u>
- Market update and portfolio review—412a
- Missing cost basis on mutual fund lot from Vanguard (Vanguard Intermediate Term Investment-Grade fund)—431a

<u>Key Discussion Items</u>
- Discuss logistics on cash needs from portfolio (timing, amount, etc.)—441b
- Revisit discussion of total spending capacity—233a
- Review of current estate plan—511a
- Review strategies for life insurance within context of overall estate plan—111a

<u>Other Items</u>
- Demo of client web site—441a

<u>Items for Next Meeting</u>
- Review of property & casualty coverage levels and deductibles—121a
- Discuss 2011 estimated tax payments—241a

v. Overview of Preparing for a Meeting

Steps in preparing for a meeting:
- Setting Agenda
- Agenda Setting Meeting
- Support Prep Work (includes Agenda email)
- IM/WM (Investment Mgmt/Wealth Mgmt) Meeting
- Lead Prep Work Review
- Deliverables and Recommendations, Tomorrow, Strategic (this is a day before meeting)
- Client Meeting
- Debrief
- Post Meeting with Support
- Discussion Letter

Other Notes

Following are some of the other important practices in our firm:

- Every e-mail interaction between a client and a staff member is kept in a journal under the client's name. By reviewing previous journals, an employee can get a sense of what the hot button issues are for a particular client as well as a sense of history regarding how the client relationship has evolved.
- We try to introduce each team member to the client since they will be working closely with them. New hires go through a training period before they are responsible for their role on a team. The advantage of our team approach is that there is always someone with institutional memory working for the client. In addition, each new client receives a "Team Card" with the names and contact information for the people with whom they will be working most directly—the principal, lead, support, analyst, and administrative people.
- There is a steep learning curve to a practice like ours. The people whom we have hired from ancillary industries such as accounting, law, or the brokerage business tend to only know a piece of what we do. It is one of the big reasons that we encourage all of our employees to get the certified financial planner (CFP®) designation (for which we will pay after they have been here six months). The students who came to us with financial planning degrees have a much broader perspective and can adapt more quickly than those students who had finance or investment degrees. While our preference is to hire people with three years of experience rather than straight out of school, the young graduates out of the financial planning programs are often more technically prepared than those people from industries that do not do comprehensive wealth management.
- One way that we help with the learning curve is that we have Strategic Planning Areas (SPA) for which all firm professionals are responsible. These are specific subjects with which a professional is supposed to go deep with their knowledge and expertise so that anyone in the firm can turn to them with questions. We think that this helps solve one of the issues that firms may have with having to be a generalist, but not being able to know all of planning's nuances.
- If you do a good job of testing your new hires, you will know what you are getting and where you may get frustrated. For example, if someone turns up as a high fact-finder on the Kolbe test, they will be slower to catch on to the program because they will want more detail before they get started. On the other hand, they will make fewer mistakes than the quick-start.

- It helps to diversify your employees just like you diversify your portfolio. If you hire too many similar people, the direction of the firm will be set by the personalities within it. Creating a more diverse group of employees will likely lead to a broader perspective. The disadvantage, though, is that people with different styles will have a difficult time working together. It is instructive to go through personality testing with the staff. Understanding people's Myers-Briggs profile helps us communicate better with each other. For example, I am someone who scores very high on the intuitive scale, which makes it very difficult for me to deal with people who are more concrete. Being aware of these differences helps me to better manage them.

Conclusion

In order to incorporate the Wealth Management Index into your practice, you need a strong way to capture and categorize all the information that you will be reviewing. Once you begin to hire employees, you will need them to learn where to find this stored data as well as how to store it themselves.

The only way to build a practice is by creating operating leverage. Each of us is limited by our time. Those who have built practices are generally better off spending time strategizing with clients. In order to do this, though, you need systems and a staff able to execute on these systems.

Notes

1. Currently, our training program is run by Kristin Whitacre and Brian Martin, two relatively recent supports who took the initiative to redo the training. We have had a couple of new hires from related fields who mentioned to us how important this program was for them. Several years ago, we invested little time in training and people learned as they went. They often felt that they were set out to sea.
2. If a gadfly is a person that upsets the status quo, there can be no higher honor bestowed upon a journalist who has been an observer and transformer of the financial services industry. Bob Veres has been doing this for over a quarter of a century.
3. Agenda setting establishes the key areas on which the upcoming meeting will concentrate. It involves the principal, lead, and support.
4. PAD is a task force that is established to regularly review our planning assumptions and create client presentation materials to be uniformly adopted for client meetings.

CHAPTER 6

The Work Plan

When a prospect becomes a client, there is much work that needs to be done. Developing a process for work flow helps you create a strategy for what areas you want to cover and when you want to cover them. The Wealth Management Index (WMI) creates the framework by which you go through these areas.

For a small practice, most of the work will be handled by the owner. As the practice grows, you can assign responsibilities for different tasks. The WMI ensures that you don't miss anything, but it doesn't require you to analyze everything all at once. Determine what the most pressing areas of concern are and start there.

Also, you don't need to be an expert in everything to utilize the Wealth Management Index. There are certain areas that you can outsource until your firm gets to a scale where you want to handle them internally. Even a firm our size provides oversight to areas where other advisors actually do the implementation. For example, we can direct what we feel an appropriate life insurance approach is to an outside advisor who runs the ledgers, puts together the proposals, and earns the commissions.

Pre-Meeting

We schedule an agenda meeting three weeks prior to our client meeting. In this session, we review any new information that we know about the client, determine the items that we will be covering in the upcoming meeting, and decide what additional information is necessary in order to analyze the items that we will be covering. The agenda meeting is scheduled with the principal, lead, and support. Another brief meeting is with the lead and investment analyst on the account to determine whether there are any cash needs that should be considered. We use I-Rebal[1] in our office, so the analyst/lead meetings are not as important because the leads and supports can establish cash guidelines directly on the system.

With existing clients, we generally meet two, three, or four times a year. For clients with whom we are meeting four times, they are generally on the following schedule:

- Meeting 1: Disabilty, income, and debt management (this is generally the cash flow, tax, and debt meeting)
- Meeting 2: Asset protection
- Meeting 3: Estate planning
- Meeting 4: Investment planning and year in review

For those we meet three times, the following schedule is used:

- Meeting 1: Disability, income, and debt management
- Meeting 2: Asset protection and estate planning
- Meeting 3: Investment planning and year in review

And for those twice-a-year clients, we collapse the meetings in the following way:

- Meeting 1: Asset protection, investment planning, and estate planning
- Meeting 2: Disability, income, and debt management

The cash-flow meeting is usually the most important meeting because this sets the table for everything from how we should invest to what numbers we will eventually use for our long-term projections. While investments are a part of every meeting, they are usually presented in an update during the first few minutes. The analyst then leaves the room so the other wealth-management issues can be covered.

Also, the meeting schedule is determined by the amount of work that needs to be covered and client predilections. We found through surveying our clients, that (no surprise) some want to meet more than others. We accommodate clients with this to the extent that there isn't a pressing concern that may require more meeting time.

We hold our meetings to an hour and a half, simply because we have found that none of us have the endurance to go beyond that.

Another aside—I have been a big fan of Dan Sullivan's *The Strategic Coach*,[2] and have tried to set up my calendar using his principles of focus days, free days,[3] and buffer days. My assistant schedules back-to-back client meetings on Wednesdays and Thursdays because each client meeting requires a similar energy. Mondays are used mostly as a buffer day to catch up on work and have internal meetings. Tuesdays are my writing days where I try not to have any meetings at all. Fridays will often include prospect meetings, but the afternoons are usually free for catch-up. This type of calendaring has dramatically increased my efficiency.

New clients have a different meeting schedule because of the tremendous work on the front end to make sure that we have facts, expectations, and objectives right. We used to meet six times a year with new clients, but have pared that down to five. The first meeting is generally a confirmation meeting where we go through the facts of their situation—balance sheets, beneficiary designations, life insurance, cash flow, and so on. We also have the paperwork signed to move their investment accounts. The purpose of this meeting is to *agree to the facts* of their circumstances and handle appropriate paperwork.

Subsequent meetings begin the process of establishing objectives. These meetings are based on the issues that were discovered from the fact meeting. We establish our priorities to work on and make sure that we are on top of those items that need immediate attention. The next four meetings will insure that we review everything on the WMI.

Post-Meeting

After the client meeting, there are two significant things that happen:

- Debriefing
- Task assignments

Debriefing

Immediately when the client meeting ends, we have arranged our schedules so that we spend five to fifteen minutes discussing what just occurred in the client meeting with those in attendance. This serves three purposes. First, since one person is typically doing more watching than presenting, it allows them to give feedback with anything that they may have noticed in how the client received the information. Second, it creates immediate clarity as to what hot-button issues need to be covered in the next meeting. Third, from a management perspective, it allows a principal to give immediate feedback as to how the presentation went and whether the materials were appropriate given what needed to be covered in the meeting. We have a formal debrief sheet which we use as a measure of how we did in the meeting:

Meeting Debrief Summary

Purpose
There are three main objectives with debriefs:

1. Ensure workload is appropriate in between meetings
2. Opportunity to give both positive and constructive feedback in a timely manner (while adhering to the four-to-one ratio[4]). This truly is a great learning opportunity for those involved.
3. Create consistency on the meeting interpretation, so discussion letters are clear and concise

Process

- Time reserved for client meeting is 120 minutes (2 hours)
- Actual client meeting is still held for 90 minutes (1.5 hours)
- Immediately following the client meeting, a debrief will occur for 15 minutes
- The following people will be required to attend the debrief:
  - Relationship manager
  - Lead
  - Support, only if attending the meeting (Lead to determine)
- The remaining 15 minutes of the allotted time is used for transitioning to the next client meeting
- If the meeting does run long, debrief could occur during staff time. However, this will be the rare exception
- Lead will have a separate meeting with the Support to discuss the client meeting details in depth and review any necessary action items

Meeting Debrief Agenda

- Overall discussion summary
  - Consider whether the investment analyst should be included in the discussions at some level
  - What worked well? Which areas could we improve upon?

- How were our communication skills? Examples to think about are: active listening, handling of emotional issues, asking open-ended questions, and so on
- Ensure action items are defined with clear expectations, including the delineation of:
  - In between meetings
  - Next meeting
- Following the meeting:
  - Lead will capture the applicable debrief items for the client's next meeting agenda as the discussion letter is completed

  For reference only:

  The six Ws for giving feedback[5]

  What happened? Describe observations or behaviors. Don't editorialize.

  Why was it good or why was it a concern? Give the big picture.

  What is the other person's perspective? Does he/she understand and agree with your concern?

  What are possible opportunities, solutions, and alternative approaches?

  When will we check in again for follow up?

  What are the consequences? (for chronic problems)

Client Feedback

We want to be sure that the client understood and processed the information that we covered in the meeting. There are three things that can get in the way of this: poor materials, poor presentation, or client stress.

Prior to each meeting, we discuss what the appropriate presentation materials for the particular client are. Different clients like to receive information in different ways. For some clients, we present with pictures; for others, facts and statistics. There is a fine line between reinventing the presentation wheel for each client and creating acceptable material for each unique client. We have developed various presentation materials that give us this flexibility.

Also, each partner in a couple often receives information differently. We may have one analytical partner who drives the decisions and one visual partner who still needs to see what things will look like once the decisions are made. It is important to reach both partners. This is a big advantage to having two professionals in most meetings.

One of the things that we talk about at the end of the meeting was whether we went into problem-solving mode too quickly. One client, who is not analytical, asked a question to me about what she should do with property that she owns with her brothers—with whom the relationship is somewhat estranged. I talked about various ideas regarding splitting up the property, what kind of agreements would be appropriate, and what tactics made the most sense for getting it done. After the meeting, one of our professionals reminded me that the property was relatively recently inherited and there were some psychic issues related to it that I didn't adequately explore before I went into my diatribe regarding splitting it up. I can go back to the client and resurrect the conversation in a way that will be more meaningful for her and also help us come to a decision that may be more appropriate than what I initially suggested.

Hot Buttons

Even though the index helps us stay steeped in process, as we establish our work plan we need to pay attention to things that may take priority over what we anticipated covering. Almost every meeting is dynamic—something new comes up that we need to tend to at the next meeting. This usually does not mean an entire overhaul of the agenda, but it does often mean a revision of what we may have expected to be covering. This flexibility is critical.

One of the biggest issues that we face concerns meeting management. We have things that we know that we need to cover to meet the client's objectives, yet either another issue comes up that can derail the meeting, or client avoidance/distraction can impact the meeting. Our job is to pay close attention to the issues that the client is bringing up while also letting them know that we have a certain amount of time left in the meeting and determine whether we need to adjust the agenda accordingly. Success is not going through the detail of all of our proposals; often, the clients don't even need to see the background work but simply want to know that it has been done. The discussion needs to be framed so that clients have enough information to make reasonable decisions, but not so much information that it impedes their decision-making abilities.

The other thing to pay close attention to with hot button issues is whether the client is still listening. For example, this happens when we go through couple cash-flow issues. Sometimes, the conversation devolves into the state of the marriage, played through their interactions over cash flow. Couples become so focused on the variability between each other that they can't hear any of the advice being rendered. Our less-experienced professionals would proceed anyway, rather than tending to the discomfort in the room. We need to sit with what is happening and guide it as well as we can before we try to move on to the presentation. One of the things that is helpful to understand in these relationships is that we are seeing only the tip of the iceberg. We are seeing the couples with their money. It is inappropriate for us to jump to conclusions regarding the state of their relationship as we work through this one primary place of relationship. For example, one wouldn't draw conclusions about a relationship if the couple was seen on vacation. We are seeing clients as they are engaged in one of the most difficult areas in any relationship. How they act in front of us will most likely not reflect on what they are like the rest of the time they spend with each other.

Immediate Feedback

The debriefing is a wonderful management tool. The meeting is still fresh in everyone's mind, so it is easy to bring up things that the other professional did particularly well and other things that may have been handled differently. Immediate feedback is much more effective than feedback a few days or weeks later. You can get agreement on what exactly happened and reinforce or redirect as needed.

In one meeting, one of our professionals asked if there is anything else that we could be doing for the client, and then jokingly said, "Lower our fee?" During our debrief, I was able to ask whether he felt that whether this was an appropriate joke given the client and the relationship that we had with them. It is likely that I may have forgotten this had we not discussed it right away, and simply been annoyed for some unknown reason with this staff person. Instead, we had a good conversation and a potentially larger issue was short circuited.

Task Assignments

After the meeting, we use the WMI to write our objectives and provide updates as to the status of items on which we have been working. We also assign who is responsible (including the client) for follow-up activities.

Post-Meeting Letter

The letter lists the objective as well as the work that has been done to date on the objective. As clients look through the activity that has taken place for the objectives, they appreciate how involved comprehensive wealth management really is. They also develop a trust in our process and our ability to handle the myriad of items. We also indicate what we are working on collaboratively with their outside advisors. Not all outside advisors are comfortable with this collaboration. For example, insurance agents may feel uneasy that we will be adjusting the life insurance that they have in force and try to work around us. At other times, we have had outside advisors drop the ball on things and try to blame us for it. Because of how we send out our letters, neither of these discrediting maneuvers can easily be done.

For example, one advisor for a relatively new client was trying to get him to purchase an annuity with money that we were removing from a life insurance policy that this advisor had sold him but he no longer needed. The advisor told the client that he had to buy it right away because the guaranteed rates were changing. There was no way that we could evaluate the annuity in time to make a reasonable recommendation, but we could note in our letter that he could apply for the annuity and we will review it while it is being issued to see whether we should use 10-day free look once it is approved. This takes a difficult situation and continues to shine a light on it in a way that the client can see that we are working for him. Also, it changes the nature of someone else's urgency into our process format.

Agenda

Prior to the meeting, the agenda gets sent to the client for their review and to see whether they have any items that they wish to have added or deleted. The agenda comes from all the assignments related to the objectives established. We don't want to surprise any client with what we plan on covering. We also want to be sure that they have a sense that they are part of the process and that we understand their hot-button issues.

Conclusion

Developing a process around the WMI is critical to delivering wealth management. Over the years, I have received calls from planners who have wanted to use the index in a free-standing fashion. While this can certainly work, it also may result in an inconsistency with your deliverables that makes using the index less effective.

The time spent in creating processes will create future efficiencies for your practice and, more important, a way for clients to be fully engaged in and appreciative of the work that you are performing for them.

Notes

1. I-Rebal is a portfolio rebalancing system that allows family level rebalancing, a way to manage cash, and selection of lots for sales of securities. We establish rebalancing parameters, run the program daily in order to put invested cash to work, and rebalance every two weeks for all clients if their investments fall outside of their investment policy.
2. Dan's web site is www.strategiccoach.com. I have used several of his products.
3. A free day is where you don't do anything work related. Truth be told, I am not very good at adhering to these. My smart phone, laptop, and curiosity often compel me to read and communicate even when I am not supposed to be doing so.
4. We are trying to maintain a ratio of four positives to every negative piece of feedback. This can be hard, because we tend to expect good performance and notice only mistakes. But there is significant research indicating the benefit of a four-or five-to-one ratio.
5. Kathy Bollerud, EdD, from Bollerud-Holland Associates created this and helped us. Dr. Jim Grubman has helped us incorporate this into our culture.

CHAPTER 7

Objective Setting

The Wealth Management Index (WMI) is organized around two simple premises:

1. Objectives
2. Solutions

The objectives are established through the big questions that come into play below each of the key areas of the index. The solutions logically follow the questions. In this chapter, I want to go through how these questions work in the context of a client relationship. If we know the "why" of any situation, the "how" becomes quite easy to solve.

As we go through the various areas, we need to remember that these are the client's objectives. While we may lead them when our experience indicates that objectives may be unrealistic or are being ignored, we need to be careful not to strongly impart our own belief system onto theirs.

In their book, *Nudge*, behavioral economists Richard Thaler and Cass Sunstein point out, "people make good choices in contexts in which they have experience, good information, and prompt feedback."[1] We can greatly enhance the success of our client's wealth management through using our own experience to provide appropriate framing as well as to give clients a sense of what is possible.

Asset Protection

The following are the philosophical questions for each category around which the technical solutions are based.

Have you articulated a life insurance philosophy?

Life insurance is one of the most incendiary areas on which we work. Some clients love their life insurance agent and therefore are extremely sensitive to any type of comment regarding the inappropriateness of their coverage. Other clients dislike anything to do with life insurance and are expecting to be sold a bill of goods. Both of these attitudes compromise good decision making.

Articulating a philosophy around needs and life events evolves the discussion from solution based to needs based. As we sit with our clients and ask them what matters most to them should they die prematurely, they can more comfortably talk about caring for their partner, or educating their children, or leaving a legacy. Insurance is only really needed if they have not yet been able to build their own resources to accomplish these things.

We tend to be very careful with allocating resources to areas that may not be necessary. We recently had a blended family prospect come into our office. When we talked with them about what they wanted for each other, one of the issues that was raised was that only one of them had grown children for whom they wished to provide. They each had their own separate assets, although they were living in a home solely owned by one of them. They wanted to be sure that each of them would not have a big disruption in lifestyle should one of them die, but they also wanted the bulk of their assets to remain separate.

The discussion centered around a transition plan for the partner who did not own the house. The home owner suggested that she could stay in the home for three years. But without a funding provision to do so, it would not make sense. If he died, she could live far more cheaply and comfortably in a smaller place of her own. The only reason for her to stay in the house would be to insure that it could be marketed and sold in an orderly fashion, thereby insuring the children maximize their inheritance.

This prospect had an existing life insurance policy in place that may be used to provide transition funds to his wife. Or not! The point is that if the goal is clear, then we can be creative with strategies for achieving it. In this instance, depending on the cost, we may actually keep insurance that given a different set of objectives, we would have cancelled.

Any discussion that is unencumbered by tactics is a more rich discussion.

What Are Your Concerns Regarding Risks of Large Losses from Medical, Long-Term Care, Property/Casualty, and Personal or Professional Liability Issues?

Clients often are aware of some aspect of liability for which they must protect themselves, but it is often from behavioral finance issues like the availability heuristic, where we remember what is most readily available. If the newspaper talked about someone being sued for a friend falling into their empty swimming pool, then liability issues may be on the forefront. I know with my own situation, I purchased long-term care insurance for my wife and I after spending several months taking care of my mother and organizing her help. While we don't rationally need the insurance, it made emotional sense for us to buy some.

The point of this conversation is to help clients understand the context and complexity of their lives. Again, the decision around which risks to accept and which to off-load can only be made once the discussion has occurred around what are financial risks that could compromise your long-term objectives. It also is useful for clients to be prompted as to how these areas can be problems.

One of our clients was sued for statements she made in the newspaper about someone. While the statements were true, she was still sued for defamation. Her property casualty insurance covered the costs of the lawsuit, but they also forced her to settle a claim that she would have rather contested. But by having appropriate coverage in place, she could choose what costs she wanted to absorb at the expense of a less than desirable, but quick and efficient, settlement.

These uncertain but significant costs can disrupt a financial plan more than any because a client may not be able to recover from the losses. Yet it is also an area that can be managed relatively inexpensively.

Have You Defined and Protected Your Business Interests?

This is an area to which almost all of us can relate because we are business owners ourselves. Even if we don't own our practices, we are probably responsible for the clients within the practice. This is also an area where front-end planning is crucial.

When we talk to clients about their business interests, it is not just the company they run. It may be the family farm in which they own an interest, the professional building in which they have invested, or the intra-family loan to their children. Many clients are unaware of the areas in which they hold an interest.

Let me share with you my personal situation as an example of how complicated things can get. I am a founder and an owner of Accredited Investors, Inc., an S-Corporation. In addition, in a separate partnership we own the building in which we house the company. We also have a partnership that funds our buy-sell agreements. My wife also has an S-corporation with a business partner. We also have an irrevocable life insurance trust established. And we have a vacation home, which, while currently not actually a business, has issues related to it should we decide to rent it out (if we can't sell it) once our girls are off in college.

The critical piece to recognize with this example is that not only are there financial considerations for each of the areas above, but there are emotional ones as well. My interest in staying involved in the business is currently unquestioned, but that may change at some point. When it does, how will that impact Wil's interest in staying involved in the business, or for that matter, Kathy's? While we want to sell the business internally, have we adequately prepared the next generation of buyers both temperamentally and financially? How will the real estate be impacted should we sell pieces of the business? Is the rental rate charged to Accredited reasonable for the buyers of the wealth-management firm? Should those buyers also automatically be part of the real estate or the insurance partnership?

On the personal front, what if we wanted to keep the cabin and leave it for our children? Would we want to set up a funding mechanism so that the annual expenses are covered to enable our kids to use the place regardless of their own financial situation? Is it right to assume that our children will want the cabin? Should there be provisions in place for when our girls inevitably use it unequally?

As you can imagine, these call for comprehensive discussions between the business owners as well as their families. Uncovering all the areas of potential decisions and overlap is incredibly important as you plan with your client. Most important, the only way to come up with reasonable solutions is through intensive questioning.

Disability and Income Protection

What Are the Income and Lifestyle Needs of Your Family Currently and Prospectively?

This broad area encompasses developing an understanding of the things on which you wish to spend money as well as communicating expectations around spending to those impacted by it.

Cash flow. This is the single most important concept in wealth management. We are accumulating money to eventually spend or distribute. When clients talk about financial independence or financial security, they are referring to the ability to live off of their portfolios without changing their lifestyle. We spend an inordinate amount of client-meeting time discussing whether client spending reflects client values and what needs to be done to bring congruity between the two. Don't think for a second that cash flow is not an issue for the wealthy.

The purpose of this lifestyle discussion is also critical because it will lead to tactics that reflect the scope of these discussions. For example, if a specialty physician is making a million dollars a year, but living off of three hundred thousand dollars, when you discuss disability protection are you protecting income or spending?

When we talk about prospective spending, we are often referring to life-style choices—things like a second home or a desire to travel—as well as upcoming commitments such as educational costs. As we all know, future cash-flow projections are much less useful the further into the future you predict. Essentially, since impermanence is the only guarantee in wealth management, how things look today may form a base from which you operate, but it only vaguely lets you look into the future. None of our clients were exactly where they thought they would be 10 years ago. Some have more money than they expected, some have less. Some have experienced traumatic life experiences such as divorce or illness. Some have reached levels of success that far exceeded their expectations.

I get quite disheartened when wealth managers attempt to tightly lay out a picture of the future that does not leave room for the vast changes that are certain to occur. This is one of the big reasons that we hate to be tied up in investments or commitments that don't enable us to recognize how much things change. Immediate annuities may be a wonderful source for generating retirement income, but they are horribly inflexible. Life changes; annuities don't.

One of the things that has happened since I wrote the Wealth Management Index is that we have experienced with clients many things for which we had planned. Several of our clients are living off of their disability insurance. Some of our clients' partners are spending the insurance proceeds generated by the death of their loved ones. Children have gone through treatment, trusts have been funded, weddings have been celebrated, and stock options have been exercised. Clients have switched careers and retired completely. Every one of these circumstances involved protecting or generating cash flow.

I think that we should carefully listen to the words of Henry David Thoreau, "This spending of the best part of one's life earning money in order to enjoy a questionable liberty during the least valuable part of it, reminds me of the Englishman who went to India to make a fortune first in order that he might return to England and live the life of a poet." We want to help our clients live the lives of poets.

One of the things that we explore is the *price paid* to meet financial independence goals. Woody Allen once said, "You can live to be a hundred if you give up all the things that make you want to live to be a hundred."

The tradeoffs involved in long-term planning are many; making realistic choices is something that we often don't do so well. For example, do you pay for your children's college education through borrowing on your home equity loan or pulling money from savings or retirement or choosing to not fund your retirement plan? Another option is to not fully pay for college or encourage kids to go to a less-expensive school. This discussion is important because you are not doing anything for your children if you pay for their schooling only to later put them in a situation where they have to provide for your needs.

Choices are often a good thing, yet we often are unwilling to make them. One of the things to which we need pay attention is how many choices and options that we are providing our clients. We know from studies on 401(k) plans, that the more investment options a plan offers, the *less* likely investors will even participate in the plans.[2] This applies to virtually all wealth-management areas. We want to provide some choices, but we also want to limit choice.

Forced-choice questions are very good tools in helping people limit choices and clarify their values. The choices need to be real and clearly serve up tradeoffs. For example, Harold Evensky uses a forced-choice question regarding risk management when he asks, "Would you rather eat well or sleep well?" In cash-flow planning, if resources are limited, a question such as "Would you rather increase your experiences today or reach financial independence sooner?" at a minimum opens the discussion around how spending impacts long-term objectives. One of our clients was a doctor who wanted to take some time to stay home with her kids when they were younger. By asking "Would you be willing to work a little longer tomorrow to allow you to work less today?" gave some perspective for her to make a choice.

Cash-flow questions cannot be stressed enough. "In the long run, people of every age and in every walk of life seem to regret *not* having done things much more than they regret the things they *did*,"[3] writes Harvard professor of psychology Daniel Gilbert. We need to straddle the line between helping our clients live well today and tomorrow.

Have You Evaluated All Current Sources of Income and Potential Changes to These Sources?

Again, this is a cash-flow discussion. From a valuation percentage when we score the index, cash flow is the single biggest factor evaluated. The sourcing of income needs to be based in reality. I love Harold Evensky's concept of "the myth of conservative assumptions."[4] He basically says that there is a tremendous cost to being too conservative in your planning. For example, clients will often say, "I am not going to count on an inheritance" even though their 98-year-old mother is on life support, has a significant estate, and has shown them how much of this estate is theirs. The price of not realistically considering this inheritance is that the client must under-live today in order to save for a tomorrow that is already accounted for.

The same thing happens in cash-flow planning. If a parent has made annual gifts regularly, you may assume that they are going to keep coming. We have called parents for our clients to ask questions that the clients are uncomfortable posing. When we do this, we simply say that we are doing our wealth management for your son or daughter and they have appreciated the regular gifts that you have made to them. We are wondering whether we should continue to incorporate them in our planning, even though we understand there to be no guarantees. To just ignore the probable gift, though, doesn't seem to make very good sense.

Any act of saving is an act of deprivation. We are putting money away today for an uncertain tomorrow. While this is obviously important, extreme behavior on either end is problematic. I always say that our two most difficult client types are those who spend too much and those who save too much. For both of these clients, money has too strong of a hold over them. In fact, over-spending can be a type of addictive disorder; under-spending may be an anxiety disorder. An appropriate balance (as determined by the client) between today and tomorrow is essential in good planning.

Are You Fully Utilizing All Benefits Available to You?

In this area we dive into all the various benefits available to our clients. Our objective here is to not only be aware of what programs our clients may participate in, but also be sure that we are picking up the nickels lying in the streets. For example, some of our clients had children later in life. If they have children under age 18 (or 19 if still in a secondary school) after they have reached full Social Security age, those children are eligible to collect a monthly benefit. For those eligible clients, this is found money.

This discussion is also important as clients are evaluating leaving or taking jobs. One of our clients was offered a new job at a Fortune 100 company and she was deciding whether to emphasize restricted stock versus stock options in her pay package. We all know that stock options provide leverage, which can result in huge gains and that restricted stock provides more of a guarantee. In her case, the ratio of stock options to restricted stock was two to one, meaning that she would get two options for each share of restricted stock. In this situation, emphasizing restricted stock over options made much more sense. Had the ratios been different, so would the recommendation.

Are You Proactively Engaged in Tax Planning for You and Your Dependants?

One of the biggest areas in which we can provide service is around tax planning. Although we have several certified public accountants (CPAs) in the firm, we choose to not do taxes for clients. We still put forth a tremendous effort on proactively providing tax planning. CPAs are often retrospective, and with our regular meeting schedule, we can be prospective. We will loop the CPA in on our planning, though, so that they stay a part of the process.

This area has become more significant given stock-market volatility and how unhappy clients can be if their portfolios generate income without accompanying gains. We also need to be in front of clients if investments are making any kinds of distributions. While I think the full value of tax-efficient investing can be exaggerated[5], it is still worthwhile to understand asset location (which assets you wish to hold where). It also is important to run tax estimates to avoid penalties.

We have found that clients really love to talk about tax planning and that they are often not aware of little things that they can do to improve their situation. As we work intergenerationally with clients, tax planning can be even more productive.

This is also an area where not being actively involved will open you up to more criticism than would seem reasonable, given that there is sometimes little that you can do to improve a situation.

We tend to not like to accelerate taxes when we don't need to. For example, Roth conversions have been one area of planning that in my mind has been totally overused. There are legitimate reasons for having some money in a Roth, but flexibility is the key. While most of us believe that total taxes paid will rise over time (at least until the deficit gets under control), none of us knows what the construct for those taxes will be. For example, if we move to a flat-tax for everyone (rather than the modified flat-tax for some that is known as the alternative minimum tax), it may be coupled with some kind of value-added or consumption tax. In this situation, income tax rates could actually fall while tax receipts increase. We prefer to have clients with the ability to draw from several buckets: already taxed, tax-deferred, and never-taxed growth.

We also are very reluctant to recommend strategies that may be inconsistent with a client's long-term planning even though they make great tax sense. We have been very comfortable using vehicles like grantor retained annuity trusts or intentionally defective trusts as a way to save estate taxes because ultimate control of the asset can still be somewhat managed. On the other hand, we have had clients who, because of qualified personal residence trusts, are paying rent to their children. This concept can be effective, but if the client develops relationship problems with the kids, it can be a disaster. Again, be careful not to get too cute in any planning that you do.

Debt Management

Have You Established Your Philosophy Regarding Using Savings or Credit?

Many of our clients come to us debt-free, but that does not mean that they should not navigate the debt maze as a way to create possibilities for them. Debt, if used appropriately, is an incredibly useful tool.

One of our clients was building a new house before they could sell their old house. Because their old house was on the market, we had difficulty taking out a first mortgage on it. We were able to use a bank to securitize a portion of their portfolio and use this as a draw on their construction loan. The rate was more attractive than a margin loan. If the securities dropped in value, we would move over more to serve as collateral. We had no restrictions as to what we could invest in, nor did we have any limitations for trading. As long as the security was there, that was all the bank cared about. The new home has been built, but the old home is being rented out because it would not sell in the bad real estate market. The cash flow from the old home is servicing the debt.

We have also at times used margin loans or home equity loans for certain investment opportunities when we knew that money either was soon to be arriving or we did not want to create a tax event for a short-term need. While we view those opportunities very skeptically, we still want to avail ourselves of them if appropriate.

We also have aggressively used home-equity loans (which we were typically able to get for our clients at very low-cost LIBOR [London Interbank Offer Rate) for unrelated purchases. While these loans are not typically deductible if they are over $100,000 or if a client pays the alternative minimum tax, the very low cost may still justify giving up the tax advantages.

When clients are retired, we tend to like to drive down their fixed costs as much as possible. This often, but not always, means that we wish for them to be debt free. This is especially true when mortgage costs exceed the spending policy on the portfolio. When Adjustable Rate Mortgages dropped to incredibly low levels, we were not as adamant about getting out of debt because we knew we could do so when the client's rates were adjusting.

Planners often view the mortgage pay-off decision as a financial one. It isn't. While most of us believe that we can beat the cost of a mortgage with an appropriate investment portfolio, the issue is about how the client perceives risk. When a client is living off of their portfolio and the market is falling, they are not thrilled that they have high fixed costs. While the decision is one to make with the client, this is a situation where the client's emotions should take precedent.

Is Your Type of Debt Appropriate Given Your Wealth Management Objectives?

Here again, using debt strategically for even the wealthiest of clients is very useful. In 2002 we would often encourage clients to take out mortgages for their second home purchases because we did not want to sell equities after some bad market years. For those clients that chose to employ this strategy, we paid off those mortgages in 2006—after significant market gains were realized. Effectively, this leverage meant that the house only cost them half of what they paid for it, due to appreciation.

This is not a strange idea. In the 1990s our Microsoft clients would sell options to make house purchases. As the stock continued to soar, they would say things like, "My $1,000,000 house cost me $2,000,000." But once the stock crashed, their $1,000,000 only cost them $500,000 (or actually less if the options would have expired worthless). I think the key to doing this though is considering the client's tolerance for risk and having a feel for stock market valuations. It is difficult to conclude that expected future returns for stocks are equal when stocks are trading at twenty times earnings as compared with ten times earnings. One can still be "wrong" taking money off the table at high multiple times, but we are looking at expected, not certain, outcomes. In 2007 and later, we were trying to use as much cash as possible for home purchases. In 2009, we started the borrowing idea all over again.

It is not only important to establish appropriate credit, but it is also important to regularly review terms, debt characteristics, tax impact, and philosophy. This may involve attempting to get clients off of personal guarantees, renegotiating interest costs, changing the length of the loans because of new circumstances, or reducing debt once a situation or attitude has changed.

I was talking to the President and CEO of a wealth-management firm in Norfolk and Charlottesville, G. Randolph (Randy) Webb, and his multi-family office firm works with people of great wealth. He was saying how credit decisions have become an increasingly large part of their services for clients who need to finance planes, for example. In the past, clients may have handled their financings through their businesses. Once those businesses are sold, clients still need to address these credit issues.

Investment Planning

Have You Developed an Investment Philosophy?

This is the area that serves as the foundation for developing an investment policy statement. It covers everything from time horizon to legal restrictions to attitudes toward risk.

Without spending the time in this area, there are good chances that when the market does not perform the way the client had hoped, the relationship could sour. By carefully going through the key areas—both technical and those of the animal spirits—you are insuring that you have agreement on what success in the investment area should look like.

A key part of this area is to try to develop an understanding of a client's risk tolerance. This has been something that has been incredibly difficult to do. While there are a number of risk-tolerance questionnaires available, the truth is that most clients have no sense of what their risk tolerance is until they are experiencing an unexpected event. While we work on defining this with the client, and even expressing potential bear market outcomes using historical numbers, it is an intellectual exercise until the client sees their portfolio falling, current events causing a psychological cascading effect, and the bad news of the day causing confirmation bias that the end is near. Daniel Gardner writes in *The Science of Fear*, "News stories routinely say there is a possibility of something bad happening without providing a meaningful sense of how likely that bad thing is."[6] Clients respond to the stories and then create their own endings. These endings are where a true understanding of client risk exists.

While the market meltdown of 2008 was occurring, it was helpful to remind clients what we had shown as possible bear market returns, but this did not alleviate their dread. What did help, though, is bringing things back to what they were accumulating money for and whether what was happening was going to cause a permanent lifestyle change. While we did not expect that to be the case, we could not promise clients that they would not need to adjust their goals or aspirations. But we could talk about money in terms of time horizon for recovery and the benefits of continuing to invest when prices have become lower.

Out of around 400 clients, five chose to sell out of the market during the crisis. We lost three of those clients, but managed to get the other two invested again over a relatively short period of time. The sad thing for the three that we lost was not only did they suffer permanent harm to their portfolios (especially since our clients were whole again by the end of 2010), but they were not invested inappropriately for their needs or time horizons. In other words, they acted out of fear against their self-interest. It's not to say that the fear was unfounded, but to say that it didn't really matter. Even if the Standard & Poor's 500 (S&P 500) fell from 670 to 450, they would not have been impacted—unless the market stayed there for several years.

We could accurately gage risk tolerance for clients who had experienced the Great Recession and reacted to it. For some, we modified their asset allocation. For others, we agreed to raise more cash at various upside targets, allowing for the fact that while market movements persist in trends, they also bounce. It is important to act upon what clients show you. After the market recovered, some of those fearful clients wanted to adjust their asset allocations back to where they were. They were responding to a perceived lost opportunity, but this was not reflective of what they showed us to be their risk tolerance. We generally did not modify their asset allocation back to higher levels of stock ownership.

Have You Determined the Mechanics for Managing Your Portfolio and the Evaluation of What Success Looks Like?

This is an area where, as a fee-only wealth management firm that usually determines its fees on a percentage-of-assets-managed model, conflict can exist. Yet it is also necessary to distinguish what is and isn't possible.

We establish with our clients those assets which we can directly manage (either through our custody at Schwab, Fidelity, or Pershing) or through outside custody using By All Accounts. In addition, there are certain assets that we simply cannot manage. Lastly, there are other assets that, for whatever reason, the clients want to manage on their own.

When we do planning, the assets that are not available to us create significant difficulties. For example, as we do retirement-distribution modeling, we can establish reasonable expectations for the standard deviation of our managed portfolios, but how do we handle unmanaged assets like company stock or an outside account managed by a small-cap growth manager? In analyzing these other areas, there is a concomitant possibility of the client doing way better or way worse with these undiversified components than they will do through us.

We need to agree with the client up front on how these assets will be used for planning purposes and allocation purposes. If someone has a significant position in their Fortune 500 company stock, we need to decide with the client whether this means we will reduce our large-cap allocation to compensate. We prefer not to do this, though, because the single stock risk is greater than the diversified large-cap stock portfolio that we would create.

The other issue is when a client has an asset that we could manage (for example a retirement plan) but, to control our fees, they don't want us to manage it. We need to incorporate this within our planning, but we do not give guidance as to its allocation.

This area also includes benchmarking returns. We benchmark in a variety of ways, none of which are ideal. Our investment performance is based on two things:

1. Our asset-allocation decisions
2. Our investments within those asset classes

It is very difficult, but not impossible, to distinguish our value in each of those areas. We show investment returns compared to a benchmark portfolio using index funds at the middle range of our asset-allocation areas. We then break down each of those asset-allocation areas to show performance against the benchmark.

Another performance metric that we use is actual return compared with expected real return (inflation plus a certain percentage). Since our clients are accumulating money to ultimately spend it, we think that this measurement helps them see how well they are doing in this regard.

We also provide two other areas that clients tend to find useful, although it is not clear how helpful they really are. We provide historic wealth created after fees in absolute dollars so clients can see how much their portfolios have grown (or shrunk) over time through investment performance. We also show their portfolio return simply against the S&P—because most clients pay closest attention to the S&P.

Our experience has been that clients will move more assets to us over time as they see our process and results, although the last 12 years have been quite good for asset allocation (unlike the decade of the 1990s).

Estate Planning

Have You a Philosophy on Wealth Transfer?

In this emotionally charged area, we spend a lot of time talking about views on inheritance and what the best ways and vehicles are for partners, children, and charity to receive money.

Our experience has not been very positive with corporate trustees, so we try to nudge our clients away from them. We also have had some issues with well-intentioned, but somewhat controlling personal trustees. One of our client's husbands had a blood disease that lasted several years, but still caused him to die in his early 60s. His law partner was named as a co-trustee on the trusts set up for this client's wife. Unfortunately, the law partner was interpreting the client's wishes in ways that were dramatically different than what we had discussed with the clients while he was alive. Fortunately, the law partner was reasonable and eventually stepped down from the position, but it did wreak havoc for a bit.

Another set of clients were in their second marriage. During the meetings, they discussed how things would be distributed to the children from their first marriages should something happen to one of them. We encouraged using trusts to ensure that their wishes would be met. They did not want to do so, in spite of our protestations. When he died, she effectively wrote his children out of the inheritance. We scheduled a meeting with her to discuss this and let her know that was not what we had heard her husband indicating that he wanted and we felt uncomfortable continuing to work with her given this decision.

The wealth transfer area is significant for discussion, because you find out much about family history and backgrounds. As you work through the various issues, you inevitably grow closer to your clients. We have helped clients establish supplemental trusts for their children with disabilities, have effectively moved millions of dollars to the next generation through the use of Grantor Retained Annuity Trusts and intentionally defective trusts, and helped clients meet their income and charitable needs through Charitable Remainder Unitrusts.

We also tend to be very pragmatic here. We prefer to use the fewest techniques necessary to meet the client's needs. Good enough is usually good enough because the price for perfection is both high and unrealistic given how much lives change.

While we often have family meetings for our clients and their children, when we know that clients stand to inherit some resources, we try to set up a family meeting for their parents as well. This can be uncomfortable because most clients don't want to appear to be greedy, yet knowing what could be coming in has tremendous ramifications for our client's decisions. We have also been able to provide guidance for clients' parents who may not have had planning available.

One of our client's 90-year-old mother was in the middle of moving the family farm into a trust for the kids with the intent of gifting the farm each year. The farm had a very low basis and she was not in a situation where she was going to have an estate tax. More important, the kids had full intentions of making sure that her long-term care was going to be paid for above and beyond the long-term care policy that she had. After one $50,000 gift, we were able to suspend the plan in order to retain what we perceived to be the more valuable basis step up.

We have found that if we call the parents for our clients and explain what we are doing for their children, the parents are often amenable to discussing their plans. While this is not always the case, nothing ventured, nothing gained.

Have You Articulated Your Charitable Philosophy or Mission Statement?

This is a category that we separated from general cash flow because we want people to directly think about whether they wish their money to serve others. This question may relate better to the clients with whom we tend to work than with what your client population may look like. It is also reflective of how we believe that one of our objectives is not simply to make our rich clients richer, but to make them feel more complete so that they can pay it forward in the world. I want to stress that this is a personal bias within our practice, yet I feel strongly that we should be broaching charitable intent directly with clients.

Again, the point is not to judge others on their philanthropy, but rather to place the concept in front of them for them to make a choice that is consistent with their own values. If one of our objectives is to help clients improve their lives, guiding them to focus on others and developing appreciation for what they have has been proven to increase happiness and satisfaction. In his book, *Authentic Happiness*, founder of the positive psychology movement Martin Seligman writes, "How important money is to you, more than money itself, influences your happiness. Materialism seems to be counterproductive."[7] Philanthropy is a great antidote for materialism.

We spend a fair amount of time on whether the client wants to leave all their charitable gifts upon death or whether they want to actually experience some of the benefits of lifetime giving.

One of our clients was providing annual support for her twin sister. This client had also been president of a children's hospital board. We established a charitable gift annuity through the hospital with the sister as the beneficiary. We were able to make a nice gift to the hospital and provide her sister with a lifetime income stream. These planning opportunities, though, can only be uncovered through intense and intentional conversations.

Have You Planned for Incapacitation, Elder Care Issues, and Final Planning Needs?

This is another area where you can provide tremendous help for the client and improve the intimacy of the client relationship.

We encourage our clients to write ethical wills (values versus valuables), write letters to their children, and use personal historians to memorialize their lives through DVDs.

I want to share with you one of our client's letters to her children, with her permission and some edits to protect privacy:

Dear Family,

It's a beautiful July evening in 2009. Dad and I have celebrated our 45th anniversary, and I am looking forward to knee surgery so I can resume some of my favorite activities like biking and gardening.

Now is probably a good time to share with you some thoughts about what I value and believe so that when I'm no longer able to speak for myself, you'll have a written statement of what was important to me.

First is my deep love for you and commitment to family. I know that before having children, I had little sense of selflessness. But once I had two beautiful babies, I knew that I would do anything to keep them safe and happy. And believe it or not, that hardly changes through the years. You are still our children and first in our hearts, and always will be. And of course the women and grandchild you have added to the family have become just as important to us. One of the rewards of growing older has been seeing you build satisfying relationships that allow you to participate in the rich human experiences that Dad and I have found in family life.

I recognize that we share some values, but we also have some different priorities. We have a love of learning and a deep respect for education. We love music, but not always the same kinds. We appreciate art and literature and theatre and film to varying degrees. We believe in social justice, though we may differ politically about how to achieve it. And we respect our heritage and our traditions, though ritual observance is not part of our daily lives.

Books, as you know, are a major part of my life. I have read most of our extensive library and because I have come to regard my books as friends, I find it difficult to part with them. I love just being in a room with my books around me, crazy as that sounds! I also take immense pleasure in the beauty of the works of art and the crafts that Dad and I have collected all over the world. Each piece has special memories for me and I treasure them all. And our house itself is the framework that contains most of our life together. We designed the house when you were small children and most of our married lives have been spent here. The various additions, the many gardens and wild areas are so well known to us, we can tell you how they have developed and grown through 30-plus years. That is another part of the beauty that we appreciate daily in each season (though I confess to liking winter less and less as the years go by).

And most important are the friendships we have made over the years. Minnesota friendships made professionally and in our neighborhood and through our community activities fill our lives. But we have also rekindled some of the old friendships from our years in other cities. Those old friendships are very special and worth nurturing. We also make special efforts to stay in close contact with family (and I include in that group some of my parents' dear friends who were like family to me as I grew up). One thing I've learned is that attending events important to our friends or family is a responsibility that brings its own rewards. Life is busy and there are always reasons to beg off from an inconvenient gathering, but life doesn't wait. You may never have that chance again and your presence is more significant than you might imagine.

One goal I have as we move into this later stage of life is to stay involved in current affairs and to continue learning. Retirement for Dad and me means time to reflect, to spend time together, and to open ourselves to new people, ideas, and experiences. Serving on the various boards and continuing to perform volunteer work, I've had the opportunity to use my skills to benefit important community organizations. After many years of teaching, I've never lost my love of being a student. Dad and I take every opportunity to study new subjects, join book groups, and invite guests for good food, wine, and stimulating conversation. And as long as we are able, we plan to learn through travel. In recent years we have found targeted travel experiences with expert guides to be one of the most exciting ways to expand our knowledge of nature and other cultures.

Finally, I want to tell you how much I admire all you are striving to achieve. You are fine human beings with integrity and high ideals. You have shown me your love and have been patient with my advice, even when you don't plan to follow it! You have enriched my life and taught me many things. For that I am deeply grateful.

Love,

Mom

This client chose to share this with her children while she was alive as a way to let them know of the things that are important to her and give some insight as to how they want to live out the rest of their lives. Often these letters may be far more intimate. We encourage them to not be prescriptive, though. We like them to be values based.

There are a number of things that are covered in end-of-life planning. The discussions and then recording of what the client wants done goes a long way in preventing confusion or poor decisions when a family is ill-equipped to be making them. We have had some clients do a wonderful job of planning for their incapacitation through both product and communication; other clients have purposely put this off, knowing that their partner or children will have to interpret their wishes. This is not only unfair, it is traumatic.

Attempting to create an atmosphere to discuss these issues can be difficult, but we keep on trying to open these discussions. Some clients feel more comfortable with their attorney present, others may wish to have fewer people in the room. We want to try to find the best approach for the client in order to achieve the results that will most benefit them and their family.

Conclusion

We form the objective discussion for the client by using the broad categories of the WMI. We are revisiting these objectives regularly throughout the client relationship. The technical specifics tend to be established underneath these broad areas. Getting to the technical too early in the client relationship makes it unlikely that you will uncover the sentiment behind decisions. Without understanding these sentiments, the plan becomes your plan, not that of the client.

Notes

1. Thaler, Richard H., and Cass R. Sunstein. *Nudge—Improving Decisions about Health, Wealth, and Happiness.* New Haven: Yale University Press. 2008.
2. TIAA-CREF Institute: Research Summary—*Plan Investment Options and Participant Behavior;* June, 2006.
3. Gilbert, Daniel. *Stumbling on Happiness.* New York: Alfred A. Knopf.2006.
4. Harold and his wife Deena Katz have written far too many books for me to mention, but it doesn't really matter what you pick up that they wrote, you can bank on something that you can incorporate immediately into your practice.
5. I am not minimizing the importance of tax efficiency, I am simply saying that the degree is often incorrect. For example, with a twenty-five percent portfolio turnover, you may be delaying taxes by four years as compared with current mutual fund distributions. This is obviously an over-simplification.
6. Gardner, Daniel. *The Science of Fear.* New York: Dutton Adult. 2008.
7. Seligman, Martin E.P., PhD. *Authentic Happiness—Using the New Positive Psychology to Realize Your Potential for Lasting Fulfillment.* New York: Free Press. 2002.

CHAPTER 8

Scoring the Wealth Management Index

When we originally created the Wealth Management Index (WMI), we thought that the scoring feature would be the area that resonated most with clients. It would allow the client and the planner to co-evaluate the work that was being performed, the progress being made, and ultimately, the success of the relationship. Implementing the scoring process could be cumbersome, but we felt the value outweighed the work.

Fast forward 15 years. While I have heard from many practitioners who like using the scoring, we have generally found for our complex, higher-net-worth clients, that the scoring often got in the way of the work. For most clients, we track progress on specific objectives which we have set based on where we are in completing the task rather than rolling everything up into a final score.

For those clients with fewer moving targets, though, the scoring can be a good way to help clients understand the many areas in which work is being done. I also think that for smaller practices, the scoring creates a sense of scale that is less important in larger practices. By this I mean that the scoring of the components of the index directly shows clients the impact that you are having on their planning, keeps the wealth manager on track, and measures joint success that may help overcome any concerns that a practice is not big enough to handle the ongoing relationship.

I think the parallel that comprehensive wealth management has with medicine that I described in the original *Wealth Management Index* book still holds true today. The secrecy of medicine may apply to the black box that people try to present in their planning:

"This secrecy is rooted in the past, when medicine was quasi-religious, and flourishes today, when it is quasi-scientific. . . . Medical secrecy is comprehensible as the almost instinctive attempt of the profession to cushion itself against its major hazard—error. . . . it is perhaps the feeling that outsiders will never understand the full context of risk and contingency that makes colleagues so tight-lipped. . . As professionals, doctors claim mastery over a field of esoteric, and patients must defer to their expertise. The professional motto {sociologist Everest} Hughes points out is not the businessman's *Caveat Emptor* but *Credat Emptor*—'Let the taker believe in us.'"[1]

In a practice, we use all of our models as a way to represent the truth, but they are not the truth. A model is exactly that—an image. Models help clients relate to the probability of different things occurring throughout their wealth management relationship, but they can't account for all the possible variations that are present in complex adaptive systems. "The mathematics of financial models can be applied precisely, but the models are not at all precise in their application to the complex real world."[2] The WMI focuses on objectives and uses models to reach these objectives. Success is ongoing, measured regularly, and adaptive. A model could prove to be wrong, but the relationship may still be successful because of other areas covered in the index. For example, for the decade from 2000 to 2009, we did not reach our target returns against inflation, but because of setting aside cash for spending, portfolio rebalancing, and clients often making changes in their cash-flow decisions, our clients who retired on January 1, 2000, still had more money after living off their portfolios than with which they started. The model may have been inaccurate, but success still was realized.

The point of the index is to measure the things that can be measured and not those that can't.

Spreadsheet

The easiest way to score the index is by placing all the categories on an Excel spreadsheet using the percentages I lay out in the book. At times I get questions about modifying or changing these percentages. I believe that what we have created gives a very good picture of all the various components of wealth management and how they relate to each other.

For example, some of our clients have no debt, so they would receive a perfect score in that area. That should not be considered a problem, though, because it is reflective of a healthy balance sheet and lifestyle choices that allowed them to become debt free. They deserve credit for this area.

Another thing to pay attention to is that the total score represents the client success. It is not a number that can be compared to other clients. The more complicated a client's situation, often the lower the score. This usually means that there are so many varying objectives that need to be worked through during the course of a year, that you simply can't complete them all. This will result in a lower score than someone with a very simple situation where execution is less complicated.

Scoring is determined by how much you have explored and completed for each objective that you discussed. The highest score comes as you complete the objective. Completion can happen without any form of implementation. You may discuss something and then dismiss it, for example. As long as the issue was explored and a conclusion reached, then that is sufficient.

For example, if the objective is that the client wants to feel secure with the situation should they need in-home care, owning long-term care insurance is not the only way to achieve this security. One could dedicate investment assets that will be used for this need. One could sell their home to pay for long-term care costs. The key is to establish the objective, explore the possible solutions, and reach agreement on what is most appropriate.

The reason integration matters is also illustrated by how this long-term care decision flows through several categories. It minimally involves cash flow, investment, and estate planning. Dollars used to purchase a long-term care policy are those that can't be invested or spent elsewhere. Self-insuring using investments for long-term care may compromise the amount of money that is left to survivors or charities.

The WMI avoids the syndrome described in the parable of the blind men and the elephant, where each of the wise blind men is led to touch a different area of the elephant and describe it to the raja. Each blind man's reality is subject to the part of the elephant that they are touching. Without integration, so too is our wealth-management reality incomplete.

Notes

1. Gingold, Judith. "Adventures in Liposuction." *Atlantic Monthly*. March, 1996.
2. Fox, Justin. *The Myth of the Rational Market*. New York: Harper Business. 2009.

CHAPTER 9

Asset Protection (Preservation)

There are a lot of points for this area of the index simply because there are no second chances with many of these categories. This does not mean that there are a set of prescriptions for how to handle the components, but it does mean that each area needs to be carefully explored.

Asset protection is about keeping what you have. If an alien landed on earth and saw this area, they would probably be very surprised. Ideas here are often counterintuitive. Why would you put all of your assets in your partner's name? Why would you create a document that doesn't allow your life partner to own your share of the business should you die? Why would someone leave their partner out of their pension by taking a life-only option? On the surface, none of these things may make sense. But incorporated into a comprehensive wealth management strategy, each of them may be appropriate.

I would say that there is no single area for the index where my experiences through being in practice for more than 25 years have had a greater impact on me. This has turned the theoretical into the practical.

We have had several clients pass away, some suffer from prolonged health issues, have seen businesses break up or be sold, have had clients go through personal bankruptcy, and seen clients sued for malpractice and defamation. We can prepare our clients for many of these things, but may not be able to prevent them. Most important, though, is that we can walk with our clients as they experience these dramatic changes to what they thought their lives were going to look like as compared to what they, at least for a brief period of time, were becoming.

In all the years in my business, the personal client characteristic that has helped them deal most effectively in this area is resilience. How clients view what is happening has a tremendous impact on how they are able to handle it.

One of our clients was a high-end developer in Chicago who started as a carpenter. Through good work and good fortune, he built up a large business—developing several projects of multi-million-dollar homes. He had split his company into multiple entities such as development, repair, and remodeling. We were one of many influencers in his business, but not the primary ones. While he relied on us for guidance on a variety of issues—whether or not to bring on a partner, how to frame discussions with his children around money, which type of retirement plan was most appropriate—we were not able to be the key advisor on issues like personal guarantees on his projects. Success begot success and he felt bullet proof until the real estate market collapsed and he was left with a few lots and a couple spec homes that he could not unload.

He eventually went through both business and personal bankruptcy. His wife was his business partner and while things were falling apart, they turned toward each other rather than on each other. What struck me the most, though, was after a conversation about all that was happening in his life, he stopped and asked me how I was doing. This was someone's whose walls were collapsing on him and he still showed an interest in what was going on in my life.

Needless to say, this client's path has been altered forever, but he is not showing regret. He is proud of the homes he built and they serve as a long-standing reminder of his impact in the area. He says that he is now back doing the things that he really loved to do when he originally got into the field. We have now been enlisted to help him regroup, salvage his home, and move on with his life. And because of his resilience, he will move on. As F. Scott Fitzgerald said, "Vitality shows in not only the ability to persevere, but in the ability to start over."

One of the things that we need to realize with our planning is that as we explore areas with clients, they still may choose to do things on their own. This may lead to problems down the road, but often it does not. While we may not agree with choices that a client is making (for example, we tend to abhor personal guarantees and do our best to negotiate for their removal), we have to decide whether those decisions are ones that as advisors we cannot live with. We are militant about not working with clients who we question ethically, although we will bring up the areas of concern so that we can hear their explanation and provide ours. But clients who make business or personal decisions against our suggestions certainly have the right to do so. We won't work with them if they are making choices that we feel show a lack of confidence in our advice, but those that feel a different strategy may be better for them often lead to fertile discussions and strong relationships.

This preservation area is one where discussions tend to provide really valuable insight into who the client is and what they feel is important to them.

Percent of Index (25 Percent) for Asset Protection (Preservation)

	Percent of Asset Protection Scale	Total Index Weight
Have you articulated a life insurance philosophy?	34%	8.5%
What are your concerns regarding risks of large losses from medical, long-term care, property/ casualty, and personal or professional liability issues?	33%	8.25%
Have you defined and protected your business interests?	33%	8.25%
Total	100%	25%

Components

The three main questions are the basis for the objective setting. As objectives are set, then subcategories are used to track tangible goals and to-dos around each of these objectives. Throughout the book, I will be going through each broad objective and then the subcategories.

Have You Articulated a Life Insurance Philosophy?

"Life insurance is a fundamental pillar of risk management in financial planning; it provides the financial means to deal with the financial impact that a death can have on a family (or business, or charity)."[1] All of our clients have different feelings regarding life insurance. It is important to recognize these feelings so that when you prepare an objective analysis your approach allows the client to actually hear what you are presenting. We try to get a clear picture of what a client's experience has been with insurance in the past. We generally find three scenarios:

1. The client views their insurance agent as their trusted advisor. In this situation, we first like to talk about the relationship and what the advisor has done to earn such loyalty. We also explore what recent decisions or suggestions have occurred in this area. Our objective is not to replace the advisor, but to work with them once appropriate solutions have been determined. These solutions may result in a new sale, a change in composition of insurance, replacement of the coverage, or dropping insurance entirely. We have generally found that the insurance agents with whom we come in contact may be defensive at first, but when they are included in what we are trying to do, they work hard with us. When they don't operate cooperatively, it puts the client in a very awkward position. While we have the club of objectivity, we don't like to swing it unless the agent is very obstructive.

2. A client hates insurance. These clients feel either like they had been sold a bill of goods in the past, or have read enough in the popular press to have decided that insurance is a raw deal. For these types of clients, we focus on the objectives that they are trying to accomplish and discuss alternative solutions for meeting them. If insurance is unnecessary, great. If it is needed, then we can go into the various kinds of insurance and the cost-benefit analysis for each. If insurance is necessary, these people do not typically have a life insurance agent, so we will either bring in a person with whom we are comfortable or buy it online.

3. A client has no feelings one way or another. For this client, we can focus on the analysis and create a solution that we think is a best fit for them.

Subcategories for have you articulated a life insurance philosophy?

	Percent of Question	Percent of Category	Percent of Index
111 Assess the living and liquidity needs of survivors and dependants	60	20.4	5.1
112 Assess the possibilities of living benefits from existing insurance	10	3.4	0.85
113 Analyze the strategy of maximizing pension income through life insurance	10	3.4	0.85
114 Assess estate tax wealth-replacement needs and wishes	20	6.8	1.7
Total	100	34	8.5

Assess the living and liquidity needs of survivors and dependants—5.1 percent

If an objective is that "I would like to be sure that my partner does not have to change her lifestyle should something happen to me", then the next step is to get a better understanding of how to evaluate this. This analysis is not cut and dried, though. When we are trying to understand the factors to consider in this type of analysis, there are a number of considerations, including:

- What is the amount of spending that needs to be replaced?
- What is the length of time for which you wish to replace this spending?
- What are the potential future sources of income that should be included in an analysis?
- What are expected real-rate-of-return objectives from the portfolio?
- What are the total assets available to meet these needs?
- How much life insurance is currently held and how is it being held?
- What are the considerations with regard to flexibility of these assets?
- What are the tax considerations or changes that would influence needs?
- What are the timing or liquidity considerations for particular assets?
- What are the costs that would be expected to change?
- What would be an acceptable range of outcomes?

Once these questions have been fully explored, then we can go deeper into the analysis and offer potential solutions. These questions are critical to understand. For example, the bulk of the portfolio for many of our physician clients is in their retirement plans. While it may seem obvious, we need to include the tax effect of the money coming out of those plans. In other words, those assets are worth far less to the client than already-taxed assets. As part of our analysis, we include a ratio of retirement plan assets as a percentage of total investment assets.

Another area where we have seen wild swings is with regard to stock options. When accounting for stock options in an analysis, it is appropriate to use a discount factor. The discount needs to incorporate the tax consequences as well as the leverage involved. Executive clients often see their insurance needs change both dramatically and frequently because of the changes in the values of their options. This is a clear example where ongoing reviews yield different results. If insurance is needed for this type of situation, we will often ladder different term insurance policies (5-year, 10-year, and 15-year) with the expectation that assets will replace the need for insurance.

Our general modeling involves Monte Carlo simulations to determine ranges of outcomes.[2] As you know, Monte Carlo simulations provide *guidance* for computations when you want to use random sampling. While this type of modeling is certainly better than the old average return analysis that we used to do, it is still very dependent upon inputs and interpretations. Monte Carlo's results are also described in confidence levels. Explaining to a client that we have a level of confidence of 85 percent is more difficult than being an oracle of exactness.

We end up with a form of survivorship needs analysis that shows the client whether they may want to increase or decrease their life insurance. Once we reach agreement on the insurance need, we then can solve for what type of insurance to be held in what type of vehicle. If a client has an agent, we will work with them. If not, we will direct an agent with whom we are comfortable to put together proposals. If there is a need that we wish to fund with permanent insurance, we will request ledgers for us to evaluate. If insurance needs to be bought and an online product is not the right product, we will call in the agent to write the policy. Since we are fee-only, they collect the commissions from this policy.[3]

Figures 9.1 and 9.2 show how we go through this with the client.

FIGURE 9.1   Life Needs Analysis—Spending.

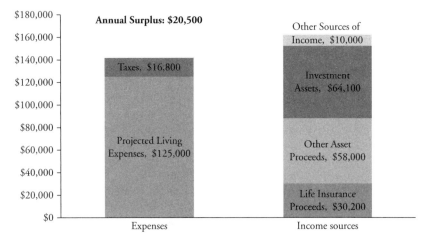

Client & Co-client
Life Needs Analysis
July 7, 2010

Projected Expenses & Income Sources

FIGURE 9.2 Life Insurance Need—Income Replacement.

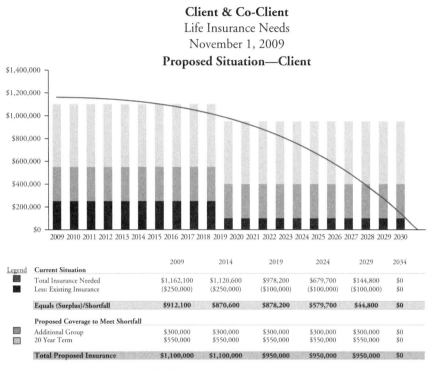

Client & Co-Client
Life Insurance Needs
November 1, 2009
Proposed Situation—Client

Legend	Current Situation	2009	2014	2019	2024	2029	2034
■	Total Insurance Needed	$1,162,100	$1,120,600	$978,200	$679,700	$144,800	$0
■	Less: Existing Insurance	($250,000)	($250,000)	($100,000)	($100,000)	($100,000)	$0
	Equals (Surplus)/Shortfall	**$912,100**	**$870,600**	**$878,200**	**$579,700**	**$44,800**	**$0**
	Proposed Coverage to Meet Shortfall						
▨	Additional Group	$300,000	$300,000	$300,000	$300,000	$300,000	$0
▨	20 Year Term	$550,000	$550,000	$550,000	$550,000	$550,000	$0
	Total Proposed Insurance	**$1,100,000**	**$1,100,000**	**$950,000**	**$950,000**	**$950,000**	**$0**

Assess the possibilities of living benefits from existing life insurance—0.85 percent

If a client does not have a need for life insurance based on our analysis, yet has existing policies in place, it does not automatically mean that we would simply surrender the policies and take the cash. There are several items to consider for this analysis:

- What is the internal rate of return on the existing policy?
- What type of policy is this?
- What is the actual cost of insurance on this policy?
- What are the opportunities for selling this policy in a secondary market?
- What is the cost basis of this policy?
- What features might this policy possess that would make it more attractive as a living benefit?
- What things may change in the client's situation that would cause us to regret surrendering the policy?
- Is it reasonable for adult children or a charity to take over this policy and are they interested?

What is the internal rate of return on the existing policy?

While we seldom suggest owning cash value life insurance, there are many reasons to stick with existing policies. The first step is analyzing what the policy is returning. This is not a simple calculation because there are so many different variables. For example, the actual amount of insurance (amount at risk) decreases as the cash value increases (unless there is a rider that entitles the policy owner to both). The premiums paid are allocated to insurance and savings. Dividends may vary. A starting point is to understand the hard costs of the policy—administrative expenses, cost of insurance, and various loads—which can give you a sense of the hurdle rate that the return must overcome. A helpful tool to use for this analysis is the web site www.policypricingcalculator.com.

If the evaluation of the policy leads you to decide to keep it, the review of the insurance still needs to occur annually because of the variables impacting return.

What type of policy is this?

Whole life and universal life (and all of its derivatives) are very different animals. A whole life policy is usually less expensive and less flexible than a universal life. The most common type of whole life policy—"continuous premium/straight life—offers the greatest amount of permanent death protection and the least amount of savings per premium dollar."[4] These are our preferred policies for permanent needs.

Universal life policies have a variety of features as well as more expense. These features may allow the client to increase or decrease their death benefits or their premiums, or may have cash value buildup occur through a regular crediting rate or through investment choices. This flexibility has a price, though, and these types of policies, if kept, must be regularly reviewed. We are less inclined to keep these policies simply because the costs tend to be too high relative to their ongoing value.

What is the actual cost of insurance on this policy?

This is an interesting question to ask. Remember, every year that you live, your expected life is longer than it was the previous year. According to the National Association of Insurance Commissioners 2001 Standard Ordinary Mortality Table, my life expectancy at 52 would be 27.4 years (or living to 79.4), but my life expectancy at 53 would be 26.52 years (or living to 79.52). This is obvious; someone in the age 52 pool died, but it wasn't me, so since I made it to 53, I am expected to live a tad bit longer.

This means that depending on the policy you are reviewing, a client may actually have a lower cost of insurance on a new policy than their existing one. That is why understanding those costs are so important. If you could do a tax-free exchange (1035) into a new life insurance policy with lower insurance costs, everything being equal, more money would be available to flow toward the cash value. The difference in mortality between age 52 and 62 is more pronounced than comparing age 52 to 53. At 62, I am expected to live another 19.06 years (or to age 81.06). While there are other costs with new policies that need to be included, understanding the cost of insurance may make changing policies desirable.

What are the opportunities for selling this policy in the secondary market?
While the validation of viatical settlements originally occurred in the 1980s with AIDS patients and devolved into the somewhat creepy stranger-owned life insurance, there is still a reasonable place to decide whether selling an existing policy into a secondary market is more attractive than simply surrendering a policy. While there are certainly some disadvantages (such as a potential reduction in Medicaid, a potential inability to purchase more insurance on your life at a later date, or lack of creditor protection) it still makes sense to explore the potential of this path. The Viatical & Life Settlement Association of America (www.viatical.org) is the first place to look if you are interested in pursuing this. By the way, you can do this on term policies as well as cash value ones.

What is the cost basis of this policy?
This is important because if a policy is simply surrendered, the owner pays ordinary income tax on the gain on the policy. But it is also important if you have a loss on the policy. "A 1035 exchange lets you defer paying income taxes on the gain {between moving the cash value of an insurance policy into an annuity}. What if you have a loss; that is, what if the surrender value of the policy is less than the total premiums that you've paid? Losses on life insurance policies are generally non-deductible, but—here's the trick—in a 1035 exchange the cost basis of the life insurance policy carries over to the annuity, and it can then be used to avoid paying income tax on future gains in the annuity."[5] We usually move dollars into low-cost variable annuity providers such as Vanguard or TIAA-CREF if we wish to make this exchange.

What features may this policy possess that may make it more attractive as a living benefit?
Depending on the policy and its riders, in addition to things like supplemental income (which must be measured against taking the money out of the policy and investing it in other vehicles), a policy may provide protection from

disability, long-term care (LTC) benefits, and business-planning benefits. In general, I would rather have my disability protection through a disability insurance policy and my long-term care through self-insurance or a suitable LTC policy, but it still makes sense to evaluate whether keeping the policy can reasonably handle these issues.

What things may change in the client's situation that would cause us to regret surrendering this policy?
We typically want our clients to get to a place where they have enough assets that their only need for life insurance may be for estate-planning purposes. But, lives change for clients. Life insurance creates an estate when you don't have one, so if a client suffered severe business losses and wanted to have an estate, their insurance may provide them with that. Divorce may cause a dramatic reduction in a client's estate and life insurance may provide assurances for new partners. Discussing what may change that would make the client have second thoughts helps solidify whatever decision is finally made.

Is it reasonable for adult children or a charity to take over this policy and are they interested?
Even if the client no longer wishes to keep on paying for their life insurance, maybe their beneficiaries would. While there may be gift, tax, and estate-planning considerations, the children may wish to take over ownership of the policies. These transactions have the benefit of removing the asset from the estate (if you gift the policy to them and live for three years) and at least starting the family discussion about estate planning. The obvious disadvantages of this are that the children's financial interest is not aligned with the client's immortality interest, especially if the policy requires ongoing premium payments.

Gifting the policy to a charity may be another way to dispense with the policy, get a nice tax deduction, and leverage the client's charitable intentions. The client can continue to pay policy premiums to this gifted policy and deduct those ongoing costs.

Analyze the strategy of maximizing pension income through life insurance—0.85 percent

Clients who have pensions need to decide what type of pension payout to take. The first decision may be between choosing a lump sum and choosing an annuity. We have helped clients choose either option depending on the annuity to be paid as compared with the lump sum to be distributed. While we have usually chosen the lump sum, we actually often went with an annuity option in the late 1980s because the expected pay out was so much larger than it was with the lump sum.

If the annuity is chosen, then the client needs to decide whether it would pay only on the client's life or that of the client and his or her partner. Any decision other than a life-only option is essentially an insurance decision. By accepting a joint-and-survivor option, the reduction in the pension benefit is an insurance policy in case the client predeceases their partner. This permanent reduction in monthly benefit is especially troubling if the non-pension receiving spouse is in poor health.

Most of the time, the pension-maximization strategy has not worked. The cost of the insurance is often too high when compared to the reduction in benefit. This analysis is relatively easy to perform, but again there are factors that don't make it a complete slam dunk. Every year the client lives, the need for insurance should drop because the assets needed to provide a lifestyle for their partner is reduced. This is almost impossible to replicate with low-cost insurance. Also, every model has to assume a certain investment rate and spend down of the insurance assets over the life of the survivor. If you are adaptive in your modeling (meaning that you decrease expected future returns after a period of strong returns or increase them after a period of weak ones), it is again difficult to find equilibrium for these insurance needs.

Assess estate tax wealth replacement needs and wishes—1.7 percent

This is an area where behavioral finance's concept of loss aversion holds clients hostage. The concept of having their estate shrink by paying taxes can be so repulsive that it creates an insurance need where no real financial need may exist.

This is also an area that is closely integrated with estate planning, because the use of asset transference, various trusts, and charitable planning influences the outcomes in this space.

We start with developing goals around broad areas to try to understand the assets needed to fund basic lifestyle, family wealth transfer, lifestyle enhancements, philanthropy, and a margin of safety. Once we understand what these amounts represent, we can determine whether a wealth replacement plan is necessary. For many clients with estates under $20 million, between asset growth freezing through Grantor Retained Annuity Trusts (GRATs) or intentionally defective trusts, gifting, and philanthropy, we can come to a place where we don't need wealth replacement. But similar to long-term care decisions, the choice is often an emotional, not financial, one.

Also, wealth replacement needs vary by state. If a client lives in a state with an estate tax, different planning may be required. If a client switches residency, then changes may need to be made.

What Are Your Concerns Regarding Risks of Large Losses from Medical, Long-Term Care, Property/Casualty, and Personal or Professional Liability Issues?

This general category is our catastrophe-planning space. While many of us are not experts in property/casualty issues, we still need to review these areas for our clients. When you think about the work that we do, avoiding financial ruin from unrecoverable risks may be the most important and least explored area in our wealth management continuum of services. We spend countless resources and hours trying to manage fat-tail risk in investing and virtually ignore it in the rest of wealth management.

Unfortunately, we have seen a number of disasters ranging from 9/11 to Katrina to Japan's earthquake and tsunami. These tragedies help create a setting in which this area can be discussed.

In working through the various issues, one of our key drivers is what are we insuring against. We want to self-insure as much as reasonable, which means that we will typically suggest greater insurance coupled with higher deductibles. The financial factors that come into play are simply the probability of an event, the consequences if it were to occur, and the costs in protecting against it.

There are emotional costs as well. We see this particularly in the long-term care area where clients are sometimes making decisions on in-home care based on the costs of such services as opposed to the needs. Several of our clients have become the primary care giver for their spouse with Alzheimer's. The cost of full-time care may be extraordinary, and the psychic cost of letting someone else take care of your partner is even more so. The Family Caregiver Alliance says, "Alzheimer's disease is often called a family disease because the chronic stress of watching a loved one slowly decline impacts everyone." This situation often leads to very poor financial decisions which possibly could be avoided if the client had insurance. If the cost of care was removed from the equation, the resultant decision could be different.

Review medical insurance including liability limits, co-pays, Medicare, and COBRA—1.65 percent

I can't tell you the number of times that I have heard clients say that they are only continuing to work because of health insurance. When we are looking at this area, we have a variety of things that we explore, including:

- Cost
- Extent of coverage

Subcategories for what are your concerns regarding risks of large losses from medical, long-term care, property/casualty, and personal or professional liability issues?

	Percent of Question	Percent of Category	Percent of Index
121 Review medical insurance including liability limits, co-pays, Medicare, and COBRA	20	6.6	1.65
122 Understand feelings regarding long-term care and evaluate needs	20	6.6	1.65
123 Determine amount of self-funding on property/casualty deductibles and limits	10	3.3	0.825
124 Understand personal liability needs	10	3.3	0.825
125 Review professional liability limits and appropriate tail insurance	20	6.6	1.65
126 Review benefits and drawbacks of asset transference and retitling for long-term care or liability considerations	20	6.6	1.65
Total	100	33	8.25

- Breadth of in-network service providers
- Specific plan benefits
- Quality of customer service
- Guaranteed renewable, non-cancellable
- Co-insurance, deductibles, and out-of-pocket maximums
- High-deductible versus low-deductible plans

These various issues are weighed differently by each client. As we all know, there are significant changes that are going to continue to occur in this area. Most recently, we have seen more of our clients (and their companies) shift to high-deductible plans through Health Savings Accounts (HASs).

These plans are interesting because they allow clients to invest their money (although the investment choices are typically not terrific) and then turn in their receipts for reimbursement. There is no time limit for this reimbursement, though. This means that clients can pay for their medical expenses out of pocket, save their receipts, let their accounts grow tax-deferred, and apply for reimbursement at a later date if they need to.

Figure 9.3 shows a spreadsheet that we use to perform this analysis.

Another key area that needs to be explored in determining everything from Medicare supplement policies to general health insurance policies is which medications will be covered. This may change year to year, thereby necessitating ongoing reviews.

Clients on Medicare have a number of options available to them for supplemental coverage. When we evaluate this, we compare premiums, deductibles, co-pays and co-insurance, coverage gaps, and catastrophic coverage to find the most appropriate solution.

We usually recommend waiting to sign up for Medicare Part B if a spouse is working and the other spouse is entitled to health coverage through their spouse's union or employer. The decision may be different for companies with less than 20 employees. For these situations, choosing Medicare Part B is often appropriate. The Department of Health and Human Services has an excellent reference brochure entitled *Medicare and Other Health Benefits: Your Guide to Who Pays First*. We also use the Social Security Administration's *Medicare Premiums: Rules for Higher-Income Beneficiaries*.

Clients are often concerned whether their pre-existing conditions will preclude them from getting health insurance. In Minnesota, we have a very

FIGURE 9.3   HAS vs. Current

Client & Co-client
Health Insurance Comparison
July 7, 2010

Scenario	Cost of Current Plan	Net Cost of Options Blue	Savings Using Options Blue
1) All family members reach their max out-of-pocket costs.	$12,097	$6,799	$5,298
2) Only one family member maximizes their out-of-pocket medical expenses.	$11,226	$6,799	$4,427
3) No one in the family incurs any medical expenses.	$9,976	$1,649	$8,327

good state-sponsored plan for those who have been rejected by private carriers. While these state plans may be subjected to the vagaries of state finances, the fears clients have are usually not matched by the reality of possibilities available to them.

Understand feelings regarding long-term care and evaluate needs—1.65 percent

One of our well-heeled clients could clearly support herself should she need extensive long-term care. Despite the fact that her assets would support almost any in-home health or long-term care situation, she found herself being extremely cautious with how she spent her money. We could not prove to her that she was fine. We finally went ahead and proposed long-term care insurance for her, which she bought, so that she could better enjoy her life. The decisions around long-term care issues are complex, emotional, and often gray.

According to a 2010 Genworth study, the median annual rate for private nursing home costs was more than $75,000. Since most of our clients don't choose median facilities or would rather opt for in-home care wherever possible, their costs are significantly more. More important, these costs had an annual compounded growth rate of 8 percent over the previous five years. According to the Center for Retirement Research at Boston College, "long-term care is the major uninsured expense for most retirees."[6]

The long-term care analysis is more or less a present-value calculation of the costs of insurance, combined with a confidence factor that would reflect the fact that a client may be paying for something that they will never use. The costs for even in-force policies may increase over time as long as the costs increase for the entire group. Since this is an area that seems almost impossible to actuarially get correct, we have continued to see increasing policy costs. We tend to like shared-care plans (where the policy can be used between the couple for whichever person needs it). If feasible, we also like to quick pay policies because of our expectation that rates will increase. Since most of our clients can afford to pay something for their long-term care, we also don't usually fully insure the benefit (unless the client emphatically asks to do so). We'll reduce the number of years, the elimination period (typically 90 days), or the monthly benefit. Lastly, we always recommend a 5 percent compound inflation adjustment. The risks in a quick-pay approach are that health care reform legislation could legislate certain protections that make private pay less necessary. (See Figure 9.4.)

FIGURE 9.4   Long-Term Care Analysis.

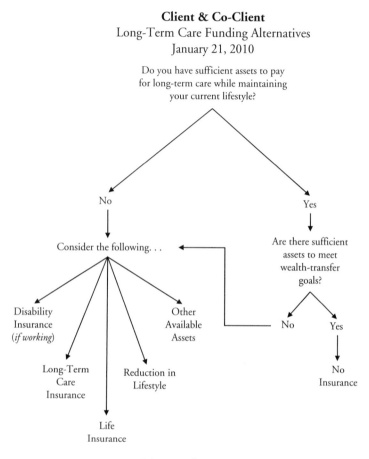

Client & Co-Client
Long-Term Care Funding Alternatives
January 21, 2010

Do you have sufficient assets to pay
for long-term care while maintaining
your current lifestyle?

No   Yes

Consider the following. . .   Are there sufficient
assets to meet
wealth-transfer
goals?

Disability   Other
Insurance   Available   No   Yes
(*if working*)   Assets

Long-Term   No
Care   Reduction in   Insurance
Insurance   Lifestyle

Life
Insurance

Other Considerations
(specific to client)
-Use of Excluded Assets (ie. Sale of Business)
-Inheritance

There are so many psychological issues regarding aging, that managing the financial aspects of this may be the least of our concerns. What is our role as wealth managers for our aging clients?

We have found that we need to help our clients in a whole host of areas ranging from helping them make decisions regarding in-home care and finding vendors (social workers and providers) for them to work with, finding assistance for them as they eventually pack up their homes and move into facilities, and working with attorneys for asset gifting and transference choices, in addition to recommending self-insurance or long-term care insurance.

There are additional life insurance and annuity products for long-term care which we consider in certain situations—in particular for those who may have underwriting issues on a regular policy.

Another key area around which discussions must take place are the attempts to become Medicaid eligible. This area is going to continue to change, but the decision to transfer assets to qualify for Medicaid should not be taken lightly. While our clients are usually not in a position to do this, we often have the discussion with them with regard to their parents. As we talk with our clients about this, some of the conversations include:

- How much of your investments are you willing to spend to provide for your care?
- Who should pay for policies that are to protect an inheritance?
- How do you feel about moving dollars out of your control today for something that may never be needed?
- Are you comfortable with relying on the state for your care?
- Have you considered the tax aspects of asset transference?
- Do you feel that these strategies are consistent with your values?

We also consider having family meetings with children as parents are making these care decisions. One of the most difficult things that we encounter is when a client is showing the early stages of dementia and we need to prepare them for what will be happening next. While some of this gets covered in the estate-planning area, a key responsibility for us is setting the stage for them to recognize that they may not be able to live independently forever and to help them explore appropriate facilities.

One of our clients handled this beautifully. She was in her late 70s and sharp as a tack. She decided that she didn't know how long she would stay this way, so she decided to sell her Florida residence and move into a facility in Minnesota so that she could be close to her kids. She spent several months looking at various options and chose one that fit her financially as well as socially. She made the move on her own terms, thereby alleviating much of the angst that comes with being forced into decisions.

Determine amount of self-funding on property/casualty deductibles and limits—0.825 percent and Understand personal liability needs—0.825 percent

We annually conduct a thorough review of property/casualty insurance (P&C). For much of this area, we partner with local P&C agents who work with products suitable for our client base. There are a number of circumstances where monitoring this coverage is vital and it may open up the need for new insurance.

- Clients with household help may require worker's comp insurance.
- Clients who have multiple properties need to be aware of the various issues such as natural disasters that may impact each property differently.
- Clients with pets may have higher liability concerns.
- Clients with art, jewelry, or collectibles need to make decisions regarding self-insuring.
- Clients may have properties that have higher replacement costs because of unique structural considerations.
- Clients who serve on boards may need to be sure that they have appropriate Director's and Officer's liability coverage.

We like to manage costs through a deductible analysis. Since our belief is that insurance should cover the things that you can't afford to cover on your own, we are predisposed to carrying large amounts of liability insurance through umbrella policies, but increase deductibles on most other coverage to help control costs. We run a payback comparison which depicts how long you would need to go before filing a claim in order to justify the increased deductible as shown in Figure 9.5. Higher deductibles also tend to be more realistic because clients are disinclined to file smaller claims and risk their costs rising or jeopardizing their renewal.

We also try to manage car insurance costs through being attentive as to whether collision insurance is needed, who the primary drivers on the cars are, what city should a vehicle be registered in, and when can coverage be lifted for those who have children off in college.

Some of our clients have fairly high profiles and many are in positions whereby they may be asked for comments related to people or issues. Through the course of their work, lawsuits or liability resulting from these comments may be covered by their employer (see Figure 9.6). One of our clients was sued for defamation for a quote regarding a person who had come to their organization on a private matter. For this client, their homeowner's insurance covered the cost of the lawsuit. Unfortunately, their carrier made the client settle even though they did not feel that what they did was wrong.

Review professional liability limits and appropriate tail insurance—1.65 percent

We rate this area relatively high on the index because the costs can be so high if the client is not appropriately covered. Roughly a third of our clients are physicians, so this is an area that impacts their operational costs as well as

FIGURE 9.5   P&C Deductible Comparison.

Client & Co-Client
Property & Casualty Deductible Comparison
May 14, 2008

Recommendation:

1) Increase the Wind & Hail and Other Perils deductible on your home to *$2,500* for an annual premium of *$921*. This will result in an annual premium savings of $684, and will help to protect against making small claims.
2) Increase the Comprehensive and Collision deductibles on the 1999 Camry and 2001 Avalon to *$1,000* for an annual premium of *$576 and $590* respectively. This will provide for a combined annual premium savings of *$340*, and will help to protect against making small claims.
3) Increase your Umbrella policy limit from $1,000,000 to *$2,000,000* for an annual premium of *$263* through Western National Mutual. We also recommend that you add Underinsured and Uninsured Motorist coverage up to $1,000,000 to your Umbrella policy. This would increase your Umbrella premium to *$453*. To add the UM/UIM coverage, you will have to change companies on the Umbrella only, to one that offers this type of coverage. The quote provided is through Navigator Insurance Company (A.M. Best rating of A). This will help to more adequately protect your net worth.

Property	Current Coverage		Proposed Coverage[1]		Payback Period in Years	Annual Premium Savings
			Premium	$1,040	1.33	$565
Home	Premium	$1,605	Deductible	$1,000		
	Deductible	$250	Premium	$921	3.29	$684
			Deductible	$2,500		
			Premium	$630	3.64	$110
1999 Camry	Premium	$740	Deductible	$500		
	Deductible	$100	Premium	$576	5.49	$164
			Deductible	$1,000		
			Premium	$650	3.45	$116
2001 Avalon	Premium	$766	Deductible	$500		
	Deductible	$100	Premium	$590	5.11	$176
			Deductible	$1,000		
			Premium[2]	$453	N/A	($303)
Umbrella	Premium	$150	Limit	$2,000,000		
	Limit	$1,000,000	Premium	$0	N/A	$0
			Limit	$0		
Total Cost	***$3,261***		***$2,540***		***N/A***	***$721***

[1] *Quotes received 8/25/05 from ABC Insurance Agency, Inc.*
[2] *The $2,000,000 Umbrella quote includes Uninsured/Underinsured coverage extended to the Umbrella for $1,000,000 through a company called Navigator. Underinsured/Uninsured Motorist coverage under the Umbrella is not available through Western National Mutual.*

FIGURE 9.6   P&C Profile.

Client & Co-Client
Property & Casualty Insurance Summary
September 21, 2010

Insurance Company: Bankers Standard Insurance Company
Agent: XYZ Private Client Group
Coverage Dates: 8/23/07 – 8/23/08

Policy	Coverage Highlights	Deductible	Annual Premium
Homeowners:[1] 9061 Gateway Lane	Dwelling: $500,000 Other Structures: $50,000 Personal Property: $265,200 Liability: $500,000	$2,500	$1,386
Homeowners: Cabin	Dwelling: $331,500 Other Structures: $66,300 Personal Property: $265,200 Liability: $250,000	$2,500	$1,124
Homeowners: 2nd Home	Dwelling: $331,500 Other Structures: $66,300 Personal Property: $265,200 Liability: $250,000	$2,500	$1,124
Personal Articles	Coverage Amount: $108,000	$0	$647
Auto	Liability: $500,000[2] Property Damage: $500,000 Un/Underinsured Motorist: $500,000[3]	Comp.: $1,000 Collision: $1,000	$4,074
Auto	Liability: $250,000 Property Damage: $500,000 Un/Underinsured Motorist: $250,000[3]	Comp.: $500 Collision: $500	$1,291
Marine[4]	Liability: $500,000 Property Damage: $500,000 Un/Underinsured Motorist: $500,000	Comp.: $1,000 Collision: $1,000	$466
Marine	Liability: $250,000 Property Damage: $500,000 Un/Underinsured Motorist: $250,000	Comp.: $500 Collision: $500	$466
ATV/Snowmobile	Liability: $500,000 Property Damage: $500,000 Un/Underinsured Motorist: $500,000	Comp.: $500 Collision: $500	$190
Umbrella	Liability: $1,000,000	$0	$462
		TOTAL	**$11,230**

The replacement coverage on the homeowner's policy is not at an adequate level.

Notes:
[1] Fraud coverage on the homeowner's insurance of $15,000
[2] Personal Injury Protection on the auto policies of $20,000
[3] Uninsured/Underinsured motorist coverage is not extended to the umbrella policy
[4] $1,000 limit on the boat trailer

their retirement plans. Depending on the subspecialty and where they work, liability costs can represent a disproportionately high cost. Insuring that they have adequate coverage once they retire (through a tail) also needs to be reviewed. One of our clients took a position with a clinic after leaving their other group as a way to gain liability insurance and a tail that would cover their previous work as well (some will not do so).

We have had clients sued who are renowned in their field. The resulting emotions from these accusations, whether founded or not, would be almost impossible to bear if the lawsuits broke them financially.

These issues are certainly not limited to doctors, though. For example, the costs of our own errors and omissions insurance (E&O) have gone up considerably over the years, even though we have never had a claim. The Madoffs of the world cause all of us to feel the pain, no matter how well run and upstanding our practices are. While the annual costs of the coverage may seem untenable, the consequences of not being covered and having something happen are far worse.

Review benefits and drawbacks of asset transference and retitling for long-term care or liability decisions—1.65 percent

Your physician client retires and you immediately roll over his or her profit-sharing plan into a self-directed Individual Retirement Account (IRA). Not so fast, buster. You may be giving up some asset protection in doing so.

When we explore the need for asset protection with our clients, we often start with the most basic approaches—we title assets in the name of the spouse least vulnerable to lawsuits, we review their insurances to determine whether their coverage is appropriate, and we try to be sure that they are operating under an appropriate business umbrella. For clients with adult children that they wish to help and are financially able to do so, we encourage them to make either outright gifts or gifts into irrevocable trusts.

There are some assets that in certain states may be judgment proof (such as life insurance or annuities). But choosing these investments for asset protection purposes creates a layer of fees and compromises flexibility.

For those clients who still feel a need to do more (and frankly, we have found this to be relatively few), establishing a properly constructed and funded family limited partnership can offer more advantages. Under the provisions of the Uniform Limited Partnership Act, *a creditor of a partner cannot reach into the partnership and take specific partnership assets.*[7]

There are many costs with asset-protection strategies beyond the legal fees in setting them up. Additional entities make life harder. Think about all the unfunded revocable trusts that you have seen or those established where the client dies and there are still assets that sit outside the trust. And revocable trusts are relatively easy. As you increase complexity, you increase noncompliance.

There are also psychic costs to asset transference. These entities encumber how we operate. It doesn't seem like a big deal, but they are a statement that a client is vulnerable, whether they really are or are not. I am not saying that these ideas should be automatically rejected. I am saying that the costs of these strategies should be carefully considered.

Have You Defined and Protected Your Business Interests?

Clients have a wide variety of business interests—everything from the small manufacturing company, to the building that houses their practice, to the endoscopy centers that are a separate part of a physician's practice, to a second home that they rent out for a few days a year.

For this part of the index, we want to thoroughly review all the potential business interests clients may have and decide how they should be structured. We also want to look at their governance. And we want to be certain that these interests have appropriate protections in place should anything go wrong.

Subcategories for have you defined and protected your business interests?

	Percent of Question	Percent of Category	Percent of Index
131 Evaluate business structure	10	3.3	0.825
132 Determine business valuation and develop succession plan	30	9.9	2.475
133 Establish/review buy/sell and business continuation agreements	20	6.6	1.65
134 Determine needs due to disability	20	6.6	1.65
135 Establish appropriate funding mechanisms for buy-out upon death	20	6.6	1.65
Total	100	33	8.25

Evaluate business structure—0.825 percent

There are many types of business structures—C and S corporations, sole proprietorships, partnerships, and limited liability corporations (LLCs) and partnerships (LLPs). Many years ago, almost all of our clients were either S corporations or personal service corporations. Today, most people are choosing limited liability partnerships or corporations because of increased flexibility with regard to ownership, ease of liquidation, and a general protection from personal liability. Essentially, with an LLC, you get to make an initial decision with how you want to be taxed (individual, partnership, C-corporation, or S-corporation).

Generally speaking, being taxed like an S-corporation is best for companies that are turning a profit and you wish to exert control over how much should be salary and how much should be dividends. Being taxed like a partnership is often the best when you are operating a business that will have losses (for example, the initial years of owning your building). Once these losses have subsided, you could then relatively easily choose to flip it into an S corporation for tax purposes. Different states may treat these differently, so when giving advice to clients with out-of-state corporations, be sure to get help from an expert in the state in which the entity will exist.

LLCs provide more flexibility than S-corporations with regard to ownership and management, as well as a better ability to non-proportionally distribute profits. You also want to consider structure for asset-protection purposes. Appropriate structure may provide another layer of protection, although it does not guarantee it.

Determine business valuation and develop succession plan—2.475 percent

This particular area scores so high on the index because any client whose wealth is tied up in their corporation will need ongoing succession planning. We worked with a manufacturing client of ours for more than 15 years on their succession plan. They were continuing to try to create the next level of ownership for people who had no entrepreneurial energies and little interest in paying for their share in the company.

Instead, we were eventually able to work on a stock appreciation rights transaction that kept the employees tied to the organization, but resulted in the clients paying capital gains on the sale of the business while the employees paid ordinary income. When the sale transaction to a strategic buyer took place, the key employees were retained with employment agreements, while our clients kept an interest in the real estate (for cash-flow purposes) and walked away with more after-tax money than if they had internally sold the business to those unwilling buyers rather than the strategic buyer.

In other cases, taking less money for selling internally is appropriate. With our own company, we are setting up for internal sales. One of my friends in the business was aghast that we may take less for the company than if we sold externally. He asked me whether I would sell my house to him for only 70 percent of what it was worth (this was before the real estate crash). I told him that I wouldn't sell it to him for that, but I may be willing to sell it to my family. There is not a right or wrong perspective, but tradeoffs exist either way.

We have had clients who have sold businesses to financial, rather than strategic, buyers and they continue to stay working. They also take a small position in the fund that the buyer has put together. For one of our clients, they stayed with the transaction for two different sales.

Succession planning discussions are both intimate and challenging. Most clients feel that their business is worth more than it really is. Many clients have a hard time understanding why they often won't have as much disposable income from their after-sale invested money than they did from the business. Clients can underestimate the amount of risk that they are taking on earn-out sales and over-estimate the desires of the next generation to take on the business. Most important, if clients stay on, they have a difficult time seeing their successful company run so differently from the way that they ran it. Loss of control, loss of significance, and grief all come into play on the sale of businesses. Yet we have also had clients who have experienced complete validation and bliss from their sales. Preparing in advance for these feelings is where we earn our keep.

Valuing the business means more than simply fulfilling the requirement of the buy/sell. Depending on the scope and scale of the company, a business valuation prepares the client for what their future will look like should they sell the business. It lets clients deal realistically with whether this is a reasonable alternative. It can also light a fire under a client to create appropriate systems and structure so that the company has value. Outside valuation consultants and investment bankers can serve as valuable resources for this requirement.

Establish/review buy/sell and business continuation agreements—1.65 percent

It took us several years to write our buy/sell. We discussed what would happen if after hearing that one of the partners wanted to quit, another one threw their chips in. We looked at the roles that we serve and how my public role would make it potentially easier for me to start a wealth-management business someplace else. We talked about how a sale of the business would create economic security for the larger shareholders but not for the smaller ones.

We spent a long time discussing what happens in the event of a disability where we are able to work, but not full time, or we don't know when we will be able to come back to work.

A buy/sell is drafted when everything is wonderful, with the hope and expectation that things will stay that way. A functional buy/sell will allow for an orderly transition of the business between partners who want the best for each other and the company.

But things can often turn ugly. One of our clients had a fantastic business and relationship with the founder/majority shareholder until the founder's child came into the business. This caused all kinds of friction. Not only did it create a financial burden, but the minority shareholder no longer felt like the favorite son—because he wasn't. While this was going on, the business started to have some problems. Personal guarantees were joint and several, so the founder was on the hook for everything should things go belly up.

The minority shareholder wanted to leave and was fighting everything from the business valuation to the non-compete agreement. Legal fees soared into the hundreds of thousands—money that went to neither party. Eventually, things became completely personal; both were willing to go nuclear to keep the other person from getting what they felt they deserved. And they were successful in crippling the business and driving it into bankruptcy. Talk about a Pyrrhic victory.

Even with well-crafted buy/sells, things may not work out as well as one might have thought, but at least they provide a firm basis for expectations. While people may react pretty emotionally, especially when their perceived livelihood is at stake, appropriate agreements may make it fruitless for someone to pursue unreasonable claims. May is the operative word. We continue to see clients act vindictively and against their self-interest by looking at what the other person is getting rather than what they are keeping.

In any event, the details regarding the type of buy/sell (cross purchase or stock redemption) and the triggering events (death, disability, retirement, and termination, even situations like divorce or insolvency) need to be accounted for as well as the special considerations for community-property states. We outline the issues for our clients with regard to their buy/sells and continuation agreements and then work with the attorneys to be sure that these issues are accurately conveyed during drafting.

Determine needs due to disability—1.65 percent and Establish appropriate funding for buy-out upon death—1.65 percent

These areas are funding and fairness issues. When an owner is disabled, how does the business take care of the owner as well as those costs associated with replacing him or her? Can the owner's income simply be taken care of with his or her own private disability policy and their distributions continue to occur from the profits of the business? Do those profits continue to be distributed proportionate to ownership even though not everyone is working equally? Should salary adjustments be made to decrease profits but treat the other owners more fairly? The answers to these questions can be vetted in the business-continuation discussion, but they are similar to risk-tolerance questions—no one knows how anyone will respond until they are experiencing the event.

In many ways, funding upon death is much easier and cleaner. Once you have established valuation measures and your mechanisms, then you are deciding how best to fund it. If a client intends to sell pieces of the business internally, then flexibility with the funding vehicle may be less critical. There is a challenge in getting this right since a growing business with few owners will result in continuously increasing funding needs.

Tools and Techniques of Estate Planning[8] published by the National Underwriter Company and written by Leimberg, Kandell, Miller, Polacek, and Rosenbloom provides comprehensive information on cross-purchase and stock-redemption plans.

Another thing to consider is which business interests overlap. For example, if a client owns a business and also owns the building in which the business operates, there is obviously an intersection of interests. There may or may not be the same owners of each business. While real estate as a separate entity is often a good idea, it will invariably create tension for owners of the business who don't own that real estate. These concepts need to at a minimum reference each other and probably call for separate buy/sells.

Life's situations continue to make buy/sell planning an invaluable tool for clients. When client's divorce, if there are not provisions in the buy/sell the client may become partners with someone with whom they don't wish to work. If a partner files for bankruptcy, it could cause a strain on the borrowing capabilities of the business and its associated guarantees. And if someone is going through a life transition and loses interest in work, then there needs to be a mechanism for dealing with it.

Conclusion

Communication is central to wealth management, and this is apparent in asset-protection planning. While technically competent wealth managers may come up with solutions that are appropriate on paper, almost each component of this area has strong emotional considerations. We have used outside facilitators in certain areas that we feel may be beyond our capabilities. For example, we are strong in family-governance issues and dealing with difficult conversations, but there are times when someone whose whole practice is spent in these situations will do a better job.

We have often used outside advisors to help clients move into long-term care facilities and navigate the maze of that world. We need to be there for our clients through all of life's transitions, and if we are in over our heads, then we may not be giving them the undivided attention that they need because we are concerned about not making a mistake.

Helping clients keep what they have and helping them to transition it when they are ready to do so has been a part of wealth management whose benefit is virtually immeasurable. Even so, it is just a piece of the much larger puzzle.

Notes

1. Kitces, Michael. *The Kitces Report*. February, 2011. *www.kitces.com*.
2. We use NaviPlan for the modeling and feed those results into spreadsheets that we developed internally.
3. I get asked all the time why don't we write the insurance ourselves and collect the commissions. We made a decision that for our practice, trying to be as objective and independent as possible was a foundation principle to us. From a business standpoint, I think operating under this premise has grown our business more than the incremental benefit of receiving insurance commissions has cost us. This thought process is what is commonly referred to as a counterfactual; I actually have no idea whether this reasoning is true or not.
4. Gitman, Lawrence J., and Michael D. Joehnk. *Personal Financial Planning*. Ohio: Thompson Higher Education. 2008.
5. Daily, Glenn S. Glenndaily.com Information Services, Inc. 2002.
6. Munnell, Alicia H., and Josh Hurwitz. *What is 'Class'? and Will it Work?* Center for Retirement Research at Boston College. Number 11–3. February, 2011.
7. Mintz, Robert. *Asset Protection*. California: Francis O'Brien & Sons Publishing Company, Inc. 2011.
8. Leimberg, Stephen, Ralph Miller, Stephen Kandell, Timothy Polacek, and Morey Rosenbloom. *Tools and Techniques of Estate Planning—14th Edition*. Cincinnati: The National Underwriter Company. 2006.

CHAPTER 10

Disability and Income Protection (Protection)

This section deals predominately with cash flow—how to view it, insuring that your client's spending and values are consistent, and how to protect it. Though this area is labeled protection, the term is being used in its broadest sense. It includes protecting the client's cash flow through disciplined and conscientious spending decisions and monitoring those actions around those decisions. It also involves reviewing and optimizing all sources of income. And it looks at ways to help clients keep more of their cash flow through tax efficiencies.

The central theme to this area is trying to strike a balance between today and tomorrow. We know that dollars that are saved today have tremendous value down the road because of time and compound interest, but those dollars ultimately need to be spent or distributed. It is as costly to under live as it is to overspend.

One of the first columns that I wrote for the *Star Tribune* newspaper in Minnesota was based on the book *The Way Life Works: The Science Lover's Illustrated Guide to How Life Grows, Develops, Reproduces and Gets Along.*[1] While the book covers the entire natural world, one of the key thoughts that struck me was that "Life tends to optimize rather than maximize. . . . To optimize means to achieve just the right amount—a value in the middle range between too much and too little."[2] This is true with our clients in every area from how hard they are working to how much they are spending. While equilibrium is different for each person, trying to establish an appropriate set point in this area is our objective.

Our clients have means, a word whose root is based on the concept of intent. Regardless of the wealth of our client, we are spending considerable time reviewing the intent of their money as viewed through the lens of how they spend it. While this entire area for the index may not represent as much as other areas, the concentration on cash flow is disproportionate to other items we review.

Gloria Steinem once said that "We can tell our values by looking at our checkbook stub." Spending time in this area unpeels the values of the client better than virtually any other wealth-management work that we do.

By the way, I intentionally did not use the word budget. Clients recoil from budgets. Think about all the symbolism of balancing the budget, budget deficits, and being over budget. Budgets are constraining. Our firm likes the concept of cash flow, because it more accurately describes how money comes in and out of our clients' lives. Money flows through our clients' hands and is directed by them into the areas that are the most significant to them. This may be semantics, but our words represent our thoughts.

The other thing to think about is not simply viewing cash flow annually. By looking out for three years, planning opportunities are created through the potential for different income taxes in any given year as well as creating a reserve for cash flow during this timeframe as a way to insulate the client portfolio from market volatility.

Percent of Index (20 percent) for Disability and Income Protection (Protection)

	Percent of Disability and Income Protection Scale	Total Index Weight
What are the income and lifestyle needs and wants of your family currently and prospectively?	35	7
Have you evaluated all current sources of income and potential changes to these sources?	25	5
Are you fully utilizing all benefits available to you?	15	3
Are you proactively engaged in tax planning for you and your dependants?	25	5
Total	100	20

What Are the Income and Lifestyle Needs and Wants of Your Family Currently and Prospectively?

At the center of each of our lives, we operate from a belief system that makes us unique and drives our behavior.

> **The Way It Is**
> There's a thread that you follow. It goes among
> Things that change. But it doesn't change.
> People wonder about what you are pursuing.
> You have to explain about the thread.
> But it is hard for others to see.
> While you hold it you can't get lost.
> Tragedies happen; people get hurt
> Or die: and you suffer and get old.
> Nothing you do can stop time's unfolding.
> You don't ever let go of the thread.
> —WILLIAM STAFFORD

Discovering what each of our client's threads may be is what will shift money conversations into values discussions. In this role, we are a trusted counselor and advisor; without these discussions we are essentially an order taker. If we don't know from where a client is operating, then we respond to their directives (or inadvertently bully them with ours).

Most of us make a much bigger deal out of these conversations than we should. When we are in conversation with a loved one or friend, we have keen radar for their values and the things that may be inconsistent with them. We lovingly and compassionately guide them toward what they feel is important. But with clients, at times we choose to play a role rather than simply be human. We had hired someone from a large financial services company who was a bad fit for our organization. This became readily apparent when, prior to a client meeting, he said, "Time to work on my acting." I was aghast. We don't act for our clients, we relate with them.

Some of us still need tools because we may not be as comfortable in pure conversation. There are several good ones that you can adapt for your own use.

The Money Autobiography

A good understanding of a client's values regarding money can come from an understanding of their relationship to money. In her book, *The Energy of*

Money,[3] Maria Nemeth, Ph.D. goes through a list of 20 questions that she encourages her clients to write about in their journals:

1. What were your family's financial circumstances when you were born?
2. When did you first learn about money? Was it from your father or your mother? How old were you? What were the circumstances?
3. Did you have an allowance? Did you have to work for it, or was it given to you even if you didn't do chores to earn it? If you have children, does this affect how you handle allowances with them?
4. When was the first time you bought something with money you had saved? Where were you? What did you buy? Was it money you earned or money someone gave you?
5. Do you remember your first paycheck? How did you earn it? What did you do with it?
6. Do you remember ever losing money? When was the earliest time? What happened? Has this happened to your children? How did you handle it?
7. Did you dream of one day having a particular job or career? Have you achieved this? Why or why not? Was the amount of money you could earn a factor in your choice of careers?
8. If your relationship with money were a personal relationship, how would you describe it? Do you fear, love, hate, depend upon, feel possessive of, or feel generous with money? Just write whatever comes to mind in this area.
9. How do you relate to people who have more money than you? Less money?
10. Do you recall your mother or father's relationship with money? If you didn't live with them, then pick people who were your primary caregivers for this question.
11. How did the above people's relationship with money affect you? Did they have expectations of you? What were they? Were there some aspects of money that were not discussed? Even though they were not discussed, you may have known what they were. If you have children, do you have similar expectations of them? Do you treat them the same way you were treated? If you are married or in a committed relationship, do these expectations affect your partner?
12. Have you ever accomplished an important task or project involving money? What was it? What did you do that made you successful?
13. Was there a time when you tried but did not accomplish a task or project regarding money? What was it? What did you do that made you successful?
14. Have you ever given or received gifts of money? If yes, how much? For what reason(s)? How did you feel about this?
15. If you were to characterize your own brand of money craziness, how would you describe it?

16. Where do you want to see yourself 10 years from now regarding money? How much in savings? How much in investing? How much do you see yourself making 10 years from now?
17. Regarding money, for what do you want to be known? If people were to talk about you and your relationship with money, what would you want them to say?
18. Are you afraid that money is not spiritual enough for you or that your spiritual path isn't compatible with financial success?
19. What do you spend money on?
20. What do you not spend money on?

Other Approaches

I love the Finding Balance exercise in Mitch Anthony's book, *The New Retirementality*.[4] Through this you look at the hours in a week and the percent of your time spent on family/friends, work/career, downtime, sleep, health/fitness, and personal growth and compare that with your desired life portfolio. Other exercises include evaluating how to collect a playcheck.

Also, Roy Diliberto's book, *Financial Planning—The Next Step*[5] includes a financial life check-up questionnaire, a tool for Dreams, Visions, Images for use of wealth, and an exercise for defining true wealth that are useful.

Subcategories for what are the income and lifestyle needs and wants of your family currently and prospectively?

	Percent of Question	Percent of Category	Percent of Index
211 Review current cash flow and budget needs	30	10.5	2.1
212 Determine the amount of income that you wish to replace if you were to become disabled	20	7	1.4
213 Determine purpose and costs of one-time large expenditures including education, vacation homes, or assistance for family members	10	3.5	0.7
214 Establish your financial independence goals and the price to be paid to achieve them	30	10.5	2.1
215 Review your annual charitable giving objectives and how they should be funded	10	3.5	0.7
Total	100	35	7

Review current cash flow and budget needs—2.1 percent

Our starting point is determining from where money is coming in and how
it has gone out. Depending on the clients' need or desire for detail, we will
set them up on Mint.com, Mvelopes, or Quicken as a way for them to gain
clarity on their flows of money. But unfortunately, most clients have neither
the discipline nor interest in tracking this closely.

Online banking can be a trove of resources, especially at a place like
Wells-Fargo, which provides a detailed 16-month spending report by category. We can also obtain this information from credit cards, which also offer
customizable solutions. Brokerage statements can give a sense of flows, but
may not give background to those flows.

Other clients will come into our offices with checkbooks and credit card
statements so that we can forensically dig into their spending. If all else fails,
we back into spending using a very simple formula:

$$\text{Annual take home pay} + \text{changes in cash balances}$$
$$+ \text{increase in debt} = \text{Net living expenses}$$

We can also try to get to numbers by backing into them from a client's
tax return.

Figure 10.1 represents the spreadsheets we have developed for this.

The problem with this model is that it doesn't provide guidance as to how
the money is spent. What percentage went to education, or charity, or food?
How do we know what the discretionary versus ongoing costs are? The data
helps us make judgments regarding what we will need to replace, what the
important components to everyday living are, and how spending is reflecting
values. This gets us to a number that has no texture.

We often get asked how does a client's spending compare with others in
similar situations. We can comment on clients who have self-selected our services, but it is difficult to describe spending in terms of a general population
of similar clients. There are places to go for data, but it all must be taken with
a grain of salt. Mint.com aggregates spending data from millions of users, but
the data is as good as the input. It is also questionable whether a Mint.com
user is a typical type of client.

If you dig below the surface with this question, a client is asking whether
they are on track, not in relation to their objectives, but in relation to their
peers. We live in a relative society, so externalities are created by how others in
similar situations spend. This type of question opens the door to a values discussion around items like where a client may wish to live, how do they want

FIGURE 10.1   Expense Reconciliation.

Client & Co-Client
Living Expense Reconciliation
1/1/2011

Net Take-home Pay	
Client wages	$125,000
Co-Client wages	$100,000
Partnership distributions	$25,000
Gross Income	**$250,000**
Less:	
Retirement Contributions	($16,500)
Other Payroll Deductions	($5,500)
FICA Taxes	($8,170)
MN Income Taxes	($16,000)
Federal Income Taxes	($65,000)
Net Take Home Income	$139,000

Expense Break Down	
Net Living Expenses	$174,000
2010 Non-Regular purchase (auto)	$25,000
Mortgage	$24,000
Property Taxes	$7,000
P&C Insurance	$2,000
Cash Donations	$2,500
Life Insurance Premium	$2,400
Other Known Expense	$8,000
Other Living Expenses	$103,100

Use this to further break down expenses based on known expenses like mortgage payments, property taxes, cash contributions, insurance, etc.

Spending Estimate	
Net Take Home Income	$139,000
Changes in Cash Balances	
Net Schwab deposits / (withdrawals)	($35,000)
Net ING deposits / (withdrawals)	$5,000
Net US Bank deposits / (withdrawals)	$5,000
Changes in Revolving Debt	
US Bank HELOC paydown / (advances)	($10,000)
Net Living Expenses	$174,000
Surplus / (Deficit)	($35,000)

to present their financial situation to the world, and how external displays of money make them feel about themselves and others. For example, when a client moves into a new home, there are not simply the costs associated with the move, but there are social costs as well. There are certain expectations or prices to move into different areas in order to feel like one fits in. It may mean a change in schools, autos, or even careers. Internal versus external motivation can create significantly different realities.

When prospects become clients, we ask them to prepare a general outline of their spending as our launching pad as shown in Figure 10.2. We fold these into our models.

FIGURE 10.2 Cash Flow Projection.

Client and Co-Client
Cash Flow Projections
April 1, 2011

Income	2010	2011	2012	2013	2014
Client					
Salary	$160,000	$160,000	$160,000	$160,000	$160,000
Pension					
Other					
Co-Client					
Salary	$105,000	$105,000	$105,000	$105,000	$105,000
Other					
Bonus	$20,000	$20,000	$20,000	$20,000	$20,000
Sub-total	$285,000	$285,000	$285,000	$285,000	$285,000
Retirement Savings:					
Less: 401 (k) Deferrals—Client	($22,000)	($22,000)	($22,000)	($22,000)	($22,000)
Less: 401 (k) Deferrals—Co-Client	($22,000)	($22,000)	($22,000)	($22,000)	($22,000)
Sub-total	($44,000)	($44,000)	($44,000)	($44,000)	($44,000)
Total Gross Inflows	$241,000	$241,000	$241,000	$241,000	$241,000
Expenses	2010	2011	2012	2013	2014
Fixed Expenses	$68,000	$68,000	$68,000	$68,000	$68,000
Discretionary Expenses	$55,000	$55,000	$55,000	$55,000	$55,000
Non-regular expenses	$40,000	$25,000			
Estimated Federal Taxes	$42,000	$42,000	$42,000	$42,000	$42,000
Estimated MN Tax	$15,000	$15,000	$15,000	$15,000	$15,000
Estimated FICA Tax	$17,000	$17,000	$17,000	$17,000	$17,000
Surplus (Deficit)	$4,000	$19,000	$44,000	$44,000	$44,000
Total Outflows	$241,000	$241,000	$241,000	$241,000	$241,000

Determine the amount of income which you wish to replace were you to become disabled—1.4 percent

This area was discussed for business owners in the previous section, but this is a huge priority for all of our client discussions. We have had several clients collect on long-term disability over the years, which include a surgeon with chronic fatigue, a plastic surgeon with multiple sclerosis (MS), a radiologist with MS, an orthodontist with a permanent hand injury, a marketing consultant with MS, a headhunter with ovarian cancer, a pulmonologist with brain cancer, and a spine surgeon with a permanent back injury. We had a 60-year-old obstetrician-gynecologist who we determined could self-insure suffer permanent impairment from a stroke a few months after dropping the disability coverage.

The first decision is whether a client wants to replace their *income* or their *spending* should they no longer be able to work (see Figure 10.3). Some clients feel that they put so much effort into their careers that they want their earnings

FIGURE 10.3   Disability Insurance Analysis.

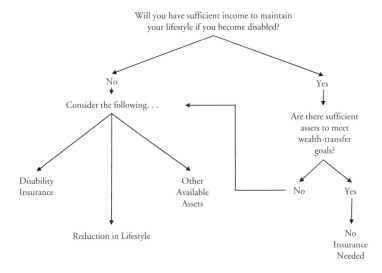

Client & Co-Client
Disability Alternatives
June 30, 2010

Will you have sufficient income to maintain
your lifestyle if you become disabled?

No

Consider the following. . .

Disability
Insurance

Other
Available
Assets

Reduction in Lifestyle

Yes

Are there sufficient
assets to meet
wealth-transfer
goals?

No   Yes

No
Insurance
Needed

Other Considerations

-Do you have the maximum amount of disability insurance through your employer?
-Are you paying your premiums with after-tax dollars (tax-free benefit)?
-Do your policies provide benefits if you are unable to do your own or any occupation?
-Do you have the option to purchase additional insurance in the future?
-Do your policies have inflation riders once you are on claim?
-Do your policies last throughyour anticipated retirement age?
- Are your policy benefits offset by other income?
-Your life expectancy may go down once disability occurs.
- You may be eligible for Social Security disability benefits.
- After disability insurance ends will your other income and portfolio withdrawals be able to support
your lifestyle?

to be covered. Other clients spend only a portion of their earnings and feel that they would rather save premium dollars and insure their spending.

Included in the template is a flow chart to go through with the client that asks some fundamental questions:

- Will you have sufficient income to maintain your lifestyle if you become disabled?
- Are there sufficient assets to meet wealth-transfer goals?
- Do you have the maximum amount of disability available through your employer?
- Are you paying premiums with after-tax dollars?

- Do your policies provide benefits if you are unable to do your own or any occupation?
- Do you have the option to purchase additional insurance in the future?
- Do your policies have inflation riders once you are on claim?
- Do your policies last through your anticipated retirement age?
- Are your policy benefits offset by other income?
- Will your life expectancy be impacted by your disability?
- Are you eligible for Social Security disability benefits?
- After the end of the disability, will your other income and portfolio withdrawals be able to support your lifestyle?

Once these issues have been fully discussed, then solutions can be offered. The areas that we modify to manage premium costs are waiting periods and length of coverage. We are rarely recommending lifetime coverage and we often extend waiting periods. Again, the decision with insurance is what risks you can afford to accept and what risks do you need to move to others. Most people can (maybe uncomfortably) live for several months off of emergency funds, credit lines, and spending reductions, but cannot live that way for several years. If it is clear that there are not enough assets to cover an extended absence from work, then disability insurance is the solution.

If a client agrees to the need but doesn't want to pay for the coverage, then that gap is reflected in their scoring on the index. It is also something that needs to be underscored annually.

Determine purposes and costs of one-time large expenditures including education, vacation homes, or assistance for family members—0.7 percent

This may seem like a surprisingly low score for the index, but most of these expenses are voluntary (although clients may not think so) and have alternative funding solutions. These costs are treated differently based on client priorities. Some clients will say that something would be a nice thing to do, but don't really view it as essential. We see this often when clients would like to help out family members.

Education

As someone who paid for my schooling by working several jobs and feels that this experience was incredibly valuable for my personal growth, it is odd that I feel compelled to pay for our daughters' schooling at private colleges. In any event, education planning is an area on which we spend a lot of analytical and emotional time.

Planning in this area is fraught with emotions. One of our clients has parents who are trying to shrink their estate but refuse to have them pay for their child's college because that is something that they wish to directly provide. It doesn't make much financial sense, but who is to question their feelings with regard to this. Other clients feel so compelled to pay for their children's schooling that they want to borrow from their retirement plans or go into personal debt to accommodate this. While we try to explain that your children can borrow for education but you can't borrow for retirement and try to help them appreciate that it may not serve your purposes if you pay for your kid's college and require them to support you in your old age, at times our clients are unmoved.

A Monte Carlo analysis is usually the starting point for determining what college costs could be and how much a client would need to set aside to fund various percentages of these costs. Many of our clients hold advanced degrees, so our education planning may include an extra three or four years for graduate school costs. The challenge with any funding analysis is projecting future costs of college in a world where the delivery of higher education needs to change dramatically. I could put myself through the University of Minnesota because the state was essentially subsidizing tuition by 80 percent. This is not realistic for today's public school students and is virtually impossible (without aid) for the private school student.

Although investment options are often limited, we still tend to favor 529 plans for the majority of our clients' education funding. We look for low-cost providers with a variety of options. There are certain advantages to using plans in one's own state, though, even if there is no tax deduction available. As states tend to look for sources of revenues, out-of-state 529 plans could be one place for them to look. If your in-state plan is reasonably attractive, then for tax risk alone, it should be your default option.

How the assets in the 529 plan are invested is something that can be covered in the investment section, but for cash-flow purposes, the way to think about it is how many years of college are being covered determines the time frame for the money. If a client has saved only enough to fund two years of college, their high school senior may begin using those funds anywhere from one to four years out. The client could choose to be more aggressive if they want to use the money for those later years. If they have partially funded plans for more than one child, they could continue to stay aggressive with the intention of using the money on child one if the markets perform, or moving it to child two or three if they don't.

Vacation homes

Clients who are looking to own second or third properties have to prepare for the initial and ongoing costs of those properties. Even the client who pays cash for a property (choosing opportunity costs rather than a mortgage) will have annual costs that are probably greater than they are thinking. Condos have association fees, homes have upkeep costs, tax rates on second homes are continuing to rise, and the ancillary costs ranging from country club memberships for the golf course property, to docks and boat costs for the lake home, are relentless.

When we discuss this area with clients, we try to create a total cost of ownership. This is particularly relevant if clients own a second home that they are reluctant to sell because of falling prices. If their $500,000 hardly used second home is worth $400,000, their annual costs may still be $30,000 or more a year (if you include opportunity costs at a 5 percent effective rate). In this simple example, the home would need to appreciate over 7 percent a year to simply stay even. If you include the limiting emotional factor that when you are ready to sell a place, you tend to get less enjoyment from being there and would rather move your recreation time to other areas, the costs of not selling climb.

When clients are preparing to make a large purchase like this, though, we try to anticipate that in the cash flow projections and begin to get a jump on raising the necessary cash.

Assistance for family members (or friends)

This is where the best-laid plans can often go awry. Wanting to help a parent is a wonderful concept, but the unintended consequences can be huge. First, a power shift occurs. When you support your parents, for example, your role has changed from being their child to being their parent. When you provide support for a friend, you may not be viewed as equals. This can be quite uncomfortable. Second, once you begin to provide support, it can become an expectation of the receiving party, thereby making your discretionary expense their permanent income item. Third, if your support is conditional, then you may be in for a disappointment.

One of our clients wanted to give their parents a travel budget with the unstated expectation that the parents would use it to fly home to see the grandkids. The parents spent it on a cruise for themselves. The clients were upset, but they were at fault for not communicating expectations around this gift. And had they communicated those feelings, the parents may have felt that the strings attached were confining.

Other items

In our customary cash-flow projections, we put money in for car purchases every five years, which the clients may choose to change, so we don't consider those one-time expenditures. We do consider things like weddings or Bar

Mitzvahs or large anniversaries where a significant dollar amount may be spent and for which funds need to be accounted.

Establish your financial independence goals and the price to be paid to achieve them—2.1 percent

Most people think of financial independence as being able to choose to work. While this is obvious, it is also incomplete. In *Walden*, Henry David Thoreau writes ". . .the cost of a thing is the amount of what I will call life which is required to be exchanged for it, immediately or in the long run."[6] We are making ongoing days-for-dollars exchanges. The price for which we sell ourselves is determined in part by the market, but more by the lifestyle choices which we have made to this point.

As I mentioned earlier, when a client chooses to add to their regular expenditures through the purchase of a larger home, for example, they are not merely adding the price of the home. They are adding all the externalities involved with this purchase. One of the externalities may be the status associated with their job, keeping them exchanging their lives in order to be comfortable within their social sphere.

In working with clients on financial independence, we want to establish what prices they are willing to pay for the choices that they are making. The choice of delaying gratification through saving may enable them to retire earlier while costing them experiences. The choice of spending money on family vacations while their kids still want to go with them may benefit their family at the cost of savings. Determining what best represents consistency between values and actions are the point of this area.

"Everything we do is ultimately aimed at experiencing happiness. We don't really want wealth, or health, or fame as such—we want these things because we hope they will make us happy."[7] This statement is the lens by which we try to help clients construct a model regarding spending. We think it is appropriate to have these discussions regarding how their spending and saving decisions impact their happiness. When clients are uncomfortable spending, we try to show them ways that give them permission to do so (see Figure 10.4).

One way to think about things is determining the areas on which a client does not wish to compromise and those things on which a client may have discretion.

Review your annual charitable giving objectives and how they should be funded—0.7 percent

We deal with charity in a couple of different areas within the index. For this particular question, we are trying to understand that annual amount

FIGURE 10.4   Cash-Flow Illustration.

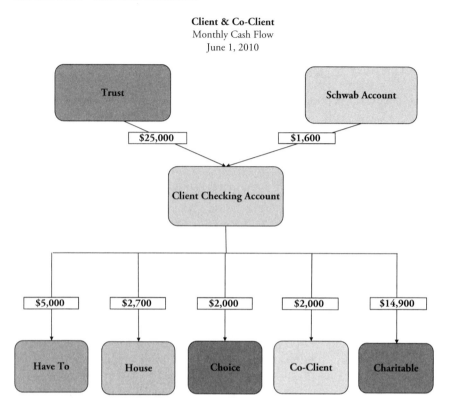

dedicated to charity, where this money is to be directed, and how best to pay for it.

Most of our clients have donor-advised funds established as a vehicle with which to meet their charitable objectives, although some of our more substantial clients have established foundations.

Generally speaking, the donor-advised fund is extremely efficient. For example, the Schwab Charitable™ Donor-Advised Fund may be established with $5,000 and allows the donor to make gifts as small as $100. This type of account allows us to easily transfer appreciated assets into the trust and avoid capital gains while getting a full deduction. This also works well for clients who have committed a certain amount of their income to charity, but either want to accumulate those assets for larger gifts or do not have charities to whom they wish to donate. Money that is not being spent is invested and continues to accumulate.

We also like community foundations for donor-advised funds for those who want the profits for the provider of the vehicle to be spent generally within the community rather than flow to shareholders of the corporate parent. Community foundations are often not as flexible or inexpensive as those established by Schwab, Fidelity, or Pershing, but often have knowledge of local charities who need support and whose missions are aligned with the donor's interests.

One of the things that we often bring up to our clients is a concept of the "One Percent Club." This group of individuals (not corporations) pledges to "try to increase philanthropy in (the) community. Specifically, to enlist people to a new standard of giving—to contribute 1 percent or more of net worth annually, or 5 percent of income, whichever is greater, to the tax-deductible cause(s) of their choice."[8] Denver, for example, has a 2 percent club. Members self-report and are not required to disclose the amounts or to whom their gifts are made. Clients who are trying to look for guidance outside the concept of tithing have found this philosophy to be quite useful.

Have You Evaluated All Current Sources of Income and Potential Changes to These Sources?

This section tries to develop an understanding of from where clients' money is coming and making timing decisions if there is flexibility on these sources. Most of our executive clients regularly have to choose between what percent of their bonuses they should receive and whether to participate in other deferred-compensation programs, the timing of exercising their stock options, and how much they should choose between restricted stock and stock options.

But timing decisions are also relevant for clients who are of Social Security age but choosing to work or married couples deciding when one or both should begin receiving their Social Security benefits. And for those clients who have cash-flow crunches, withdrawal decisions from Individual Retirement Accounts (IRAs) (even with penalties) are things that need to be explored.

One of our clients was a former consultant who became a writer. We needed to fund his lifestyle out of his retirement plans until he could get published. We weighed the decision between taking regular withdrawals out of his retirement plan on an as-needed basis or a 72(t) election where we may be stuck taking more money than we eventually needed, but could avoid the 10 percent penalty on early withdrawals. We went through a comprehensive

Subcategories for have you evaluated all current sources of income and potential changes to these sources?

	Percent of question	Percent of category	Percent of index
221 Understand current and projected earned income for your family	20	5	1
222 Review all pass-through income from S-corps, LLCs, or Partnerships	20	5	1
223 Review the cost/benefits of various pension pay-out options	15	3.75	0.75
224 Analyze social security income options including those for children under 18	15	3.75	0.75
225 Understand required minimum distributions from retirement plans	10	2.5	0.5
226 Determine the amount of portfolio withdrawals to fund expected three-year cash-flow shortages	10	2.5	0.5
227 Objectively consider any expected gifts or inheritances	10	2.5	0.5
Total	100	25	5

analysis and determined a 72(t) election made sense and which of the available elections would be best for him. After several long, dry years, he received a relatively large advance for a novel. He can offset the unneeded taxable income by funding a new and separate retirement account with the earnings from the novel, but since he is not yet 59 and a half, he will still be taking distributions from his previous plan.

Understand Current and Projected Earned Income for Your Family—1 Percent

This analysis impacts cash flow as well as taxes. For clients who receive straight W-2 income with little or no bonuses, this exercise is remedial. But many clients get paid a salary plus bonus by which we have to manage cash flow based on total earnings that are not received in a regular manner. This impacts tax planning, debt management (as some clients borrow money until those bonuses arrive), and cash flow.

Most of our physician clients receive production bonuses that are paid regularly but are irregular in amounts. For these clients, we construct a cash-flow analysis that is based on expected production, but if this changes, we need to have a back-up plan in place to manage costs. These bonuses were particularly volatile during the Great Recession when people lost jobs and their medical insurance and therefore put off medical procedures. With the continued growth in high-deductible plans (as well as the great unknown regarding future health care reimbursements) cash flow could be compromised by patients putting off care to grow their plans or procedure reimbursements getting drastically cut.

Our executive clients also have wide divergences in their annual income. Many must qualify for bonuses based on not only their ratings, but that of their particular department or the company as a whole. Often, while the metrics seem pretty straightforward with regard to measuring success, they still may create unknowns until year end.

Our lawyers also tend to take modest draws throughout the year and have significant partnership distributions at year end. Cash flow needs to be subsidized either through savings from previous years or through credit lines. Each strategy represents either potential opportunity costs or real carrying costs.

Each person feels differently about uncertainty. Within couples, each partner also feels differently. It is somewhat shocking to go through these income analyses with couples only to discover that the non-working spouse had little understanding of how their partner was paid. It also is surprising to see the non-working spouse trying to make ends meet on current take-home pay that is not at all reflective of actual pay. Our objective is to try to normalize earnings so that people are better able to make decisions based on realistic earnings expectations.

Review All Pass-Through Income from S-Corporations, LLCs, or Partnerships—1 Percent

The tax return provides valuable information on the various entities in which a client is involved and what income they produce. These entities can create tax exposure unequal to the cash distributed from them. This may be positive, for example, when the early years of a real estate investment may shelter some of the income produced by this investment, or negative, when flow-through income on S-corporations may not produce cash flow.

This entity analysis also may lead a client to treating certain income differently than what may be typical. For example, trading gains and losses from a hedge fund may be better handled through Schedules B and D rather than through the hedge fund's K-1.

This review may also create awareness (in conjunction with the tax planning component) for the unexpected sheltering of certain income as passive gains and losses offset each other. Obviously, this sheltering is a positive for cash flow. When we have clients who have some flexibility with regard to distributions from their various entities, getting a jump on trying to distribute cash flow equal to tax liabilities removes some of the cash-flow pressure clients feel when their tax liabilities are disproportionate to their cash flow.

Review the Cost/Benefits of Various Pension Pay-Out Options—0.75 Percent

For the ever-diminishing number of clients who have pensions, this analysis is becoming increasingly important. For example, some of our clients had substantial expected pensions that got dramatically reduced when their companies filed for bankruptcy. This was not nearly as bad as those clients with unfunded deferred-compensation plans that lost a significant amount of their value when their company filed for bankruptcy.

There tend to be a number of factors in considering how to handle pensions:

- What is the lump-sum benefit versus the monthly pension amount?
- If a client were choose to take their pension monthly, which is the spousal benefit that they should choose?
- How do clients feel about having their portfolio pay them a check each month rather than their pension pay it to them?
- What are their assets outside the pension plans?
- Do they have charitable objectives?
- Do they feel strongly about leaving assets to their heirs?
- Are they insurable?
- How do they weigh an irreversible but predictable decision with a flexible but uncertain decision?

When interest rates were quite high several years ago, we would often recommend to our retiring clients to take their pension as a monthly payment. As interest rates have fallen, the lump sum has become more attractive (it takes more money to provide the same benefit in a lower interest rate environment). But as you can see from the questions listed previously, the decision is far more complicated than calculating rate-of-return comparisons.

Our preference, everything being equal, is to maintain client flexibility with as much of their portfolio as possible. If a client has substantial assets outside of their pension plan, we may opt for a monthly income stream. If a client has no one to whom they wish to leave their assets, we may choose an income stream. These variables tilt the decision in a particular direction, but do not form the entire basis for the decision.

I know that lately there has been a lot of talk about the advantages of annuities, and a pension is an annuity. The most often cited reasons for annuitizing are the greater payment from the mortality benefit as compared with a bond that comes coupled with the predictable income stream that one can't outlive, which is produced in a chaotic world. While I think both of those things are true, I am still reluctant to permanently and irrevocably tie up client's money. A client's life is often equally chaotic. They get ill, get divorced, have windfalls or setbacks. Merely looking at the financial benefit that annuitization *may* bring is very short sighted. Also, each year a client waits to annuitize will bring a greater income stream should he or she choose to do so.

Analyze Social Security Income Options Including Those for Children under 18—0.75 Percent

There are many considerations in evaluating when a client should begin taking social security income:

- What are current income needs?
- What is full retirement age?
- What are partner's income needs upon death?
- What assets are available to support those needs?
- Is there an expected inheritance that may provide for income in the future?
- What is the age difference between partners?
- What are the clients' health history, their current health, and their family health history?

What are current income needs?
The social security question begins with what does a client need in order to be comfortable today? If a client has ample resources and does not need the cash flow from social security, then the decision is more about present value of the income stream coupled with life expectancy. We show this through a break-even analysis of how long a client would need to live before delaying social security makes sense.

The income-need question is a lifestyle question. We like to see clients spend more on experiences in their early retirement years while they physically can do things that poor health (or premature death) would preclude them from doing in the future. If drawing on social security provides them a level of comfort with their cash flow that they would not otherwise have, then the scales tilt to taking the benefit.

When clients are still working, though, we would rather use assets to supplement their spending needs so that we can let their benefit grow at full retirement age by currently 8 percent and, if they are not at full retirement age, avoid benefit reductions.

Another caveat to this is if a client has children under the age of 19 (if full-time students still in high school). The decision to take social security earlier so that they are entitled to a children's benefit needs to enter into the equation.

What is full retirement age?

Full retirement age is significant due to the taxation of benefits from other earned income. We may encourage a non-working spouse to collect his or her benefits early and delay those of the working spouse as long as possible. This would entitle the non-working spouse to the partner's higher benefit should the partner die first. While a widow or widower under full retirement age still gets a reduction in benefits, if the working spouse had delayed taking social security, this benefit is on a higher amount. We may encourage the higher wage earner to still take their spouse's benefit until they reach age 70 and then switch to their own benefit as a way to leverage overall benefits.

What are partner's income needs upon death, and what assets are available to support those needs?

Again, especially in situations where one spouse is significantly older than the other, delaying social security may mean a much longer and higher benefit for the younger spouse. This is essentially a form of life insurance similar to a pension offset. The 8 percent annual increase in benefits through delaying beyond full retirement is an awfully attractive guaranteed return to pass up.

In performing our analysis for withdrawal planning, if possible, we will carve out assets needed to fund this delay in taking social security. This carve out would mean spending in a particular year may be much higher than what any appropriate withdrawal rate should be, but it is more than made up for by the permanent increase in benefits.

Is there an expected inheritance that may provide for income in the future?

If a client is going to have a significant amount of money coming in the future, we would most likely suggest to them they take their social security sooner. The income will be made up down the road by the inherited assets. An alternative may be for them to delay taking the social security and use more of their current assets for a carve out, but unless there is a compelling reason to do so (such as no need for the revenue), they may be able to experience things more freely by taking the money.

What is the age difference between partners?

Large age differences make a difference in strategies because the total expected payout will change given a longer joint life expectancy. Also, often our couples with large age differences are second marriages. They may be keeping their assets somewhat separate or the older partner may be planning to put a large amount of his or her assets in a trust for the benefit of children from a previous marriage. Delaying social security for the older partner will mean a larger income stream for the younger partner should the older partner die first. This higher income stream may take some of the pressure off of the trusts (or the trustees) with regard to creating income for the survivor.

What are the clients' health history, their current health, and their family health history?

The social security calculation is based on total expected value of future payments. Obviously, health considerations play a significant part in this estimate. Current health and family longevity factor into the expected-outcome equation. When we run our analysis (see Figure 10.5), the crossover age is a simple calculation based on expected returns and payment amount. The client needs to make the bet as to whether he or she will live past that crossover age and at what point would longevity have a material effect on their total payouts.

Understand Required Minimum Distributions from \Retirement Plans—0.5 Percent

Not only does a mistake here carry huge penalties (50 percent on the amount of the required minimum distribution (RMD) that was supposed to be distributed, but wasn't), this is also one of the most common mistakes that people make. "Unless you are a more-than 5 percent owner for the plan year ending in the calendar year in which you reach age 70 and a half, your required beginning date is generally the later of these dates: (1) April 1 following the year in which you reach age 70 and a half *or* April 1 following the year in which you retire."[9]

FIGURE 10.5   Social Security Analysis.

Client & Co-Client
Social Security Analysis—Lower Earner Spousal Graph
January 21, 2010
The Lower Earner's decision is based on the life expectancy of the first spouse to pass away.

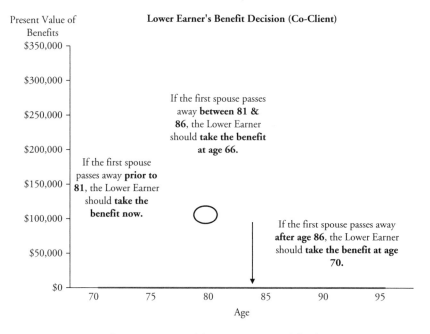

Average Life Expectancy Tables: 13 years until the first spouse
passes away (Co-Client's age 76)

Age	Early	FRA	Late
70	$0	$0	N/A
75	$0	$0	
80	$0	$0	
85	$0	$0	
90	$0	$0	
95	$0	$0	

This decision is a tax, investment, and cash-flow decision. It is a tax decision because, depending on the year, a client may choose to make charitable gifts directly from their retirement plan thereby satisfying their RMD, avoiding income limits on charitable deductions, and, for higher-income taxpayers, reducing their adjusted gross income and therefore potentially more itemized deductions. It is also a tax decision for someone who turns 70½ on July 1 or later, because they get to decide how much of their initial RMD they can spread over the current year and the next tax year (see Figure 10.6).

It is an investment decision because preparing for the RMD may mean that cash is raised in anticipation of the need. It may also mean that a client with multiple retirement plans, since withdrawals do not need to take place pro rata from *the same type of plan*, takes their RMD from the poorest performing plans or the ones with the worst investment options.

It is a cash-flow decision because an RMD is the least that one takes out of a plan. Clients in need of cash may take more out of their retirement plans. On the other hand, clients who are still generating income may choose to

FIGURE 10.6 RMD and Withholding Summary.

Client & Co-Client
Retirement Distributions and Tax Withholding

January 1, 2011

RMD Summary	Required	Distributed[1]
IRAs—Client	$69,631	$121,502
IRAs—Co-Client	$20,361	$0
TIAA CREF—Co-Client	$12,534	$12,534

[1] *Each RMD category must be satisfied separately. TIAA-CREF distributions occur automatically on a monthly basis.*

Tax Withholding Summary	Federal	Minnesota
Safe Harbor Target (per CPA)	$44,000	$11,000
Less: Taxes Withheld[2]	($10,425)	($3,706)
Additional Withholding Needed	$33,575	$7,294

[2] *Includes year-to-date withholding plus what will be withheld by year end from automatic monthly payments.*

Recommendations
1) Distribute $42,000 from Co-Client's IRA by year-end. Withhold all for taxes.
2) Consult with CPA at end of year regarding additional tax withholding distribution.
3) Increase monthly payments from Client's IRA in 2011 to cover living expenses.
4) Continue to dedicate Co-Client's Schwab RMDs to year-end tax withholding.
5) Adjust withholding rates once 2011 tax rates and 2010 tax liability are known.

take their RMD and still put money back into a plan through a retirement contribution.

Determine the Amount of Portfolio Withdrawals to Fund Expected Three-Year Cash-Flow Shortages—0.5 Percent

While this is an investment decision, we view this also as a cash-flow decision. We do not want to sell investments in a bad market to meet cash-flow shortages of which we were aware. Getting a firm handle on all sources of income will give us an estimate of how much cash we will need to raise from the portfolio in anticipation of these cash needs. Once this money has been raised and set aside, the decision to refill this bucket is dependent upon the markets. If markets are soft, the three years may get drawn down; if they are healthy, the bucket may get replaced annually.

Objectively Consider Any Expected Gifts or Inheritances—0.5 Percent

Clients are constantly telling us that they don't want to count on an inheritance. While their caution is admirable, it is also unfortunate. "Conservative assumptions are a dangerous myth. . . . A conservative assumption may well result in an inappropriate and aggressive solution. We believe in making intelligent assumptions, not relying on fundamentally unsound, conservative defaults."[10] One of our clients receives annual gifts from her very wealthy father. She and her partner get $26,000 a year, which, since she does not work in a high paying job, is used to supplement her housing costs. Given our model of raising three years worth of cash in advance of those needs, if we did not factor in those gifts, we would need $78,000 sitting unproductively in a money market fund. One thing that we will do is talk to the family members who are making these gifts so we can judge their predictability. It is often hard for the recipient to do this for fear of seeming greedy, but it is easy for us to do this as a way to get our arms around the significant planning issues.

This is also true of inheritances. These may be more problematic because their timing and amount is uncertain. Still, a plug-in number as a starting point may help provide more realistic scenario planning.

Are You Fully Utilizing All Benefits Available to You?

When we work with clients from a particular company, we scan and store their benefit booklet with a hope and expectation that if we do good work, we will continue to get business from this company. The learning curve on executive compensation for each company is steep; there are many different methods that corporations use to try to retain and reward their key personnel.

While all employees have access to things like 401(k) plans, stock purchase plans, and cafeteria plans, higher-level executives begin to benefit from stock options, restricted stock programs, and bonus structures. As people climb up the ladder, we get into more complicated work involving company-owned life insurance, long-term incentive plans, deferred compensation, stock option reloads, and supplemental employee retirement plans.

It has been our experience in working with executives that the company human resource people dedicated to the executives are extremely seasoned, smart, and have their fingers on all the various methods of compensation as well as any significant legal issues or expectations. They are there to serve the executive and usually are amenable to working closely with the executive's wealth manager. We still need to have a good understanding of the various programs for our clients, but the HR professional will usually sit down with us and go through the nuances.

We are constantly balancing our executive and business-owner clients undiversified investment in their companies with the leverage and tax advantages those risks provide. Bill Gates didn't get rich selling Microsoft and buying mutual funds. Our executive clients build their net worth rapidly—far more quickly than we can diversify them away from their companies. When we consider issues like holding requirements for stock in their company, their balance sheets will inevitably have a disproportionate amount invested in their business. Many of our executives recognize this and are willing to gradually reduce this exposure. There are, at times, people who believe so strongly in their companies that they want to magnify their positions. We de-risk their portfolios by emphasizing where it makes sense to hold stock and where it doesn't.

One of our clients had a large position in a family-owned private business in which the family was going to be exploring ways to split the business off. For this client (who was not a family member) we actually encouraged them to not exercise any of their options and had them accept their bonuses in this stock. The valuation of the company was about one-third of similarly traded public companies. Given that the patriarch of the company had already decided to pursue a liquidity event, our feeling was that we could not control the timing (be it one year or two), but even with dramatic negative corporate events, a strategic or financial buyer would pay far more than the current stock price. When the company got sold within a year, our client got three times what they would have received had they exercised their options. While there was no guarantee that this event would occur, the expected value of the stock should anything happen was so great that diversification would have been imprudent.

A different client was an executive at Enron who had a significant exposure to Enron stock. We had no idea that Enron would become Enron, but we knew that the client could exercise enough stock options to become financially independent when combined with his other assets. He was extremely reluctant to do so and ended up only exercising a small piece of what he could have. He believed in the company and felt like he had a far better handle on it than we did. While in many ways this was true, we still explained to him that if he was right about the stock, he would participate with his unexercised options; if he was wrong, he would still be "a little" rich. He was not persuaded. When the stock collapsed, his options were worthless.

Subcategories for are you fully utilizing all benefits available to you?

	Percent of question	Percent of category	Percent of index
231 Review participation in pre-tax reimbursement and cafeteria plans	25	3.75	0.75
232 Determine levels of participation and type of company retirement plans (qualified and non-qualified)	25	3.75	0.75
233 Review all available stock purchase and stock option plans (including necessary filings)	25	3.75	0.75
234 Evaluate whether any form of IRA contributions, rollovers, or supplemental retirement plans on self-employment income are appropriate	25	3.75	0.75
Total	100	15	3

Review Participation in Pre-Tax Reimbursement and Cafeteria Plans—0.75 Percent

The only questions that matter regarding cafeteria plans are the amount of participation and in which areas do you allocate dollars. While highly compensated and key employees may not be able to participate, involvement for any other client is a no-brainer. These plans are not subject to federal, state, or Social Security taxes. And for employers, they save on FICA, FUTA, SUTA, and Worker's Compensation taxes. The risk for an employer is that someone quits before they had fully funded their flexible savings account and had withdrawals greater than their contributions. This may be offset by the use-it or lose-it nature of the plans whereby employees who don't spend the money that they set aside annually forfeit it back to the corporation. We check with our clients to be sure that they have fully utilized the money that they set aside each year. For clients with higher incomes, using the cafeteria plan for dependent expenses will generate a greater savings than the dependent care credit.

Many of our clients are also participating in Health Savings Accounts. Depending on the clients' cash flow, we may use these as long-term savings vehicles (even though the investment options are often not very good).

There are other pre-tax reimbursement plans for clients that may be available such as qualified parking or commuter expense programs that are easy to overlook, but can create tax savings of close to $1,000 a year. Also, for many of our clients who are paying for their children's graduate school (even though the child is working), they may not be aware that their child's employer offers a tuition reimbursement plan. The child must pay and apply, but the parent could gift the child dollars for those costs not covered by the plan.

Some of our business-owner clients are ineligible to participate in these tax-qualified plans themselves. There are programs such as Benicomp which can provide insured medical reimbursement for a monthly fee or a surcharge on their medical costs.

Determine Levels of Participation and Type of Company Retirement Plans (Qualified and Non-Qualified)—0.75 Percent

The level of client commitment to their company retirement plans is a cash flow decision, but it is also an investment and tax decision.

It is difficult to come up with a reason why someone would not contribute at least to the match level for an employer sponsored plan. Beyond that, though, clients need to see if they qualify for other programs. Most of our clients are only eligible for their company's 401(k) and are not eligible for deductible IRAs. Generally, we have recommended Roth 401(k)s as a way to build up different buckets of taxation—already taxed personal investments, tax deferred 401(k)s or deferred-compensation programs, and ultimately tax-free Roth 401(k)s. Having tax diversity creates the best opportunity for tax arbitrage opportunities down the road. We generally tend to favor deferring taxes, so have not been huge proponents of Roth conversions, but building some assets in the Roth 401(k) is a sound strategy until flat-tax optics become clearer.

Many of our executive clients participate in Supplemental Executive Retirement Plans (SERPs) that were created to pick up where qualified plans left off. Because there are income and contribution limits for qualified plans that impact highly compensated employees, supplemental plans restore some of the benefits that were lost by the Employee Retirement Income Security Act (ERISA) rules. Clients have the right to pick payment dates, which we often choose to coincide with life events—such as college. Most of these plans are held in Rabbi Trusts, which help protect the client's benefit should a takeover of the company occur, but don't provide insulation if the company files for bankruptcy.

Clients also often have decisions regarding split-dollar life insurance offered as a quasi-retirement plan. These programs need to be evaluated based on the expected career life expectancy for the client. More important, split-dollar rules have become far more complex and far less attractive as vehicles.

Review All Available Stock Purchase and Stock Option Plans Including Any Necessary Filings—0.75 Percent

Many employees, regardless of their position within a firm, have stock-purchase plans available to them. In these programs, an employee uses withholding from each paycheck to pay for company stock, typically priced at a 15 percent discount based on the lower price at the annual start or end date of the program. The stock must be held for two years to qualify for capital gains, but regardless of tax treatment, these programs can generate an immediate return (with the risk being the time-frame between the grant of the stock and the client's ability to sell it). While there is always a risk that clients may own too much of their company stock, this is certainly a risk worth taking with these plans.

Most of our executive clients receive the rights to stock in the future either through stock options, stock appreciation rights, or restricted stock grants. We are seeing more of our executive compensation be through stock grants. The advantage of these is that regardless of what the stock does when the grant is made, there is some value when the restrictions are lifted. These plans don't provide the leverage (or upside) of stock options, but are much easier to manage. We fold restricted stock into our cash-flow analysis because we need to account for the tax on the stock as the restrictions are lifted and make decisions regarding whether this asset will be an investment or a use asset. Some of our executives run a fairly tight cash-flow account for their options or restricted stock in spending plans. For others we suggest deferring compensation (which often allows investment into a range of investments) and replacing the deferred compensation by selling the restricted stock—a cash-flow-neutral transaction which helps them diversify.

Stock options for clients are either non-qualified or incentive stock options. We handle these differently because they are very different animals. Non-qualified options are simply the right to buy a certain number of shares of stock at a future date for a predetermined price. The difference between the current price and the exercise price is the gain to the client. There is a decision tree that needs to account for when a client should begin exercising their options after they have started to vest in them. The decision tree as it relates to cash flow (as opposed to diversification) should include a variety of considerations:

- What is the purpose of the money?
- How much time is left before the options expire?
- Are there significant issues that may impact tax rates?
- Is there other company stock that can be used?
- What level of regret will a client feel regarding exercising and spending (as opposed to exercising and diversifying)?
- Are other vehicles more appropriate?

What is the purpose of the money?

This question is to try to get an understanding of how the stock option money is going to be used and whether it will be an ongoing item (which would suggest taking more off the table to reduce the volatility) or whether it is for special items. The leverage that stock options provide are a double edged sword—for those with reasonable time horizons, allowing for the options to appreciate can increase wealth quickly and dramatically. Think about it this way: If a client owns an option exercisable at $40 on a stock that is trading at $50, a $1 increase in stock price (2 percent or 1/50) represents a 10 percent increase in option values (1/10).

This leverage creates significant risk as well as huge psychological hurdles. In the example above, if a client exercised 10,000 shares for their $10 gain (or $6.50 after tax) in order to purchase a new car, and the stock subsequently went up by merely another dollar, the cost of that car increased by 10 percent. This is not a very useful way of thinking about it, but when clients have options that increase rapidly shortly after their exercise, they tend to view things in those terms. The risk, though, comes from how quickly the spread can disappear on those options.

Clients who do not view their options as a necessary component of their annual cash flow tend to feel better about exercising their options for something that can create longer-term value for them, such as children's education or a second home.

Some of our clients work at companies where a significant portion of their compensation comes in the form of stock options. For those clients who receive relatively modest income but significant long-term benefits, creating a method for spending some of those longer-term benefits today becomes more important. Ideally, clients would live off their salaries. For some of our executives, though, their positions within their companies coupled with pay packages that are incentive laden, may make it difficult for them to do so. With these clients, we develop regular exercise strategies.

How much time is left before the options expire?

We tend to like our clients to let their options run for as long as possible using either price or cash-flow targets for exercising. Once a client is three years away from expiration, we will begin to more aggressively take money off the table. The price target piece is logical in the sense that as the price of a stock increases, the leverage with the option decreases. Therefore, the benefit of continuing to hold them diminishes. Cash-flow targets help clients deal with some of the emotional aspects of the options. We often create an exercise plan for certain options at predetermined prices to create cash targets. This removes some of the psychological hurdles of balancing short-term company status with long-term wealth. For some of our executives, we file 10b5–1 plans using price and/or time triggers. We establish price targets, but if the stock does not hit the target by a certain date, then some shares will automatically be sold, regardless of price. We use these programs most frequently with executives who have expiring options and we don't want to be prevented from selling if they later are aware of material non-public information.

Are there significant issues that may impact tax rates?

Pending tax-law changes may affect our exercise timing. We may create plans to exercise based on whether a client will pay alternative minimum tax thereby capping the tax rate on the option exercise. Alternately, we may accelerate the ordinary income from options to avoid our client's AMT.

Is there other company stock that can be used?

We may want to use company stock for reloading options, but generally, our preference is (absent holding requirements) to sell shares that have long-term capital gains while we keep our options. Again, the options provide leverage that existing stock does not. Also, a drop in the value of the stock is subsidized at a higher rate by the government with options than it is with existing stock. Since options are taxed at ordinary income rates, a one-dollar drop in stock price costs the client 65 cents with options (if they are in a 35 percent federal tax bracket) but 85 cents for stock held more than a year. While it is also true that gains are only 65 cents, the leverage works in the client's favor.

What level of regret will a client feel regarding exercising and spending (as opposed to exercising and diversifying)?

This is a difficult question because clients may feel regret when they exercise and the stock goes up or they don't exercise and the stock falls. We work on framing the discussion by showing pictures of ranges of outcomes with the stock at various prices. When clients are exercising options for other investments, the psychology may be especially difficult because there is a guaranteed immediate loss through taxes currently paid as compared to the potential benefits of a less-volatile and potentially higher-returning diversified portfolio. The issue becomes easier when we are working on areas like spending on retirement because for our projections, even keeping returns the same between the individual stock and a diversified portfolio, we have to increase the standard deviation. This means that the single stock may have significantly better outcomes than a diversified portfolio on the edges, but it will also have more Monte Carlo failures.

Clients who are exercising and spending their options can get into trouble if the growth of the underlying stock slows or falls, and the value of their spread on the options diminishes. Relying too much on option income is not a sound long-term strategy.

Are other vehicles more appropriate?

Depending on the client, home equity loans or margin loans may be more appropriate than exercising options. This is especially true if a client has a large restricted stock grant vesting soon or deferred compensation paying out. Rather than sell long-term options, short-term borrowing until the grant matures or the deferred compensation pays may be a better, albeit riskier, decision.

The complicating factor for incentive stock options is that a client receives long-term capital gains treatment on the spread if they hold them for a year after exercising them and more than two years after being granted them. The gain is an add-back for alternative minimum tax (AMT) purposes so we try to exercise incentive stock options early in the year with the expectation that if the stock drops before the year is over, we will sell it, thereby forgoing the potential for long-term capital gains, but also negating the impact of the AMT. I read with horror the stories back in early 2000 and 2001 about people who exercised their incentive stock options, watched the stock crash, and paid AMT on the spread rather than perform a disqualifying disposition. While someone can carry forward the AMT capital loss, they can only use it against other capital gains plus an additional $3,000! Some employees of technology companies lost hundreds of thousands of dollars by not handling this area correctly.

The other thing to consider when working with executives is whether they will have black-out periods during which they are precluded from selling stock. These black-out dates surround earnings announcements and can be obtained in advance from the human resources manager. They may occur intermittently for material non-public information. A trading plan allows you to sell during these periods if the plan was established prior to knowing anything.

Evaluate Whether Any Forms of IRA Contributions, Rollovers, or Supplemental Retirement Plans on Self-Employed Income Are Appropriate—0.75 Percent

Clients have a number of retirement-planning options. While general retirement planning gets captured in the cash-flow and tax areas, clients who have additional income through their self-employment (typically board work, speaking, or writing) have increased options open to them.

Contribution limits on defined-benefit and some defined-contribution plans are much higher than what an employee may be able to make simply through their 401(k) plan. While we don't often use defined benefit plans for clients (although we have in situations of significant positive cash flow, a predictable income stream, and a favorable employee census), clients who have significant outside income and are not subjected to aggregation rules often benefit from starting a Simplified Employee Pension.

Are You Proactively Engaged in Tax Planning for You and Your Dependants?

Tax planning garners a lot of attention. It has caused some of our clients to choose to switch domiciles, it has certainly caused some to hold onto stocks that we had encouraged them to sell, and had led clients into buying bad investments with little economic purpose. Yet, good tax planning can result in saving dollars that certainly don't need to be spent. For example, one of our clients had a large gain in a private stock that was going through a liquidity event. We were able to find a local foundation that would accept the stock, even though there was a chance that the event may not happen. This entitled the client to meet their charitable obligations while avoiding capital gains tax. So how do you work on tax planning that is beneficial for the client and does not become the focal point rather than a piece of the entire plan?

There are a few things that we consider when going through tax planning:

- How does a tax-planning suggestion fit into the client's long-term objectives?
- Is there a good financial reason to pay a tax up-front rather than delay paying it?
- Is the strategy legitimate?
- Is there an easier way to do it?

No tax decision should be made unless it clearly fits into the client's plan. Several of our clients who would not be considered philanthropic but had large holdings in low-basis securities have been approached by insurance agents seeking to set up a charitable remainder trust for them and use insurance as a replacement for the assets gifted. Why? We have often used this strategy for clients who want a portion of their estate to go to charity, but how can someone justify doing this for someone without those interests? It is financially impossible to benefit more from implementing a strategy like this than it is to do nothing. Someone who is not philanthropic may be willing to do something like this if the perceived value is greater than their net cost, but there will be a cost.

Some of our clients are interested in establishing residency in states other than Minnesota, in part because of the high state income taxes here. For those clients who have built legitimate lives in other places, this is a fine idea. But for those who are merely interested in saving state taxes it may be silly. There are social costs associated with no longer being a resident in addition to the practical costs.

One of our clients was describing how his old business partner did this prior to their sale of the business. This person moved his family to a no-tax state in order to avoid income taxes as he exercised stock options granted to him from the acquiring company. By chance, these options became worthless and this guy ended up stuck in a state for which he had no affinity with a portfolio that had shrunk to a point where he didn't feel he could afford to move back to Minnesota. One tax decision had a cascading effect on all aspects of his life.

Most things are not this black and white. The question to ask the client is how this will impact them. Most decisions should be based on more good than bad rather than right or wrong. Tax decisions should be part of the planning process, but not the only part.

We also think it makes sense to avoid paying taxes too soon. Several years ago, there was a tax that was introduced on excess annual withdrawals from retirement plans beyond $150,000. A 10 percent excise tax was imposed. One of the planning ideas at the time was to take massive withdrawals from the retirement plans before this tax went into effect. I thought that was a stupid idea for several reasons including: The client will be incurring ordinary income tax rates up front and it is always uncertain as to whether federal income tax rates will go up or down (they do both); and, there was no guarantee that the law would stay in place (it didn't); and, there are other things that can be done with retirement-plan assets that may create better planning opportunities (such as using for charity or creating a stretch out); and, the client is permanently giving up the deferral rights on that money.

In fact, we saw something similar in 2010 when everyone knew that tax rates were going to go up so advisors suggested tax-gain harvesting rather than tax-loss harvesting to pay income taxes at lower rates today in anticipation of higher rates tomorrow. Guess what? Rates didn't change and people unnecessarily paid taxes.

The world is dynamic. Tax law changes just like everything else. When the government first relaxed the income limits on Roth conversions, people got all excited simply because they could spread the tax over two years. Some did massive conversions. If income tax rates rise, there certainly is an advantage to getting money into a Roth sooner. But what if they fall or stay the same? Good advice becomes bad advice. Can anyone unequivocally say that there won't be reduced federal income tax rates but a significant value-added or consumption tax? A more reasonable approach may be to develop a plan for partial conversions over time, thereby diversifying your tax risk.

The legitimacy of the tax-planning strategy also needs to be evaluated. I have been around long enough to be a real skeptic on aggressive tax-saving strategies. I have seen stock option tax shelters explode, aggressive insurance strategies blow up, and aggressive discounting on estates get called into question. It's easy to say after the fact that the headaches that these good ideas gone bad wreaked on people who used them were not worth it. But I can also say that before the fact the stress regarding doing something that these people knew to be incredibly aggressive was generally not worth it.

And one of the first questions that needs to be asked: Is there an easier way of doing this? It almost doesn't matter what the issue is, but the most complicated answer is not necessarily the best answer. Are there things on the margin that may be better for the client even if it doesn't garner every last nickel of tax savings?

Isaiah Berlin once wrote an essay comparing foxes to hedgehogs. He said, "The fox knows many things, but the hedgehog knows one big thing." In wealth management, we need to be foxes. When it comes to tax planning, unfortunately, we are often hedgehogs.

Subcategories for are you proactively engaged in tax planning for you and your dependants?

	Percent of category	Percent of question	Percent of index
241 Determine appropriate levels of withholding and estimated tax payments	15	3.75	0.75
242 Determine whether tax-loss harvesting is possible and appropriate	15	3.75	0.75
243 Review gifting opportunities and strategies	20	5	1
244 Determine whether to accelerate or defer income and/or deductions for tax bracket or AMT reasons	30	7.5	1.5
245 Evaluate the recharacterization or conversions of IRAs to/from Roth IRAs	20	5	1
Total	100	25	5

Determine Appropriate Levels of Withholding and Estimated Tax Payments—0.75 Percent

Running tax projections for clients enables us to get a sense of what reserves we need to set aside for taxes. Since our asset-management minimums are relatively high, most of our clients have to supplement their withholding with estimated taxes (unless they want end-of-the-year withholding to come completely out of their paychecks). This can be problematic at times, because it is often difficult to know exactly what investment income will be—especially if clients hold mutual funds whose distributions are unknown until the last couple of months of the year. While estimates can be set up to be based on income actually received at the time the estimates are due, thereby eliciting a large fourth quarter payment when distributions are understood, some clients would rather pay proportionately each quarter.

We need to operate with certain assumptions for tax planning as well as verifiable information, as shown in Figure 10.7.

FIGURE 10.7   Tax Projection Assumptions.

Client & Co-client
2010 Income Tax Projection
January 1, 2010

Action Plan

- **Recommended Planning Options**
  - **Planning Assumptions**
    - Roth IRA Conversion Income: **$xx,xxx**
    - Additional Capital Gains/Losses: **$xx,xxx**
    - Other income opportunities (Be specific): **$xx,xxx**
    - Contribution to Donor-Advised Fund: **$xx,xxx**
    - Other deduction opportunities (Be specific): **$xx,xxx**
  - **Federal Tax Liability**
    - Projected tax liability is expected to equal total payments
    - Projected tax refund is **$x,xxx**
    - Projected tax due by April 15, 2011 is **$x,xxx**
    - Based on your projection, you may want to consider reducing your withholding by **$xxx** per paycheck
    - Based on your projection, you may want to consider increasing your withholding by **$xxx** per paycheck
    - Based on your projection, you should pay your **$x,xxx** fourth quarter estimate by January 15, 2011 as set up by your accountant
    - Based on your projection, you should **increase** your fourth quarter estimate to **$x,xxx** and pay it by January 15, 2011
    - Based on your projection, you should **decrease** your fourth quarter estimate to **$x,xxx** and pay it by January 15, 2011
  - **State Tax Liability**
    - Projected tax liability is expected to equal total payments
    - Projected tax refund is **$x,xxx**
    - Projected tax due by April 15, 2011 is **$x,xxx**
    - Based on your projection, you may want to consider reducing your withholding by **$xxx** per paycheck
    - Based on your projection, you may want to consider increasing your withholding by **$xxx** per paycheck
    - Based on your projection, you should pay your **$x,xxx** fourth quarter estimate by December 31, 2010 / January 15, 2011 as set up by your accountant

- Based on your projection, you should **increase** your fourth quarter estimate to **$x,xxx** and pay it by December 31, 2010 / January 15, 2011
- Based on your projection, you should **decrease** your fourth quarter estimate to **$x,xxx** and pay it by December 31, 2010 / January 15, 2011
- **Base Projection**
  - **Federal Tax Liability**
    - Projected tax liability is expected to equal total payments
    - Projected tax refund is **$x,xxx**
    - Projected tax due by April 15, 2011 is **$x,xxx**
    - Based on your projection, you may want to consider reducing your withholding by **$xxx** per paycheck
    - Based on your projection, you may want to consider increasing your withholding by **$xxx** per paycheck
    - Based on your projection, you should pay your **$x,xxx** fourth quarter estimate by January 15, 2011 as set up by your accountant
    - Based on your projection, you should **increase** your fourth quarter estimate to **$x,xxx** and pay it by January 15, 2011
    - Based on your projection, you should **decrease** your fourth quarter estimate to **$x,xxx** and pay it by January 15, 2011
  - **State Tax Liability**
    - Projected tax liability is expected to equal total payments
    - Projected tax refund is **$x,xxx**
    - Projected tax due by April 15, 2011 is **$x,xxx**
    - Based on your projection, you may want to consider reducing your withholding by **$xxx** per paycheck
    - Based on your projection, you may want to consider increasing your withholding by **$xxx** per paycheck
    - Based on your projection, you should pay your **$x,xxx** fourth quarter estimate by December 31, 2010 / January 15, 2011 as set up by your accountant
    - Based on your projection, you should **increase** your fourth quarter estimate to **$x,xxx** and pay it by December 31, 2010 / January 15, 2011
    - Based on your projection, you should **decrease** your fourth quarter estimate to **$x,xxx** and pay it by December 31, 2010 / January 15, 2011

Assumptions:

Income

- **Client's Projected Income**
  - Wages / Self-employment income: **$xxx,xxx**

- State tax refund: **$xx,xxx**
- Rental income / Pass-through income: **$xxx,xxx**
- IRA / Pension income: **$xx,xxx**
- Social Security income: **$xx,xxx**
- Other income (alimony, non-investment interest, etc.—be specific regarding source): **$xx,xxx**
- **Co-client's Projected Income**
  - Wages / Self-employment income: **$xxx,xxx**
  - Rental income / Pass-through income: **$xxx,xxx**
  - IRA / Pension income: **$xx,xxx**
  - Social Security income: **$xx,xxx**
  - Other income (alimony received, non-investment interest, etc.—be specific regarding source): **$xx,xxx**

Investment Income

- Aii-Managed Accounts:
  - Taxable interest income: **$x,xxx**
  - Ordinary dividend income: **$xx,xxx**
    - Qualified dividend income: **$xx,xxx**
  - Long-term capital gain distributions: **$xx,xxx**
  - Realized capital gains are projected to be the following:
    - Long-term gains / losses: **$xx,xxx**
    - Short-term gains / losses: **$xx,xxx**
- Other Accounts (not managed by Aii):
  - Taxable interest income: **$x,xxx**
  - Ordinary dividend income: **$xx,xxx**
    - Qualified dividend income: **$xx,xxx**
  - Long-term capital gain distributions: **$xx,xxx**
  - Realized capital gains are projected to be the following:
    - Long-term gains / losses: **$xx,xxx**
    - Short-term gains / losses: **$xx,xxx**
- Limited partnership income: **$xx,xxx**

Adjustments

- Health Savings Account deduction: **$x,xxx**
- Self-employed SEP/SIMPLE/qualified plan deduction: **$xx,xxx**
- Self-employed health insurance deduction: **$x,xxx**
- IRA deduction: **$x,xxx**

- Other adjustments (alimony paid, domestic production activities deduction, etc.—be specific regarding source): **$x,xxx**

Itemized Deductions

- Medical expenses: **$x,xxx**
- State income taxes paid (prior years): **$xx,xxx**
- Real estate taxes: **$x,xxx**
- Home mortgage interest: **$,xx,xxx**
  - Points paid to refinance: **$x,xxx**
  - Points not amortized from prior refinance: **$x,xxx**
- Investment interest: **$x,xxx**
- Charitable contributions: **$x,xxx**
- Miscellaneous deductions: **$x,xxx**

State Additions / Subtractions

- Additions to State taxable income:
  - Tax-exempt interest income from non-resident states (if significant): **$x,xxx**
  - Domestic production activities deduction: **$x,xxx**
  - Federal bonus depreciation addition: **$x,xxx**
  - Federal Section 179 expensing addition: **$x,xxx**
  - Other addition (if significant—be specific): **$x,xxx**
- Subtractions from State taxable income:
  - U.S. Bond interest (if significant): **$x,xxx**
  - Education expenses for qualifying children in grades K-12: **$x,xxx**
  - Federal bonus depreciation previously added back: **$x,xxx**
  - Federal Section 179 expensing previously added back: **$x,xxx**
  - Railroad Retirement Board benefits: **$x,xxx**
  - Other subtraction (if significant—be specific): **$x,xxx**

Federal Tax Payments

- Client's projected withholding: **$xx,xxx**
- Co-client's projected withholding: **$xx,xxx**
- Estimated tax payments:
  - Overpayment of 2009 tax applied to 2010: **$xx,xxx**
  - First quarter estimate paid by April 15, 2010: **$xx,xxx**
  - Second quarter estimate paid by June 15, 2010: **$xx,xxx**
  - Third quarter estimate paid by September 15, 2010: **$xx,xxx**

State Tax Payments

- Client's projected withholding: **$x,xxx**
- Co-client's projected withholding: **$x,xxx**
- Estimated tax payments:
  - Overpayment of 2009 tax applied to 2010: **$x,xxx**
  - First quarter estimate paid by April 15, 2010: **$x,xxx**
  - Second quarter estimate paid by June 15, 2010: **$x,xxx**
  - Third quarter estimate paid by September 15, 2010: **$x,xxx**

We then run a template for a safe harbor calculator to be sure that clients are not in a penalty situation from improper withholding as shown in Figure 10.8.

Our basis for this is the analysis that we run that reviews all the sources of taxable income and incorporates expected deductions. We use plug-in numbers for capital gains and dividends generated by the investments that we own.

This area can be a source of frustration for clients, though, because they may not like getting tax refunds on money that they sent in for estimated taxes based on investment-income estimates that did not match up with reality. It can also be a frustration because at times accountants may not have been aware of the investment income that was going to be realized and are frustrated (and panicked) that a client may owe money at year end.[11]

We get permission from our clients to share our numbers and projections with their accountants. We can load information through our web site to an advisor vault to which the accountant has a password. One of the responsibilities of the staff is to communicate to accountants as numbers come in so that everyone is aware of the tax situation.

Determine Whether Tax-Loss Harvesting Is Possible and Appropriate—0.75 Percent

These are two areas over which we have some control that we watch closely. As clients have losses on their portfolios, we try to realize them through selling those assets at a loss and purchasing similar assets in their place. This is essentially a time-value-of-money strategy. We would rather gather those losses to use to offset future gains, than—everything being equal—hold onto the asset until it recovers. Now I know that nothing is ever equal. If we have an investment that we like, isn't it short sighted to sell it? Our trigger is a 3 percent loss (or a dollar amount due to transaction costs in smaller accounts, in larger accounts due to magnitude) in the taxable account. We can buy that investment back after 30 days to get back into it. If the replacement investment has appreciated by the 3 percent, we may not choose to do so.

FIGURE 10.8 Safe Harbor Calculator.

Client & Co-client
Safe Harbor Worksheet
2010 Tax Year

Safe Harbor Calculation

	Federal Safe Harbor		
Current Year	110% of Prior		

Federal Summary Table	90% of Current	100% of Current	Prior Year
First Quarter Required Payment	$11,000	$12,000	$38,000
Second Quarter Required Payment	$8,000	$11,000	$62,000
Third Quarter Required Payment	$6,000	$11,000	$87,000
Fourth Quarter Required Payment	$5,000	$10,000	$115,000
Current Year Tax	$56,470		
90% of Current Year Tax	$50,823		
Withholding Taxes	$9,500		
Prior Year Tax	$143,928		
Prior Year AGI	$1,019,869		
Prior Year Safe Harbor	$158,321		
Required Annual Payment	$50,823		

	90% of Current	100% of Current	Prior Year
First Quarter Estimate			
Required Payment	$12,706	$14,118	$39,580
25% of Withholding	$2,375	$2,375	$2,375
Remaining Required Payment	$10,331	$11,743	$37,205
First Quarter Estimated Taxes Paid	$(13,000)	$(13,000)	$(13,000)
First Quarter Shortfall	$-	$-	$24,205
First Quarter Excess	$(2,669)	$(1,258)	$-
Second Quarter Estimate			
Required Payment	$12,706	$14,118	$39,580
25% of Withholding	$2,375	$2,375	$2,375
	$10,331	$11,743	$37,205
Prior Shortfall / (Excess)	$(2,669)	$(1,258)	$24,205
Remaining Required Payment	$7,662	$10,485	$61,410
Second Quarter Estimated Taxes Paid	$(12,000)	$(12,000)	$(12,000)
Second Quarter Shortfall	$-	$-	$49,410
Second Quarter Excess	$(4,339)	$(1,515)	$-
Third Quarter Estimate			
Required Payment	$12,706	$14,118	$39,580
25% of Withholding	$2,375	$2,375	$2,375
	$10,331	$11,743	$37,205
Prior Shortfall / (Excess)	$(4,339)	$(1,515)	$49,410
Remaining Required Payment	$5,992	$10,228	$86,616
Third Quarter Estimated Taxes Paid	$(12,000)	$(12,000)	$(12,000)
Third Quarter Shortfall	$-	$-	$74,616
Third Quarter Excess	$(6,008)	$(1,773)	$-
Fourth Quarter Estimate			
Required Payment	$12,706	$14,118	$39,580
25% of Withholding	$2,375	$2,375	$2,375
	$10,331	$11,743	$37,205
Prior Shortfall / (Excess)	$(6,008)	$(1,773)	$74,616
Remaining Required Payment	$4,323	$9,970	$111,821

There are two disadvantages with aggressive tax-loss selling:

1. A client dies with the losses
2. Transaction costs

If a client dies with unused losses, the beneficiary cannot use them beyond the decedent's last tax return and only to offset gains or $3,000 of income. But if the client held the stock and died with the loss, the beneficiary's basis is the value at the date of death or alternate date. The only time that aggressive tax-loss selling creates a disadvantage is if a client had an asset for over a year, had a loss in it, we swapped out of it, the asset rebounded so that it would have had a gain had we held onto it thereby losing the basis step-up, and the client dies within a year of the replacement. And even this situation is really only a problem if the client dies so suddenly that we could not match the assets that had a loss with other assets that may have had short-term gains.

Transaction costs certainly need to be considered because of the friction that they create on returns. Transaction costs have dropped considerably but still form a hurdle before initiating the transaction.

Review Gifting Opportunities and Strategies—1 Percent

While non-charitable gifting is covered under estate planning, it is a cash-flow item as well. We look at gifting in a number of ways using a variety of strategies. Gifting is especially useful in non-legally married couples with disparate tax situations. We often try to create ways to pass income through to the partner in the lower tax bracket through gifting low-basis assets or establishing intentionally defective trusts.

After the stock market crash in 2008, it was easy to pass significant assets to client's partners or children through grantor-retained annuity trusts (GRATs). The interest rates on those trusts were modest, so all appreciation beyond the interest rate went to the beneficiary of the trust. Taxes on the gains within the trusts were paid by the grantor, so it effectively increased the size of the gift. We used multiple trusts with various maturities with different investment styles. Since a failure to meet the interest rate simply meant the trust was ineffective, it was better to have non-diversified portfolios to carry-out the terms of the GRAT. One GRAT was funded with value stocks, a different one with growth stocks, one with bonds, and one with international equities. While the client's portfolio stayed diversified, the GRATs did not. All strategies worked after the crash, but think about the benefits of multiple GRATs this way with a $2,000,000 portfolio: If large stocks are up 10 percent for the term and international stocks are down 10 percent, a combined GRAT equally divided between asset classes would not have met any hurdle rate. Two individual GRATs would have resulted in the international GRAT failing to pass assets, but the large-cap GRAT would pass the difference between the 10 percent and the hurdle interest rate.

Using these strategies becomes a long-term cash-flow issue, though, because if too much money goes into GRATs, and all of them appreciate, the client has a good and a potentially bad outcome. The good outcome is that the client transferred a bunch of money to their partner or other family members; the bad outcome is that returns often come in clusters and if those good returns were passed on to the next generation, then the retained portfolio growth may not be sufficient to meet the client's long-term needs. One way that we have dealt with this when children are the ultimate beneficiary is by using spousal access trusts from which the spouse can use the money if they need to, but if not, it gets passed on. The disadvantage of this is when the spouse with the spousal access trust dies, the money moves to the beneficiary.

Determine Whether to Accelerate or Defer Income and/or Deductions for Tax Bracket or AMT Reasons—1.5 Percent

Tax bracket arbitrage can be one of the easiest ways to improve cash flow as viewed over a three-year period. Clients who have stock options, or have both qualified and non-qualified assets (and are of the age or inclination to draw from the qualified assets), or clients who move in and out of AMT, all create multiple year planning opportunities.

For various reasons, we may have clients in exceptionally low tax brackets in any given year. For example, if a client is living off of their portfolio and we have excess losses generated from a poor investment year, the client may have little taxable income. We can use this situation to write calls on low-basis stock, sell low-basis stock, accelerate withdrawals from qualified plans, or look at converting some of the qualified plan to a Roth. In any event, we try to use up as much of the lower bracket as feasible.

We have clients that retire in other states which may not have any state income tax. Since Minnesota's tax rates are relatively high, we need to provide tax forecasts that determine from which assets to draw or sell given residency issues. The decision may be to incur short-term borrowing costs at a lower rate than the state tax costs of distributions or the concomitant state taxes on the exercise of options.

Since AMT rates are lower than ordinary income tax rates, deciding how much income we wish to bring in once we know we are in AMT is a cash-flow decision. For clients who have large purchases on the horizon for which they will need cash, we would accept bonuses rather than defer them in AMT years in order to create the cash necessary for the purchase. We would rather defer when their marginal tax bracket is more onerous.

Evaluate the Recharacterization or Conversions for IRAs to/from Roth IRAs—1 Percent

As I mentioned earlier, I think converting into a Roth is an area where people need to be far more deliberate than guidance often offers. I love Roths for a few reasons:

- They are a great asset to pass on intergenerationally
- They are wonderful as a way to create tax diversity
- Clients only withdraw from their plans what they want to spend rather than being forced to take out more because of RMDs.
- You can withdraw your contributions at any time without penalty.

While these benefits are terrific, there is a key cost associated with them—you have to pay an immediate tax on the money going into the vehicle.

To think about this simply, if tax rates stay the same throughout the holding period (and you don't care about the RMD issue) you are neutral between the Roth and a tax-deductible qualified plan. If rates go up, you are better off with the Roth. If rates go down, you were better off with the qualified plan.

The only tax rate that really matters is your client's. If your client is in a high-tax state and intends to move to a low-tax state, their tax rate may go down. If we move into a flat-tax or your client will be in AMT, their tax rate may go down. If your client has flexibility with regard to how they manage their cash flow (withdrawals from various buckets), their tax rate may go down.

We know with certainty the tax that a client is paying on a conversion or the deduction they are losing through a contribution; we have no certainty regarding the client's future tax rate. In other words, don't drink from the Roth hose, sip from the faucet. Roths are great tools, but they should not be the only one.

Once a client converts, there may be a couple of reasons why they wish to do a recharacterization:

- Something came up and they don't have the money to pay the taxes.
- The market tanked and they would rather convert at a lower valuation.

Since a client has until the due date of their tax return (including extensions) for this do-over, once the conversion decision has been made, you want to continue to review it until the time has expired for this irrevocable decision.

We have also had prospects come in who have had huge losses in their IRAs. If a client has basis in their IRA (Roth or non-deductible contributions), they can take a deduction (subjected to the 2 percent miscellaneous itemized deduction rules) if they close out of all their IRAs of the same type. There are a number of things to think about, though, including AMT considerations, early withdrawal penalties, and the fact that this money taken out cannot go back in later. This strategy really is for those who are just starting the conversion process or whose portfolios were decimated (Madoff and tech bubbles come to mind).

Conclusion

Cash-flow planning forms the basis for wealth management. Either the person at work is creating cash flow or investments at work will ultimately create it. In any event, building cash-flow models and managing to them is the first step in delivering planning.

This area flows through everything. It will lead to discussions that bring you closer to your clients and create a level of professional intimacy on which individual planning is based.

Notes

1. Hoagland, Mahlon, and Bert Dodson. *The Way Life Works*. New York: Three Rivers Press. 1998.
2. Ibid.
3. Nemeth, Maria. *The Energy of Money*. New York: Ballantine Wellspring. 1997.
4. Anthony, Mitch. *The New Retirementality*. Chicago: Dearborn Financial Publishing. 2001.
5. Diliberto, Roy. *Financial Planning—The Next Step*. Denver: FPA Press. 2006.
6. Thoreau, Henry David. *Walden*. New York: Houghton, Mifflin. 1854.
7. Buettner, Dan. *Thrive*. Washington, D.C.: National Geographic. 2010.
8. The Minnesota's chapter's web address is www.onepercentclub.org.
9. Lasser, J.K. *J.K. Lasser Your Income Tax 2011*. New Jersey: John Wiley and Sons. 2010.
10. Katz, Deena. *Deena Katz's Complete Guide to Practice Management*. New York: Bloomberg. 2009.
11. For some reason, certain clients seem to judge an accountant's talent based on whether or not they get a refund. And accountants who sense this may throw us under the bus if a client owes money due to investment gains—regardless of how well investments performed.

CHAPTER 11

Debt Management

One would think that in working with people of affluence, debt would not be an issue. Au contraire! Understanding and appropriately using debt is something with which we are constantly engaged. Businesses have always managed their balance sheets; clients need to do this as well.

Utilizing credit solutions for housing, financing of capital equipment, short-term cash flow needs, or investments are tools in which every wealth manager must become involved. Leveraging a client's balance sheet is a way to create flexibility and help them manage their cash flow. For large clients, credit solutions and credit spreads can create wealth-building opportunities that must be explored. One of our clients has more than $12 million of investment assets, some of which includes municipal bonds with varying maturity dates. We have a line of credit for her because if we have short-term cash flow needs a few months before a bond matures, it may make more sense to access the credit line than to either sell investments or keep too much cash on hand.

Practices that are not associated with an investment bank or commercial bank will outsource this area. This represents both a drawback and an opportunity. It can be a drawback in the sense that one-stop shopping may be convenient for the client. It can also be problematic in the sense that when you shop for credit for a client, you are going to be engaging another firm that would love to make a run at that client's wealth management. The benefit, though, is that by offering independent and objective credit solutions, you have the ability to shop rates and terms, bargain on collateral, and provide a credit solution that is optimal rather than simply convenient.

This area represents a relatively small piece of the index, but its importance surfaces often at unexpected times. For example, clients who had sterling balance sheets ended up needing credit solutions because they were stuck with two houses when the real estate market collapsed. If this area had not been reviewed, they would have had to sell other assets at inopportune times to manage this short-term shock.

Debt Management begins with two open-ended questions:

Percent of index for debt management—10 percent

	Percent of Debt Management Scale	Percent of Index
Have you established your philosophy regarding using savings or credit?	30	3
Is your type of debt appropriate given your wealth-management objectives?	70	7
Total	100	10

Have You Established Your Philosophy Regarding Using Savings or Credit?

Discussing with clients their feelings regarding owing money may unknowingly provide keen insight into their family-of-origin issues. Our clients' feelings around debt are often responses to their parent's feelings about money. Depression-era babies are often loath to borrow. Children of parents who made a lot of money using leverage (for example real estate developers during the boom times) are often comfortable borrowing—regardless of whether they should or shouldn't be. Clients of parents who had a tough time with money are often less inclined to seek bank financing.

In order to establish appropriate objectives within this area, we must overcome but not ignore these long-carried emotions. Interestingly, in our own practice, different people within the firm feel differently about debt. My background was one where my family was not financially successful and I had to support myself early on. This has led me to two distinct views which certainly influence the advice that I may render:

1. Since I feel like I have the same level of happiness with money as when I was without, I don't feel that money decisions are a big deal, and therefore,

2. I don't have a desire to take on much debt because servicing those loans could change the importance of money in my life.

On the other hand, my founding partner, Wil, came from a farm background where debt was a constant. His parents were farmers and entrepreneurs and passed down views about using borrowing to expand their opportunities. He feels more comfortable using debt than I do.

Neither of these approaches is necessarily right, but each of them may impact the way we discuss these issues with our clients. "We don't see things as they are, we see them as we are."[1] Debt management is an area in which we need to sit beside our clients to experience their view of the issue—regardless of where we come out on the topic.

This question represents 30 percent of this piece of the index and incorporates the following three questions for analysis.

Subcategories for have you established your philosophy regarding using savings or credit?

	Percent of Question	Percent of Category	Percent of Index
311 Determine desired level of emergency fund and credit lines	35	10.5	1.05
312 Evaluate appropriate credit cards for limits and benefits	25	7.5	0.75
313 Develop a strategy for when you wish to be debt free	40	12	1.2
Total	100	30	3

Determine Desired Level of Emergency Fund and Credit Lines—1.05 Percent

The rule of thumb for emergency funds of three months' expenses is inadequate. Developing rules for each particular client's needs and situation will result in different levels of emergency funding for various needs. For example, clients living off their portfolios may have three years, not three months, worth of expected spending set aside to avoid selling assets during market downswings.

Clients who have inconsistent earnings streams (salespeople, for example) may require more liquidity than those with predictable cash flow like salaried physicians. For clients whose earnings are quite variable, we often like to have six months of credit or cash available to them.

The decision is really one of opportunity costs. Is a client better off establishing accessible credit lines such as home equity lines as their emergency funding source rather than keeping cash set aside for events that may never occur? Most clients feel differently about things depending on their stage in life or their success in investing. Opportunity costs only exist when there are opportunities.

We almost always establish large home equity lines for clients. Through negotiating with the banks, they generally have no costs and interest rates set at London Interbank Offer Rate (LIBOR) or LIBOR plus a small margin. Recently, banks have pared back on renewal for clients who are not using their lines, but for most clients with reasonable balance sheets and good credit scores there still is ample access to this debt.

There are secondary financing sources available through unsecured debt or margin loans, but we tend to view using these for special situations where selling investments doesn't make sense and other debt has been fully extended or not available.

Evaluate Appropriate Credit Cards for Limits and Benefits—0.75 Percent

We work with clients on which credit cards will be the most attractive for them. This is a wealth-management need because credit card usage can generate significant cost savings. Since our clients do not typically carry balances, we look for credit cards with reward programs.

For example, since Delta Airlines has a Twin Cities hub, clients often like a Delta American Express card which gives clients free checked baggage, saving them around $50 for each individual flight. Additionally, they have promotions that give clients Medallion Qualifying Miles for charges above certain levels. These enable clients to board a plane earlier or be on a list for upgrades. And depending on the type of card, access to sky clubs may also be available—which provides a quick payback for the annual cost of the card.

Schwab was offering a Visa/Mastercard that deposited 2 percent of all purchases each month into the client's Schwab account. The Chase Freedom no annual fee card at the time of this writing offers 5 percent cash back in rotating categories such as gas, groceries, and so on, and 1 percent cash on everything else.

The key thing to understand is the client's intention. If a client carries a balance on his or her cards, then rewards features may be secondary to lower interest costs. Some cards are not appropriate for business use.

There are enough reward cards out there without annual fees that paying an annual fee is usually not necessary. We review this annually with our clients. A couple of web sites that we currently like in this category are www.cardratings.com and www.creditcards.com.

Develop a Strategy for When You Wish to Be Debt Free—1.2 Percent

When our clients are retired, we like to drive down their fixed costs as much as possible to help them feel more secure when they are living at least partly off their portfolios. Low interest rates have changed this strategy for certain clients. For example, if a client is spending 5 percent of the portfolio and the mortgage financing costs are less than 4 percent, we would consider maintaining the home debt.

Some clients want to be free of debt earlier than they reasonably should. Younger clients with excellent cash flow may improve their long-term position by actively using credit. The challenge is whether we should convince them of this. Over the years, we handle this by incorporating a host of behavioral observations in addition to their proclamations. For example, if a client is regularly mentioning discomfort around their debt and keeping huge balances in cash as a protective measure against the apocalypse, that's a pretty good tell that we need to pay down the mortgage. Plus, the cash hoard wipes out the spread advantage of long-term investing as compared to long-term financing.

A key thing to pay attention to with regard to ultimately paying off the mortgage debt is that because of acquisition indebtedness rules, we can't access that money later in a tax-favorable manner. It's important to distinguish between a client's temporary risk aversion during a bad market and real ongoing concerns. While there are other forms of debt that could be structured in a tax-advantaged manner, mortgage indebtedness provides the best long-term rates.

Another consideration in this category is whether there are assets that may be coming in with which to pay off debt. If a client is likely to inherit assets, it may not make sense to liquidate other investments to pay down debt. This is especially true if you consider that often clients are inheriting a certain amount of non-stock investments, yet it is stocks that often need to be sold to arrange for the payoff.

For couples, each person's view of this question may be different. We were in a meeting where one of the couple was suggesting that they buy a new home before they sell their old one. While we solved the question of how both could be financed, we offered our view that this would not be a good idea because of how cautious the other person was. In this case, the husband was very comfortable managing the debt load, but the wife was far more conservative. Distinguishing between what is financially viable and emotionally feasible is no small feat.

Is Your Type of Debt Appropriate Given Your Wealth-Management Objectives?

This is a category that needs to be looked at annually because the tracing rules for deductibility require the right debt to be associated with the right asset. For example, using a margin loan to fund home improvements would not be deductible. If you increased your stock holdings through margin and subsequently sold some of that stock and withdrew the funds to pay for the improvements, the margin interest would still be deductible as investment interest.

We not only care what type of loans clients are creating, but we also regularly review their credit scores. We have had a couple of clients become victims of identity theft, so ongoing monitoring of credit reports really hit home.

The analysis for the question above represents 70 percent of the index in the proportion shown here.

Subcategories for is your type of debt appropriate given your wealth-management objectives?

	Percent of Question	Percent of Category	Percent of Index
331 Review the best financing terms on all properties considering time horizons, interest rates, and deductibility	34	23.8	2.38
332 Review the best financing and deductibility terms on lines of credit and alternative debt	33	23.1	2.31
333 Determine current ratio as well as credit ratings	33	23.1	2.31
Total	100	70	7

Review the Best Financing Terms on All Properties Considering Time Horizons, Interest Rates, and Deductibility—2.38 Percent

Matching financing to time horizons reduces ongoing carrying costs of properties. Clients who indicate that they will only be staying in their home for another three years, should not bear the excess burden of a higher interest rate associated with a 30-year mortgage, if rates have fallen on adjustable rate mortgages (ARMs). Clients who intend to stay in their property for a relatively short time frame may choose to also use zero cost refinancing and accept a slightly higher interest rate in order to avoid paying closing costs. And some clients may want to choose a 15-year mortgage if the spread justifies it and they intend to be in their home for several years—this decision may fit nicely with their feelings about either being out of debt or their wish to free up cash flow when children are starting college (even though a 529 plan may make more financial sense!).

FIGURE 11.1   Mortgage Refinance Analysis.

Joe and Jane Doe
Mortgage Refinance Analysis
April 15, 2010

	Current	Scenario A
Mortgage	**1st Loan**	**1st Loan**
Loan Type	30-Year Fixed	30-Year Fixed
Interest Rate on Loan	4.500%	4.500%
Loan Amount	$333,700	$649,545
Closing Costs of New Loan	N/A	$15,845
Cash Flow Payback	1st Loan	1st Loan
Monthly Payment	$3,251	$4,291
Months until Mortgage is Paid Off	167	225
Interest Over Remaining Life of Loan *	$62,906	$188,177
Annual Cash Flow Savings vs. Current (pre-tax)	N/A	($12,477)
Principal Reduction in 1st Year (savings)	N/A	($1,271)
Cash Flow Payback (tax adjusted in months)	N/A	0
Interest Cost Payback		
Interest Savings in 1st Year (tax adjusted)	N/A	-$8,578
Interest Cost Payback (tax adjusted in months)	N/A	360

NOTES:
1) Origination fee is assumed to be fully tax deductible immediately (rather than being amortized over the life of the loan).
2) Closing costs may include an escrow account (if desired), third party fees (i.e. title insurance, appraisal, etc.), or other prepaids not fully considered in this estimate.
3) Any cash TO borrower at settlement is presumed to be used to buy, build, or improve home. If otherwise, then interest on debt may be not be fully tax deductible.
*Interest Over Remaining Life of Loan is tax adjusted.

Developing a database that allows you to screen for clients' mortgage rates enables you to let them know between meetings when a refinancing is appropriate (see Figure 11.1). Since interest rate movements do not necessarily coincide with client meetings or phone calls, creating a strategy around contacting clients who are candidates is a tremendous service.

Since there are almost always lower initial costs for using an ARM, the decision on terms is a combination of time horizon, spread, cash flow needs, and client personality.

- Time horizon. As mentioned earlier, it does not make sense to have long-term financing in place for properties that you intend to own only for a few years, but the converse may not be true.
- Spread. The difference between one-, three-, five-, seven-, and 10-year ARMs as compared with 15- and 30-year mortgages have narrowed recently, but still cause choices to be made. For the last couple of decades, buying shorter-term ARMs and continuing to refinance resulted in the lowest carrying costs on mortgages. Most of the time we were using zero-cost refinancing options so that clients could redo their mortgages multiple times without incurring costs. If clients had to pay anything, then before we would recommend refinancing, we wanted them to be able to pay back their costs with reduced after-tax mortgage savings in less than three years (depending on how long they would be in the home). The spread call is one on prospective rates, though. Locking in 15- or 30-year fixed rates becomes more attractive if you are forecasting rising rates. For commercial buildings which clients leased back to their businesses, banks would often provide two-tier financings—a five-year fixed rate with prepayment penalties amortized over 20 or 30 years coupled with a floating rate loan tied to LIBOR which adjusted monthly. Often the short-term loan could be paid down without penalty. Both notes would be rewritten (with the bank charging new origination fees) after five years. We usually suggested clients take the minimum amount on the fixed note and (often through a triple net lease) pay down the shorter-term note more aggressively.
- Cash-flow needs. Some clients have temporary cash-flow issues for which a debt restructuring may be appropriate. It is difficult to justify a long-term decision for a short-term problem, but at times this is exactly what needs to be done.
- Client personality. Things are changing because interest rates are at historic lows and most likely will creep up, government-backed agencies

are in turmoil and may not survive, banks will likely be required to hold more of the mortgages which they originate, and tax laws could be changing impacting deductibility of mortgage interest. All of these factors may change the environment enough whereby the predictability of fixed-rate mortgages at a higher initial rate is preferable to an adjustable. For some clients, regardless of what happens, they do not like the uncertainty of rates moving against them, even if you can show them how far rates would need to move in order for them to justify taking out the higher-costing mortgage. Other clients want 15-year mortgages. If there is no rate differential, we would prefer a 30-year mortgage with the intent of paying it off over 15 years as a way to maintain client flexibility. Some clients would still prefer to be locked in for the 15 years as a discipline.

Another consideration in this area is whether intra-family loans are appropriate as a way to increase the relatively safe income that a parent may be receiving on their term deposits while providing lower-cost financing to their children. While some clients don't want to be their kids' lender, this option can be a positive for both parties if executed well and each party is responsible. If we are working with the children, we will ask whether we can propose the idea to their parents.

Review the Best Financing Terms and Deductibility Terms on Lines of Credit and Alternative Debt—2.31 Percent

Regularly reviewing terms and agreements on all debt gives a client a chance to change and improve their situation in many ways. For example, being able to change a note for a partnership investment from joint and several to proportional liability decreases the risk of a client with a strong balance sheet supporting the partner with a weaker balance sheet should a project run into trouble. For clients who have pledged securities as their collateral on loans, monitoring the account to take back securities as the market improves so as to not have too much coverage on any loan frees up their balance sheet for other purposes.

Regular review allows you to look at when you can move high-expense debt for better terms or rates. There are times when clients may have had a stretched balance sheet that becomes unencumbered after an event, thereby improving their financing options.

It is astounding the number of wealthy people with whom we work that have credit card debt that can easily be paid off from their assets or from alternative financing. Some clients prefer the mental accounting of keeping money in short-term instruments even though they have consumer debt. If they won't let us pay it off by reducing their assets, they may allow us to refinance. The one thing that we watch for is simply counseling clients to use alternative financing as a way to pay off credit card debt if we don't have a good explanation for how this debt was built in the first place. For example, one of our clients is comfortable carrying levels of debt on their home equity line. If we pay this credit line down, they end up using it again. Even though it may make financial sense to bring that down to zero, we tend to keep it at a higher balance because they don't go beyond their limits in that category.

At times we run into situations where a client's adult child may have credit issues. We meet with them to find a number of maxed-out credit cards on which they are paying the minimums. For them, we typically do a credit-consolidation plan where we reduce their number of cards, change to lower-carrying-cost cards, and create a spreadsheet where we target which cards we will pay off first. We may not choose to pay off the highest interest first, but rather work on cards based on minimum payments. If they pay a little more interest, but don't have as big of a monthly obligation, we may keep that card until we pay off lower balance/higher monthly payment cards, after which we can double up.

Determine Your Current Ratio as Well as Credit Ratings—2.31 Percent

A current ratio is current assets divided by current liabilities. This is a simple metric that we use to measure how liquid a client is. We would like for this to be infinite, meaning no current liabilities, but at a minimum, we are looking for a two-to-one ratio. Most clients have no short-term debt, but for those who do, calling this item out to them is the potential canary in the coal mine for other issues.

The bigger issues that we confront are client credit reports and credit scores. Every year, we help our clients obtain their credit reports through the credit reporting agencies so we can see early on whether there may be issues that need to be resolved. We suggest requesting a report every four months to take full advantage of the free reporting from the three agencies, but many clients just ask for them once a year.

While we look at this as a way to see if we need to work on rebuilding client credit, its real purpose is protecting clients from identity theft and being aware if there is anything strange that appears on their scoring.

Conclusion

Clients may use credit strategically or desperately. There are a number of tools to help clients get the most out of their balance sheets by developing credit planning. While this item only accounts for 10 percent of the total index score, it still represents an area where tremendous value can be created.

Note

1. Nin, Anais. *The Diary of Anais Nin*. Vol. 3. Boston, MA.: Harcourt. 1971.

CHAPTER 12

Investment Planning (Accumulation)

Many prospects come into our offices wishing to have their investment itch scratched, not realizing that hives cover all aspects of their wealth-management bodies. The assets-under-management model has, maybe inadvertently, made wealth management a euphemism for asset management. While no one can denounce the importance of managing investments as an integral piece of meeting long-range planning objectives, it is still just a piece.

For a young doctor with $200,000 of investment assets, is it more important to capture an incremental 1 or 2 percent of return or to insure that they are saving the tens of thousands of dollars in their retirement and personal accounts? There are certainly stages and incidences when investment planning is the key focal point—often when a portfolio has been incorrectly invested for a clients' risk tolerance or lifestyle objectives; the key is to make sure this area holds its place in the wealth management area but no more.

Investment planning is not simply about delivering higher returns. It needs to be about discovering a client's attitudes about risk, understanding their time horizons, developing a philosophy of what success should look like, and creating a mechanism for managing back to agreed-upon allocations. We all have investment styles—only some of which fit our client's expectations of how investments should be run. Selling prospects on returns through a style that does not fit the prospects may create a short-term relationship filled with frustration for both parties. At times, the breadth of planning can overcome this discomfort, but bad markets or bad performance in the client's mind will eventually win out.

One of our very good clients was the chief financial officer for a large private company. When he retired, he split his assets evenly between us and another investment manager. In his words, "a horse race" is always a good thing. Depending on the assets, this may be a reasonable proposition (although virtually all of our clients prefer us to manage all of their assets). It doesn't seem totally fair to us, though, because we provide a whole lot more for the asset-management dollar than does this investment house.

When a client is living off their portfolio, though, a horse race can be a very difficult thing. If one firm thinks the track is a mile long and we feel the track is significantly longer, there will be huge dispersion of returns, varying tax consequences, and significantly different risk factors. If return is all that matters, that may be fine. But it isn't. How those returns come may be equally significant. Simply stated, a client who starts with $1,000,000, is spending $50,000 a year from their portfolio, and receives a sequence of returns like this: 10 percent, –5 percent, –10 percent, and 25 percent would have around $776,000 (presuming all money comes out at the end of the year), yet their compounded investment return was better than 4 percent annually. On the other hand, if the portfolio earned a steady 4 percent (with the 5 percent withdrawal rate) then the client would have more than $950,000 at the end of the period. The chance for outsize returns may not adequately compensate the client for the additional risk. Each portfolio may have similar expected returns, but the variance of those returns causes very different results.

This example holds true for undiversified stock positions as well. A single stock, regardless of how much a client knows about that stock and loves it, is always riskier than a portfolio of stocks, bonds, cash, and alternatives. This may be a fine risk to accept during different times in a client's investment life, but it is generally not attractive at the time that they are living off of their portfolios.

In other words, the horse needs to be retired when it is time for it to go to stud! Living off the portfolio is equivalent to living off past accomplishments; going forward the portfolio needs to be optimized to handle certain expenditures in an uncertain future. A horse race pitting someone with diversification among asset classes and, therefore, lower volatility against someone with a particular investment style and higher volatility, must end when the client is living off their portfolio. The negative compounding of bad returns coupled with withdrawals is simply too much to overcome. The bad result (outliving the portfolio) is so significant, that it is not a risk worth taking.

There are different stages in a clients' life where taking on additional risks, while not wise, may be acceptable. Some clients don't want to regret diversifying out of a single stock position only to have that stock have extraordinary returns. By incorporating a cash-flow analysis, we can show how much the client needs in a diversified, more predictable portfolio as compared to the more volatile, single-stock investment. We may suggest selling enough of the single stock and diversifying for them to meet their lifestyle needs and let the rest ride (because no matter the odds, it is still a gamble).

Going through the investment piece on the Wealth Management Index™ will help determine how a client should be invested, but in many ways more important, why they should be invested.

Percent of index (25 percent) for investment planning (accumulation)

	Percent of Investment Planning Scale	Total Index Weight
Have you developed an investment philosophy?	60	15
Have you determined the mechanics for managing your portfolio and the evaluation of what success looks like?	40	10
Total	100	25

Have You Developed an Investment Philosophy?

An investment philosophy needs to be determined outside the confines of the news, the markets, and the neighbors. The first step in managing a client's portfolio consistent with their objectives has to come from an understanding of those objectives and issues that may impact them.

The client-investment philosophy will be influenced by your own. "You need to go soul searching and formulate your own investment beliefs: a clear view on how you perceive the way capital markets work, and how your organization can add value and strive for excellence."[1] Most clients cede investment decisions to us by agreeing to the asset allocation we establish or the investments we use to meet their allocation. Clients who choose to work with us buy in to our philosophies as they understand them. Our approach may not completely replace theirs, but it certainly influences it.

Philosophy plays into a client's understanding of risk. In 2008, many clients realized that their capacity to accept risk—whether they were financially able to accept portfolio swings—did not match their appetite for risk—how much of those swings they could stomach. And no models or metrics could have accurately predicted how their behavior matched their feelings about risk. Some with a terrible risk appetite refused to open their statements, others got angry, some became sad or anxious. These varying responses were to the same stimulus.

Ironically, as clients are building portfolios they should crave bad markets. "In brief, rational investors should only want stocks to be low in price and should be pleased to see stocks going down—so they can buy more. We should only want stock prices to be high when we are selling. . . most long-term investors will be net buyers in future years, not sellers."[2] Only when they are net sellers of stocks should they wish for markets to go up. Many people's reaction to risk is against their self-interests.

The asset allocation is the last thing that is developed because it is born from the philosophy coupled with needs. Needs compete. A client with low risk tolerance and low savings will need to change their picture of what the future will look like because they will have to save more today, spend less tomorrow, and work longer. Yet the client can't be strong armed into an allocation that they will regret. Experience may lead clients to accept greater levels of risk, but experience cuts both ways. Clients who experienced huge volatility in their portfolios before they came to us may view a lower volatility portfolio through their lens of experience—making them reel when the markets are swooning, even though the portfolio doesn't drop as much.

Subcategories for have you developed an investment philosophy?

	Percent of Question	Percent of Category	Percent of Index
411 Define your attitude toward investment risk	10	6	1.5
412 Determine whether the portfolio return objectives are consistent with these attitudes	10	6	1.5
413 Define the various time horizons for which you are saving	10	6	1.5
414 Determine legal, investment, regulatory restrictions or unique circumstances impacting your portfolio	10	6	1.5
415 Determine a suitable asset allocation	60	36	9
Total	100	60	15

This area of the index is one that is regularly addressed. While the performance monitoring is obvious, it is this philosophy section that is more mutable as clients discover things about themselves and the markets. Also, this is the area where time horizons are explored. Time horizons have a huge influence over policy decisions.

Define Your Attitude toward Investment Risk—1.5 Percent

Attitudes toward risk are certainly easier to define looking backward than looking forward. There are a number of risk-tolerance and risk-capacity materials that are available, but we have not found them to be effective. We discuss ranges of returns with clients and worst-case situations as a way to gauge how they may react to market volatility, but clients really do not know until they are immersed in it. This does not make the discussion of risk moot, though.

There are several ways to talk about risk with clients. Also, we need to agree that any rejection of one risk is an automatic acceptance of another. For example, rejecting volatility risk often means accepting purchasing-power risk. This is not always true, because at times returns are so compromised through poorly managing volatility that purchasing power drops. Being solely focused on outliving one's assets increases the likelihood of under living one's experiences.

By now, we are all familiar with the field of behavioral finance and its implications regarding how it impacts our decision making. Behavioral finance gives us the keenest insight into how we view risk, because at its basic level, heuristics are mental shortcuts created to help increase our pleasure or reduce our pain. Accepting or avoiding risks does the same. If all decisions came from the rational brain, we would weight risk proportionately to its expected outcomes. No one does this.

We rely on emotional decision making:

- "When the problem is ill structured and complex.
- When information is incomplete, ambiguous, and changing.
- When the goals are ill defined, shifting, or competing.
- When the stress is high, because either time constraints and/or high stakes are involved.
- When decisions rely on interactions with others."[3]

Basically this is anything that has to do with a client facing wealth management. Therefore, perceptions of risk are going to be carved by reactions to our experiences or expectations regarding those experiences—regardless of how likely they are to occur.

We know from behavioral finance that losses are far more painful than gains are pleasurable. This makes discounting a client's interpretation of their willingness to trade gains for losses appropriate.

This awareness of loss aversion is problematic when the market is going up and anything that balances the portfolio hurts performance, which is why general discussions of risk should be framed around the cost of not meeting objectives, rather than only rates of return. When we report returns, we not only report them relative to benchmarks, but also to the Consumer Price Index (CPI), because ultimately client investments need to be spent to pay for future costs.

The big advantage for the client of bringing risk back into the context of spending power is that it changes the magnitude of both gains and losses. If a client suffers a $200,000 portfolio hit, that may mean $8,000 to $12,000 less spending in a given year. Clients can take something over which they feel like they have little control—the markets—and substitute something over which they have more control—their spending. If you set aside cash to meet spending requirements, then clients don't even need to sell at low prices to meet their obligations, again giving them control over timing decisions.

Another risk that is often not considered is maverick risk. This type of risk is when a client's portfolio is so different from what they are used to hearing about that underperformance causes the relationship to be jeopardized. We experienced this throughout the late 1990s when the Standard & Poor's (S&P) and particularly the NASDAQ were hitting new highs and any diversifying feature in the portfolio—value stocks, international stocks, and bonds—caused a drag. This was a noteworthy problem at the time because clients were being inundated with how great the stock market was doing. We lost a couple of clients to themselves—they could buy Microsoft or Intel or Cisco and do way better than our portfolios were doing. Unfortunately for those who left us, those stocks blew up with the tech bubble and our portfolios held up well.

We do not give clients a risk-tolerance number. It is a judgment based on personal experience, interactions, and whatever wisdom we may have assembled over the years. Since we are in constant discussions and meetings with clients, we are managing face to face their risk concerns. This doesn't ameliorate them, but it helps somewhat alleviate them. While this is not satisfying to someone who wants metrics, it is certainly more authentic.

Determine Whether the Portfolio Return Objectives Are Consistent with These Attitudes—1.5 Percent

John, who was in financial difficulty, walked into a church and started to pray. "Listen God," John said. "I know I haven't been perfect but I really need to win the lottery. I don't have a lot of money. Please help me out." He left the church, a week went by, and he hadn't won the lottery, so he walked into a synagogue. "Come on, God," he said. "I really need this money. My mom needs surgery and I have bills to pay. Please let me win the lottery." He left the synagogue, a week went by, and he didn't win the lottery. So, he went to a mosque and started to pray again. "You're starting to disappoint me, God," he said. "I've prayed and prayed. If you just let me win the lottery, I'll be a better person. I don't have to win the jackpot, just enough to get me out of debt. I'll give some to charity, even. Just let me win the lottery." John thought this did it, so he got up and walked outside. The clouds opened up and a booming voice said, "John, buy a lottery ticket."[4]

We have clients looking for the free lunch. While some say diversification is investing's free lunch, it isn't. It may reduce risk, but it doesn't make it go away. The lunch is subsidized, not free.

So when clients want to know what the cost of avoiding volatility risk is, we try to show it through prospective returns. When we do our long-term planning for clients, we vary our expected returns as well as the standard deviation of those returns based on a combination of historical and prospective data. When we spell out expected returns over the next seven years in our annual investment-policy review, we change those returns based on what has transpired over the last few years. We base these expected returns using a mid-point asset-allocation weighting for our categories and a combination of historical returns and volatility coupled with forward returns and volatility obtained from a variety of sources. The following chart represents how we modified our prospective return as the markets improved. The quick read of this is that during this period mean reversion was clearly working—we had our highest prospective returns when the markets were the cheapest and continued to lower them as the markets improved (see Figure 12.1).

When we talk about volatility, we use Ibbotson's historical numbers. Clients (as well as many financial journalists) will judge the risk of a portfolio by the weight of bonds to stocks. First, there are many categories of stocks—not each of which is equally risky at any particular point in time. Second, bonds can be used offensively or defensively and again represent varying degrees of risk based on valuation measures. Third, alternatives fall somewhere in between stocks and bonds and can change the risk profile

FIGURE 12.1   Mean Reversion.

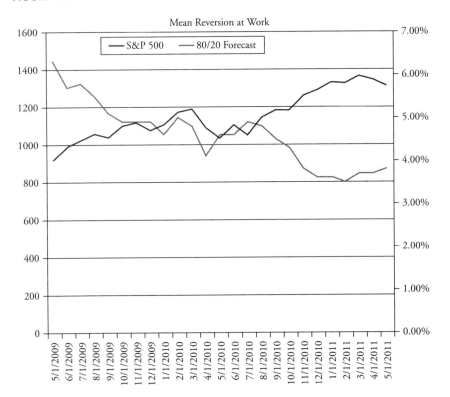

of a portfolio. In other words, making a judgment about the riskiness of a portfolio based on its stock-to-bond weighting is like deciding where someone is from based on where they are standing. If you are in the middle of a suburb, you may have a better chance of being right than if you are in the middle of a national conference.

Clients must choose the amount of volatility that they are willing to accept for their desired returns. We make valuation decisions that would over or underweight a portfolio in particular categories, which gives us room to maneuver within the 80/20 or 70/30 framework. During the meltdown of 2008, for clients who wanted to own less stocks, we substituted high-yield bonds as a way to stay invested but increase their bond exposure. Once the markets recovered, we kept clients at the new stock-to-bond allocation because they proved to us that they couldn't handle the ups and downs of stocks in the amount that we held for them. While they will forgo future upside for reduced volatility, it didn't cost them on the rebound because of the stock-like characteristics of high-yield bonds.

The choice to reduce portfolio weightings is a cascading decision because it leads to needing more money saved or invested to create the same expected future lifestyle. It also leads to lower spending policies when the client is living off their portfolio. For some clients, this may mean not only is there no free lunch, but they won't be able to afford to eat out.

Clients ultimately need to decide where they are on this risk-versus-return tradeoff. If a client is more aggressive than we think is appropriate for the risk tolerance that they showed us, we communicate that to them. It may mean that we cannot continue to manage their portfolios because we don't want to be in the situation where they are not going to have their needs met and yet hold us responsible for it. Or worse, they won't make the necessary lifestyle changes (spending less and saving more) to meet their new possibility and we don't expect them to be successful in their planning.

There has been a lot of discussion in the industry regarding whether expected returns should lead to changes in allocations. We don't believe that a market trading at 20 times earnings will have the same expected returns as the same market trading at 10 times earnings. Yet we also don't know when the expensive market gets cheaper or the cheap market gets rich. We manage this by changing expected seven-year returns (as I previously explained) and by allowing us the latitude in our investment policy to have ranges within categories. These ranges are governors so that we don't eliminate categories in which we probably should have some exposure or that we don't over emphasize other categories. I prefer to call this market managing rather than market timing, but it is certainly different than a rigid buy-and-hold strategy. We also use the opportunities that expensive markets give us to more aggressively fund donor-advised funds with appreciated stock. At times, we have modified our cash policy for clients spending their portfolios to increase the money set aside for expenses beyond the original three-year target.

Tax considerations also play into whether portfolio returns can meet objectives. Returns tend to be reported before tax, but the dollars left for a client are dependent upon where a client's assets reside. Clients who come to us with large retirement portfolios and little else lose the benefits of capital gains and tax-free income from municipals, but they pay no taxes until withdrawals. These clients do better annually with their taxable bonds until it is time to spend the money.

The difficulty in looking at annual after-tax returns is that tax rates are unpredictable. Clients whose parents die with large gains may pay no capital gains tax on the sale of those investments. Clients who move to other states may see different tax rates. Clients who own variable annuities see long-term capital gains turn into ordinary income. These factors need to be included in the solution for how a portfolio should be invested.

The best way we have found for people to become comfortable with portfolio volatility is by showing them what percentage of their portfolio is invested in which manner for which time period. We call this bucketing and actually use buckets for the illustration. For some clients, we may run separate portfolios with different asset-allocation strategies depending on how they view the money being invested. But the easiest way to think about the bucket is that we fill up the spending bucket with three years worth of cash. The second bucket is a cash-flow replacement bucket or lifestyle bucket and in it we hold all of our bonds and alternatives. The last bucket is the long-term replacement or legacy bucket and this is where we use equities. Visually, clients can see in a bad market how much of their portfolios could be sold before they have to spend their equities. This has given great comfort to nervous clients.

Define the Various Time Horizons for Which You Are Saving—1.5 Percent

Clients have a variety of time horizons for which they put away money. Unfortunately, in good and bad markets investors conflate the purpose of the money with their gains and losses. When markets are strong, clients hate having cash sitting around—even if it is going to be spent in the next few months. When the markets are falling, clients forget that they still need exposure to stocks to meet their long-term obligations.

The bucket approach helps client see things more clearly. A thorough cash-flow analysis reveals what expected expenses will be incurred in the next three years as well as what large planned expenditures will be made. This money is in cash or short-term instruments with little or no market risk.

Clients at times have multiple horizons for the same money. A partially funded 529 plan may mean that the dollars will be used for one or two of the four college years. If the client knows that they are going to pay for the first year of college, then that money needs to be in the guaranteed account. But if the client wants to be aggressive with the money, they can use it in the outlying years if the market is accommodating. It's the same money only with different time horizons. Some clients will make purchases if their investments allow them to do so. Again, this money has a different time horizon than set-in-stone spending. The more discretion with regard to spending, the more volatility a client's portfolio is able to take.

Recently a prospect came in with several million dollars from a divorce. She was told that she would be fine. What does that mean? How do we know unless we tie her assets into her objectives into her spending? She had a few million dollars sitting in cash, because she could not yet see how this money could be used effectively for her, yet she felt that she was spending principal. I talked with her about the various buckets, but let her know that we couldn't decide how to invest the money until we were aware of her various needs for her various time horizons.

Now when I talk about time horizons, I know that I am venturing into the subject of time diversification. I also know that Paul Samuelson and several others have shown that the probability of incurring a loss increases over time and that the magnitude of the potential loss increases with a longer time horizon. While standard deviation may drop with time, the reason that the potential loss increases with time is because the portfolio is larger. But our experience is that clients can handle the large losses if their spending and time horizons match. The counterargument to the larger potential loss is that each year that loss does not incur, there is a larger potential gain that is being compromised. This leads me to the discussion of spending policies.

Spending policies[5]

People who are living off of their assets have multiple time periods and multiple objectives. Their short-term time horizon is for the money off of which they will be living for the next few years. Their long-term time horizon may be for legacy purposes. Everything in between is creating a way to keep filling up the three-year bucket while meeting the other agreed-upon long-term objectives.

The first thing we establish is how long the client wishes the portfolio to last. For most clients, a joint life expectancy of 95 feels appropriate to them. The interesting thing about any distribution planning is that you are exaggerating the importance of bad outcomes. If you think about it, the percentage of clients who live to 95 is relatively small. The number of consecutive bad market periods used for modeling is unprecedented. This means that almost always, clients will have more money than they thought they would at the end of their lives.

The second piece we evaluate is the amount of the clients' investment portfolio that they wish to leave to either heirs or charity. For this analysis, we exclude real estate in which they are living. We may include real estate if it is anticipated that there is a date when it will be sold and invested. We may also include an expected inheritance in this amount.

After these first two areas have been agreed upon, we then determine what the allocation is. The stock-to-bond allocation will determine prospective returns and prospective volatility, both of which influence the amount of money available to spend. We take these three areas and incorporate a spending percentage.

The spending percentage was determined by using a Monte Carlo simulation for various investment rates. We use distinct periods—1928 to 1957, 1953 to 1982, and 1978 to 2007 to illustrate how the spending policy would have fared during each of these periods. The Monte Carlo was run based on returns and standard deviation using Ibbotson historical data and standard deviations as well as expected future returns using our forecasts. Spending percentages get adjusted annually to account for the forecast. We use a three-year portfolio balance (rolling average) to determine the value of the portfolio. With the Monte Carlo, we normally pick a success rate ranging from 89 percent (for 50-year time horizons) ramping up to 95 percent (for 10-year timeframes).

The result is a spending number, when paired with Social Security and pensions, that gives the client an annual spending level. But this spending level is not permanent. It can increase over time if the portfolio grows in value; it can also decrease if the portfolio falls. It is not tied to inflation because we view inflation as a long-term problem more than a short-term one. In other words, a properly invested portfolio will grow over time, thereby allowing for greater total withdrawals. Inflation will cause the spending power of the portfolio to erode, but those effects are cumulative. If we are able to control spending in the ways described, then protecting against inflation becomes a natural byproduct rather than a driver. We use two distinct controls on the spending—floors and alarms.

A floor is where spending can drop by no more than 5 percent from the prior year. This reduction can occur only once every three years. We hold this floor in place until the portfolio surpasses the level that triggered the floor or an alarm is triggered. Floors occur when the annual portfolio spending is greater than 10 percent of their assets for a client with a time horizon longer than 15 years, and greater than 12 percent with the time horizon longer than 10 years but less than 15 years. The alarm results in a 5 percent cut each year until they are no longer in that situation. In no year can the spending drop by 10 percent. While we have never experienced a market where successive alarms would be executed, we cannot eliminate the possibility. It is important to be a little conservative because Monte Carlo simulations are based on Gaussian probability, thereby understating the likelihood of extreme events. "If you are going to use probability to model a financial market, then you had better use the right kind of probability. Real markets are wild."[6]

This approach means that the client's spending does not increase with inflation, but rather with their average rolling portfolio movement. We have found that this allows clients to have a larger initial spending rate and is also more reflective of client behavior. Our experience has been that clients spend less when they feel poor. If their investments have fallen, they may not buy the car or take the trip. It is up to us to drive down fixed costs so that they are in a position to make those choices.

We have also found that some clients may have periods where they spend too much. We keep track of this in a phantom deficit account, which they need to pay back. If they don't do so, then there will need to be a complete spending policy reset—which means a lower floor and a decrease in spending ability. If a client doesn't spend enough, we create the phantom surplus account for future large items.

The spending policy maximizes spending, but this means that the client needs to set aside money from their monthly cash flow for larger purchases.

When a new client comes in, we use our returns over the prior three years to establish the set point for investment policy purposes (see Figures 12.2 and 12.3).

FIGURE 12.2 Goals-Based Allocation.

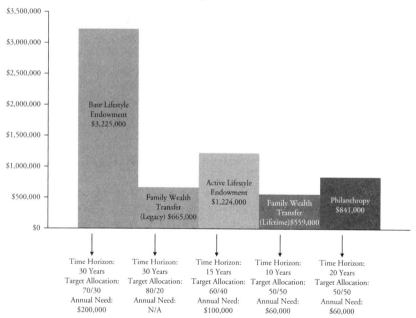

DISCLAIMER: Information is based on a Monte Carlo analysis run for 5,000 random iterations with a success rate that varies between 89%–95% based on time horizon. Success of wealth-preservation goal is measured by terminal value at end of the defined time horizon. Spending is based on portfolio returns and is not guaranteed to maintain purchasing power.

FIGURE 12.3 Spending-Policy Deliverable.

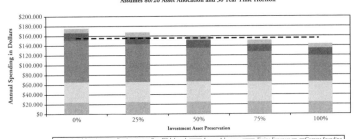

Client & Co-Client
Determining Annual Spending Amount

Time Horizon
Today to Age 95

Investment Asset Preservation
% of Assets to Meet

Asset Allocation
Stock-to-Bond

Initial Spending %

X

3-Year Portfolio Balance (Rolling Average)

Future
Withdrawals
Supported By

FLOOR   **ALARM**

Client & Co-Client
TOTAL Spending Based on Legacy Goals
May 11, 2010

Investment Asset Preservation	0%	25%	50%	75%	100%
Income from Portfolio					
Social Security Advance	$20,000	$20,000	$20,000	$20,000	$20,000
Mortgage Expenses	$10,000	$10,000	$10,000	$10,000	$10,000
Other Withdrawals to Meet Base Spending	$103,100	$93,100	$83,100	$73,100	$64,000
Other Income Sources					
Social Security	$30,000	$30,000	$30,000	$30,000	$30,000
Pension	$50,000	$50,000	$50,000	$50,000	$50,000
Less: Expenses					
Projected Taxes	($38,400)	($36,200)	($34,200)	($32,600)	($31,000)
TOTAL Spending (Net of Taxes)	**$174,701**	**$166,900**	**$159,400**	**$150,900**	**$143,000**

Assumes 80/20 Asset Allocation and 30 Year Time Horizon

DISCLAIMER: Information is based on a Monte Carlo analysis run for 5,000 random iterations with a targeted success rate of 92% based on a time horizon of 30 years. Success of wealth preservation goal is measured by terminal value at end of the defined time horizon. Spending is based on portfolio returns and is not guaranteed to maintain purchasing power.

Determine Legal, Investment, Regulatory Restrictions or Unique Circumstances Impacting Your Portfolio—1.5 Percent

Many clients have certain issues which impact how their money is invested. They may be corporate insiders with either holding requirements or restrictions as to when they can sell their company stock. They may be a socially responsible investor who wishes to exclude certain types of investments for personal or religious reasons. They could possibly have low-basis stock that may limit diversification opportunities. They could be expecting an inheritance from a parent who has considerable assets in a particular stock.

These restrictions impact the expected returns of the portfolio as well as issues regarding how cash will be raised. Any restriction that limits the amounts or types of investments we own will inevitably either increase the risk or decrease the expected return of a portfolio.

Holding requirements result in similar limitations. While a client may do incredibly well hanging onto their company stock, they do so by accepting greater risk and, most likely, a higher standard deviation on their portfolio.

Limitations are not quite so clear on low-basis stock. When a client has a significant holding in very low-basis stock in a large company, any choice to diversify is going to automatically decrease the portfolio by the immediate (within 12 months) capital gains cost. This cost must be considered when evaluating how and when to diversify. There may be ways to synthetically reduce the portfolio risk while not triggering the capital gains tax. For example, can a client with a large holding in a large-cap oil company stay neutral in that position by pairing the stock with a sector exchange-traded fund (ETF)? Is the client able to enter into a pre-paid forward contract to give them more flexibility with regard to their sale date (and their taxes due), even though they can no longer couple this with an immediate share loan tendered for cash?

There are other ways to diversify with low-basis stock. Companies such as Parametric (www.parametricportfolio.com) can integrate a low-basis stock position with a portfolio around this position that attempts to track a particular index. While there will be tracking error, the cost of it may be less than the cost of creating the sale of the position and investing the proceeds.

Determine a Suitable Asset Allocation—9 Percent

This is the mother lode of this area because each of the aforementioned areas rolls into this ultimate decision.[7] And this decision will likely dictate the future value of the portfolio more than any other investment decision. "Although investment strategy can result in significant returns, these are dwarfed by the return contributions from investment policy—the selection of asset classes and their normal weights."[8] Basically, the decision of how much of your portfolio to distribute between stocks, bonds, cash, and alternatives is going to be the main driver of your returns.

We establish ranges for our portfolios among the various asset classes. We describe these ranges in the context of our investment policy statement.[9] Also within the investment policy is our forecast for expected returns given the asset allocation chosen. We change this forecast monthly and try to have our clients sign new investment-policy statements annually.

For our portfolios, the ranges within asset classes serve three purposes:

1. It provides a discipline and insures that we will always have a certain percentage of the portfolio in large, mid, small, and international stocks as well as cash and bonds. We tend to use alternatives for defense, so there are times when we may not choose to own any in our portfolios.

2. It protects us from our hubris in the sense that even if we are certain that large stocks are the absolute best asset class for the time being and therefore we should put all of our money in large caps—we can't. This is a very good governor for a firm that is trying to generate consistent and somewhat predictable returns so that clients can spend the money that they want to spend when they want to spend it. More important, the consistency that this strategy produces has created more terminal wealth for clients from January 1, 2002, through March 31, 2011, than a benchmark portfolio of index funds and vastly more than simply the Standard and Poor's (S&P).

3. It helps us adhere to our fundamental investment belief of reversion to the mean among asset classes. While it generally makes sense with stocks to let your winners ride and sell your losers, this is not the case for asset-class investing. We allocate our dollars among the asset classes using a combination of active and passive funds. We will take money out of categories or funds that have performed well and allocate to those that have not done as well. We may be overweight or underweight an asset class given our expected future returns for this class—but we will not be completely out of the assert class. While we are big believers in mean reversion, we also don't know when things will revert.[10]

Our asset-class investing has continued to develop over time. Some of the major changes include:

• Creating an *alternatives* asset class and increasing the allowable allocation into it. We typically use regular open-ended mutual funds for this area.

Now that mutual funds can go both long and short, we have found that we can get lower fees, marketability, and more transparency using mutual funds than we can get through either individual hedge funds or funds-of-funds hedge funds. We include many types of investments for this category including real estate, commodities, market neutral, risk arbitrage, and any other vehicle to which we don't wish to have a permanent allocation. We also tend to use this area defensively rather than offensively.

- Collapsing *Bonds* and *Cash* together rather than in discreet categories. This has given us broader flexibility to have more or less invested in bonds depending on the opportunities that we see. A key point is that when we have clients living off of their portfolios, the cash that we set aside is generally unmanaged, and in this market environment, often out of our custody, sitting in an online bank account.

- Modifying various ranges of investments to reflect the incorporation of the alternatives.

One of the things that we have explored modifying is whether we want to split asset classes by risk characteristics rather than distinct investments. This would allow us to room to expand beyond our current bands if we feel particularly good about foreign as compared with United States, for example. We have been reluctant to do so because this can put us in a position where our overconfidence may lead us to sub-optimal decisions.[11]

Figure 12.4 is an example of our investment-policy statement that shows the ranges as well as other information we wish to convey to the client. We use historical returns for best and worst case scenarios. Even in 2008, our numbers did not hit the worst case represented.

FIGURE 12.4 Investment-Policy Statement Sample Page.

Investment Policy Statement
Client and Co-Client
Month Day, Year

I. Potrfolio Objective:

The focus of the portfolio will be **Appreciation or Aggressive Growth.** *(Time horizon is long and/or the portfolio is not needed to support living expenses)*
The portfolio will be structured to provide both **Appreciation & Income or Growth.** *(Cash is needed from portfolio to support living expenses, but*

time horizon is long and/or client wishes to leave inheritance. 70/30 Model where cash is not needed from the portfolio)

The portfolio will be structured to provide both **Appreciation & Income or Moderate Growth.** *(Cash is needed from portfolio to support living expenses, but time horizon is long and/or client wishes to leave inheritance. 60/40 Model where cash is not needed from portfolio)*

The focus of the portfolio will be to provide **Income or Conservative Growth,** while preserving purchasing power. *(Cash is needed from portfolio to support living expenses. Time horizon is short, and there are no major inheritance goals. Also used for 50/50 portfolios and below where client is not taking cash from the portfolio but whose main focus is maintaining lifestyle needs)*

II. Risk Objective:

(This section will be personalized to each client by the Investment Analyst.)

III. Return Objective:

Given anticipated cash needs, time horizon, and ability to accept risk, the portfolio will be constructed to achieve an expected return of **3.8% above the inflation rate** over a 7-year time horizon. There is no guarantee this objective will be met. *(80/20 portfolios)*

Given anticipated cash needs, time horizon, and ability to accept risk, the portfolio will be constructed to achieve an expected return of **3.3% above the inflation rate** over a 7-year time horizon. There is no guarantee this objective will be met. *(70/30 portfolios)*

Given anticipated cash needs, time horizon, and ability to accept risk, the portfolio will be constructed to achieve an expected return of **2.9% above the inflation rate** over a 7-year time horizon. There is no guarantee this objective will be met. *(60/40 portfolios)*

Allocating investments

We manage portfolios using mutual funds and ETFs. We have not used separately managed accounts (SMAs) because we have not felt a need to. While SMAs may give certain tax advantages if a client rigorously adheres to stock selling at year-end, we have found that we can manage for taxes using highest-in, first-out (HIFO) accounting on our mutual fund lots. Since our portfolio turnover is in the neighborhood of 25 percent, any distributions that the mutual funds pay have accelerated gains by around four years. This is not ideal, but we think that the benefits of low-costs, maneuverability, and targeted approach far exceed the disadvantages.

We are agnostic between passive and active management. Our view has tended to be more passive during strong markets and more active during more volatile markets, but we are never all one way or another. What has been interesting for us is that when we have reviewed performance metrics over the last 10 years, our greatest benefits in active over passive management have come from international (no real surprise), large cap, and bonds. Large cap is a bit of a surprise because one would expect those markets to be the most efficient. In the mid-cap categories, our active managers have tended to trail. Our small-cap managers have done much better in down markets. In other words, while the research on active versus passive is meaningful, it is not necessarily definitive. "The research in favor of passive management is compelling but not overwhelming. Many of us are attached to passionate money managers. We are unprepared to reject their possible contributions to our clients' well-being."[12]

We do a thorough screening prior to introducing a new mutual fund. We have weekly investment meetings with our analysts to go over various asset classes, valuation metrics, world events, and research. We also begin to make decisions regarding which investments we want to change and why. We have a three-day rule between when a decision is made and when we implement. Once a month, we review all the decisions that we have made over the last two years to determine which ones worked out and which ones didn't. We then try to determine what may have caused a decision to not work out. At times, we may have made a bad decision; but we also may have made a good decision with a bad outcome. This distinction is not cute or self-serving. For example, our decision to underweight technology in the late 1990s was a good decision, but for a couple of years it had a bad outcome.

There are very few rules that we have when beginning a screen, but here are two:

Size is the enemy of performance and we will handle the diversification. Some asset classes, such as small cap, are more susceptible to the problem, but none are immune. In the recent past, we have sold managers of the year for no other reason than, in our judgment, they were too big to be effective. The second sin is hiring a manager with a diversified portfolio. Diversification is an extremely cheap asset (index funds have expense ratios as low as 0.09 percent), so do not pay for it. We prefer concentrated managers. Managers with 20 percent in a single stock, 15 names, or 25 percent of their portfolios in cash do not scare us. Only by hiring managers who are truly different from the benchmark can you get excess returns and, as alphas generally do not correlate, end up with even more diversification.

We are also careful between our reliance on data versus our reliance on instincts. Both are important. For example, when the markets imploded in 2008 and 2009, Treasury Inflation Protected Securities (TIPS) were providing an inordinately high fixed-rate return (plus inflation), that made them appear very attractive. But everything at that point was attractive! So if a wealth manager only focused on that aspect of the portfolio, they would have lost the 40-percent returns that high yield produced.

One constraint that we place on most portfolios (it gets relaxed with those allocations that have higher than 50 percent in bonds) is that we don't allow a single managed investment to represent greater than 15 percent of the portfolio. We again view this as protection against our believing so much in a particular manager that we would dedicate too many resources to them. If we would be right in our enthusiasm, the client could greatly benefit. But if we are right, but early, the client may leave before the benefits are realized. We believe in mean reversion, so a clients' departure for performance reasons would almost assuredly result in them going to someone whose recent results are not replicable. While it is obviously in our best interests to keep our clients, we also feel it is in our clients' best interests to stay with us. A way to protect the client and the relationship is to not bet too much on any one manager or style.

We created an internal weekly document from our Bloomberg terminal that compares our total return against the benchmark, the distribution of this return, and various measurements including standard deviation, semivariance, beta, correlation, r-squared, Sharpe ratio versus risk free, and tracking error.

Have You Determined the Mechanics for Managing Your Portfolio and the Evaluation of What Success Looks Like?

There is a tremendous amount of paperwork and review in order to successfully manage portfolios. Gaining agreement on what is going to be managed, how things will be evaluated, and where assets should be held in the beginning of the relationship will help avoid conflict and confusion later on.

Decide Accounts to Consolidate, Transfer, or Maintain Separately and How They Will Be Handled for Policy and Advice—5.5 Percent

When a client comes with a portfolio of assets, we don't feel that they should automatically have us manage them, nor do we force them to have us do so. We would prefer to be responsible for all of their assets, but if they meet our minimums, they may choose to keep assets elsewhere.

This creates problems, though. We don't want to provide advice on assets which a client chooses to not have us manage, yet the performance on those assets has an effect on their wealth management. This is the fundamental

Subcategories for have you determined the mechanics for managing your portfolio and the evaluation of what success looks like?

	Percent of Question	Percent of Category	Percent of Index
421 Decide accounts to consolidate, transfer, or maintain separately and how they will be handled for policy and advice	55	22	5.5
422 Determine asset location	15	6	1.5
424 Review portfolio performance relative to appropriate benchmarks	30	12	3
Total	**100**	**40**	**10**

conflict confronted by a fee-only planner who charges based on assets under management.

When a new client comes into our fold, we review all of their assets to determine which ones are appropriate for us to manage. We exclude assets for billing purposes that a client intends to keep. These may be things like municipal bonds intended to be held to maturity, low-basis stock, or investments with too high of penalties or with too little liquidity to change. We perform a comprehensive cost-basis review prior to making any investment suggestions or performing trades to insure that we can justify incurring tax costs.

With many clients, we can use a service like byallaccounts (http://www.byallaccounts.com/) to manage their 401(k)s or other assets that they cannot move. These investments take more work because we are not as familiar with the investment options and trading must be done manually rather than through our automated process.

Once we agree to what we can manage, we establish our fee.

There are certain assets that we cannot manage. For those assets, we provide advice once a year.

If the client chooses to exclude assets from us or use multiple investment managers, we run into the problem described earlier in the book in that we have a hard time legitimately doing planning around those outside assets. We have a responsibility to incorporate them into our planning, but we simply cannot use our own measurements for portfolio volatility or expected portfolio taxes. This is where we must work with the client and communicate to them the limitations with regard to the multiple-wealth-management-advisor approach. We also need to lay out in our policies, what we agreed to with the client.

This area has created the most issues with our client relationships. It tends to be the most discomfiting with clients with low-basis stock that we are keeping, but not providing advice. While the clients appreciate that these assets are excluded from their fees, if something happens to the investment, they may wonder why we didn't do something about it. The reason is simple—we can't. If a client is going to keep a particular investment, we can't dedicate the resources of our investment team to monitor all the things going on with it. We can create news alerts, but it is difficult to do more than this. If we imply that we can, then I think that this is unfair to the client. If it is our decision to keep low-basis stock and manage around it, we are doing so because we don't think that their effects adversely impact the clients' objectives. But if they wish to keep it, then they must ultimately be responsible for it.

Determine Asset Location—1.5 Percent

Which assets to hold where is a tax consideration. But it is one based on probabilities as well as a client's situation. In order to answer this question, you need to think about expected future returns and the tax construct of those returns. You couple this with a client's changing circumstances—moving from a high to a low tax bracket, or life-expectancy changes. The objective is to try to create the greatest lifetime after-tax wealth for the client.

In a research paper published by *The Journal of Financial Planning*, Chris Cordaro and Gobind Daryanani posits that their "proposed location approach is shown to provide an average 20-basis points-per-year, after-tax return benefit over simply using identical allocations in the multiple accounts with different characteristics."[13] The paper discusses the characteristics of different investments. Some investments may offer high returns but are tax inefficient. It is more effective to hold those within a retirement plan. Some investments may have more modest turnover and growth potential. These types of investments can be in either taxable or non-taxable accounts, depending on the range of investments or the client's profile.

We create a priority list of investments ranging from most tax efficient (and therefore to be held outside of retirement accounts) and least tax efficient. We use this list as our building block. Judgment also needs to intercede, though. Some of the least tax-efficient investments may also be those more likely to create trading losses—which we obviously cannot use in a retirement plan.

Here is how we categorize the investments:

Most Efficient/Growth (optimally held in after-tax accounts)
Tax efficient mutual funds

Certain index funds
Most Efficient/Income (held in after-tax accounts)
Municipal bond funds
Average Efficient/Growth (neutral)
Most equity mutual funds
Certain index funds or ETFs
Least Efficient (optimally held in retirement accounts)
Most alternative investments
Bond funds
Commodities
Less-efficient equity mutual funds

Review Portfolio Performance Relative to Appropriate Benchmarks—3 Percent

Communicating to the client how well they are doing is rocket science. We are taking complicated information with a variety of influencers and trying to create something clients can intuitively grasp and easily understand. "Excellence in statistical graphics consists of complex ideas communicated with clarity, precision, and efficiency. Graphical displays should:

- Show the data
- Induce the viewer to think about the substance rather than about methodology, graphic design, the technology of graphic production, or something else
- Avoid distorting what the data have to say
- Present many numbers in a small space
- Make large data sets coherent
- Encourage the eye to compare different pieces of data
- Reveal the data at several levels of detail, from a broad overview to the fine structure
- Serve a reasonably clear purpose: description, exploration, tabulation, or decoration
- Be closely integrated with the statistical and verbal descriptions of a data set

Graphics *reveal* data."[14]

When we decided what and how we wished to communicate performance *to cli*ents, we used Tufte as our guide. The information that we thought relevant to display was:

- Our funds in broad categories against the appropriate benchmark

We break down performance of how we have done relative to an equivalent index fund (which we felt was a buyable benchmark and therefore appropriate) in each asset class. We show this in two ways: 1) the actual percentage returns as compared to each benchmark for the entire previous year as well as current year to date. 2) Bar charts that show the same results, but for year-to-date only. This shows how our stock selection did.

We also show how the aggregate portfolio has done relative to an aggregated benchmark return using the midpoint of our investment policy ranges. This shows how our combined asset allocation and stock selection decisions did.

- Historical inception to date performance relative to inflation and the S&P

We produce a chart that shows how a client's portfolio did against inflation—the yardstick against which their portfolio must grow in order to produce spending power, and the S&P—the most recognized benchmark for equities.

- Historical actual wealth created

This area shows the amount of dollars originally invested, the total dollars withdrawn or added to the portfolio, the dividends earned, the capital gains earned, the fees and expenses taken out, and the wealth created after fees and contributions/withdrawals.

- Market commentary

We provide an overview of our expectations for different market areas. This also explains why we may be over or underweight particular categories.

- Asset allocation

We show the clients a pie chart that indicates how much of their holdings are carved up into each individual asset class. This pie chart is a visual representation of diversification.

- Scale

We display via a scale whether we are under or overweighted relative to our benchmarks on the three main categories of investing: stocks, bonds/cash, and alternatives. We also give a description as to why we have made these choices.

The sheet is printed on legal size paper, in color. On the back, we provide a graph of the S&P with commentary regarding what was going on during significant periods for the rolling three-year graph. The sheet allows clients to quickly and easily see how their portfolio has performed, in both absolute and relative terms over both short-term and long-term time periods. It also shows their current portfolio positioning and rationale behind our decisions—all on a single page.

Figure 12.5 shows our report.[15] This is for illustration purposes only.

FIGURE 12.5 Sample Performance Handout.

ACCREDITED INVESTORS, INC.
Real. Life. Planning.®

PERFORMANCE REVIEW - As of 05/31/2011 (Managed Only)*

Category	Benchmark	BENCHMARK 2010	YOUR PORTFOLIO 2010	BENCHMARK 2011	YOUR PORTFOLIO 2011
Foreign Equity	iShares MSCI EAFE	8.1%	15.7%	6.6%	4.6%
Large Cap Equity	iShares S&P 500	15.1%	15.8%	7.7%	7.1%
Mid Cap Equity	iShares S&P 400	26.7%	20.1%	10.6%	13.3%
Small Cap Equity	iShares Russell 2000	26.9%	25.8%	8.7%	11.0%
Alternatives	1-Yr LIBOR	1.0%	10.6%	0.3%	-0.4%
Fixed Income	Vanguard Total Bond	3.0%	30.9%	2.9%	5.5%
TOTAL PORTFOLIO		**14.5%**	**14.8%**	**6.8%**	**5.8%**

PORTFOLIO VALUE: $737,800

YEAR-TO-DATE INVESTMENT GAIN: $39,692

YEAR-TO-DATE PERFORMANCE BY ASSET CLASS

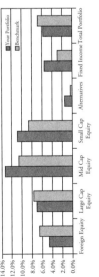

MARKET & PORTFOLIO COMMENTARY

Equity markets, posted volatile but positive performance in 2010, and the first quarter of 2011 delivered more of the same. Investors have, for the most part, focused attention on strong corporate profitability and gradually improving economic fundamentals while shrugging off the potential impact of higher oil prices stemming from unrest in North Africa and the Mid-East, higher food prices due to global shortages and increasing demand, and the impacts of the earthquake, tsunami, and nuclear power plant crisis in Japan.

Within domestic equities, we continue to prefer large companies, while maintaining lower allocations to mid and small-sized firms. The valuations on large US companies appear significantly more attractive, and the larger companies tend to have stronger balance sheets, with better access to capital and more exposure to international markets.

Our foreign equity allocation is currently near the lower end of our targeted range. At the beginning of 2010, we substantially trimmed our exposure to China and India, due to increased valuations and inflation concerns. These issues remain, and we are currently in the process of shifting out of our dedicated emerging markets funds entirely. In their place, we are adding to our European exposure, specially to stronger countries such as the U.K., France, Germany, and Switzerland.

The fixed income portfolio reflects a balancing act between limited opportunities in corporate bonds, the threat of higher interest rates, and alarming sovereign debt levels in the industrialized world. Yields on many types of high quality bonds dropped significantly in the summer of 2010, primarily due to an almost insatiable appetite from retail investors. More recently, investors have become more discerning. Bond funds experienced outflows in November for the first time in 2010, we foresee challenges ahead, and as such we continue to position portfolios accordingly.

We continue to maintain positions in alternative investments, which generally have lower corrections to traditional assets classes like bonds or equities due to their ability to bet on falling as well as rising prices.

CURRENT ASSET ALLOCATION

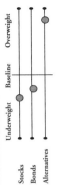

Foreign Equity, 24.5%

Large Cap Equity, 24.3%

Mid Cap Equity, 5.6%

Small Cap Equity, 15.3%

Alternatives, 9.1%

Cash, 4.5%

Fixed Income, 16.7%

PORTFOLIO WEIGHTINGS

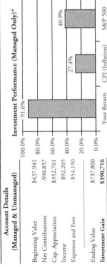

Underweight   Baseline   Overweight

Stocks

Bonds

Alternatives

We are currently underweight equities, relative to our baseline allocation, reflecting the impact of the recent stock market rally, and the resulting impact on overall market valuations.

Within the fixed-income asset class, we maintain a slightly under-weighted allocation, and we have taken steps to more conservatively position your holdings.

We continue to increase our exposure to alternative investments that we believe offer significant benefits given our current expectations.

Account Details (Managed & Unmanaged)

Beginning Value	$437,941
Net Contributions	-$90,857
Cap. Appreciation	$352,701
Income	$92,205
Expenses and Fees	-$54,190
Ending Value	$737,800
Investment Gain	**$390,716**

Portfolio Review: 12/31/2001 - 05/31/2011

Investment Performance (Managed Only)*

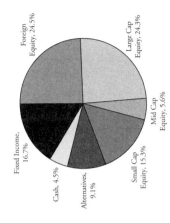

Your Return   CPI (Inflation)   S&P 500

* Note: Fees are reflected in returns only when fees are paid directly from "managed" cash within accounts

I think one of the things to stress is what is *not* shown.

- We don't break down individual investments in each asset class. As investment managers, we are discerning which investments in each asset class complement each other. We also know that at certain times, different investments in the same asset class may produce variant returns. With our old reporting, client eyes would immediately move to underperforming investments, even if the portfolio as a whole was doing well. We would explain that the underperforming investment was doing exactly what it was supposed to be doing, but it always created a conversation that, to me, seemed counterproductive. This style of reporting has changed the discussion.
- We don't show after-tax returns on this report. Tax planning is a key component of our work, but different clients assets are in different places and their situations change. We discuss the portfolio tax impact as we go through our tax work. We also provide supplemental reporting for gains and losses taken year to date.
- We don't show percentages in any one investment. Since we don't show the individual investments, we don't show the percentages in any one investment. We don't think that in managing a total portfolio this is meaningful to the client.
- We do not include risk measurements. While we evaluate these in making investment decisions and structuring a portfolio we do not communicate these to the client on our presentation material. This is, in part, because things like Value-at-Risk and drawdown do not accurately reflect what happens in the world. Theory meets reality and reality wins.

Anyone who creates portfolio report will make judgments regarding what are the essential pieces to communicate and what fairly represents returns commensurate with the risks a portfolio is accepting.

Conclusion

Many prospects come to us because they have been dissatisfied with how their investments have performed. Some prospects come because they don't feel comfortable with their investment advisor because of communication problems. And some come because they don't like the vehicles that are being used to manage their portfolios.

While it is tempting to take the new client and immediately put their money to work, going through the process described above and identifying all the key areas in creating an investment plan will give you the greatest chance of the client being successful in their outcomes.

We have found that we need to constantly be questioning what we are doing and how we are doing things in order to continually affirm our methods and strategies or to alternate them based on structural changes in the environment. Alternatives are an example of a structural change that we felt compelled to introduce into our portfolios. Index funds obviously represented another structural change. But there is a difference between structural changes and valuations. There were people who professed early in the decade that technology was forever going to change the world (true) and therefore growth stocks were the only way to take advantage of this (untrue). Planners who had been solid in their views on asset allocation untied themselves to move to the false god of growth stocks.

What we believe to be intellectually honest—that over time some asset classes will temporarily perform better than others but they will return to equilibrium—means that a type of stock picking will always have a single-year return higher than a portfolio of asset classes. But that type of stock picking is not as enduring.

In order to win the investment planning game, it is important to know what game you are playing and communicate that clearly, succinctly, and honestly to your clients.

Notes

1. Koedijk, Kees, and Alfred Slager. *Investment Beliefs—A Positive Approach to Institutional Investing*. New York: Palgrave McMillen. 2011.
2. Ellis, Charles. *Investment Policy—How to Win the Loser's Game*. New York: Dow Jones. 1985.
3. Montier, James. *The Little Book of Behavioral Investing*. New York: John Wiley & Sons. 2010.
4. Old joke copied from jokes.com.
5. Two of our employees, Chris MacBean and Steve Gilbertson, spent hundreds of hours creating our spending-policy program. The process, like everything we do, was iterative. They start, get feedback from a small group, improve it, and continue to get feedback from larger groups (and clients) until we are comfortable with the end result.
6. Mandelbroit, Benoit, and Richard L. Husdon. *The (Mis)behavior of Markets*. New York: Basic Books. 2004.

7. If you want to really get a fantastic overview on the whole investment area, there are a couple of books that I really encourage you to read. A more technical book on asset allocation strategies is *The CFA Institute Investment Series—The New Wealth Management* written by Harold Evensky, Stephen Horan, and Thomas Robinson. A book that is a terrific read and is almost like a novel is Justin Fox's *The Myth of the Rational Market: A History of Risk, Reward, and Delusion on Wall Street*.

8. Brinson, Gary P., Brian D. Singer, and Glibert L. Beebower, "Determinants of Portfolio Performance II: An Update," *Financial Analysts Journal* (May/June 1991).

9. We got our start on investment policies several years ago but were helped quite a bit from the work of Norm Boone and Linda Lubitz. They later put their thoughts together in their book *Creating an Investment Policy Statement*.

10. The Callan Periodic Table of Investment Returns (www.callan.com) provides a great and colorful illustration of this concept.

11. Jacob Wolkowitz, CFA, is in charge of our investment meetings and has created the structure by which we review performance, determine what data is appropriate to consider, and which investments to consider. He also is responsible for the interview format we use for evaluating fund managers.

12. Evensky, Harold, Stephen Horan, and Thomas Robinson. *The New Wealth Management*. CFA Institute. New Jersey: John Wiley & Sons. 2011.

13. Daryanani, Gobind PhD., CFP®, and Chris Cordaro, CFP®. *FPA Journal— Asset Location: A Generic Framework for Maximizing After-Tax Wealth*. January, 2005.

14. Tufte, Edward R. *The Visual Display of Quantitative Information*. Cheshire, Connecticut: Graphics Press. 2001.

15. One of our analysts, Sean P. Smith, created this after spending time at a Tufte workshop. We have trademarked the material for our use.

CHAPTER 13

Estate Planning (Distribution)

My wife and I were walking with friends who had recently sold their business and were discussing their situation. This is their second marriage. They each came into this long-term marriage with children, although one set of kids was essentially raised by both of them. The business sale generated several million dollars; enough money to insure that they would live more than comfortably without ever invading the principal.

They always helped the set of children that they jointly raised, but mostly through bringing them on trips, providing business guidance and, at times, loans, and helping out in emergencies. The children have never had much money, but they would be described by the parents as very happy.

How much should these children inherit? How should it be passed down to them? What is the price to pay for this inheritance?

As we walked and talked, I mentioned that in my opinion I don't think that someone can inherit too little money, but they could inherit too much. I said that "rich social workers have a group of people with whom they spend time who are in a very different financial situation than they are. They end up with a foot in two distinct camps—those with money and those without. That is a crevice that is difficult to straddle."

The conversation went in the direction where if the kids were happy now, then how much money should they get to enhance their happiness rather than begin to obstruct it. This question is ponderable, but also unanswerable. But it is a fundamental question that must be approached in order to effectively provide wealth management.

The mistake that we almost automatically make is to assume that transfering the most wealth to the next generation results in the best outcome. This presupposes that maximizing gross family wealth is the most desirable outcome. Is it?

We have children fighting over cabins that are not equally used. We have clients renting their homes from their estranged children because of a successful Qualified Personal Residence Trust (QPRT) strategy. And we have clients who have transitioned their estate in thoughtful, intentional, and consistent ways which have resulted in a clearly communicated and understood intergenerational plan that is consistent with the family's values and intentions.

Estate planning is more than just figuring out a way to distribute what you have earned or protect what you have made from the ravages of long-term care costs. It involves passing on a money legacy that can catapult the heirs happily into a new financial situation or corrupt their money experiences. We have clients of inherited wealth who have felt both liberated and imprisoned by their money. Some felt that people loved them for their money and some felt unloved by the parents or grandparents who created the wealth. So this area in the index is technically and emotionally complicated.

Percent of index (20 percent) for Estate Planning (Distribution)

	Percent of Category	Percent of Index
Have you a philosophy on wealth transfer?	70	14
Have you articulated your charitable philosophy or mission statement?	10	2
Have you planned for incapacitation, elder care issues, and final planning needs?	20	4
Total	100	20

Have You a Philosophy on Wealth Transfer?

Clients have a very diverse view on this subject. Some clients have a dollar amount in their mind that they would like their children to inherit. Others have a maximum amount on which they are willing to be federally taxed. Some believe that they want to use their estate as a way to engage their children in philanthropy. Others care mostly about insuring that their spouse doesn't run off with the cabana boy or girl and either disinherit their children or frivolously spend it.

Warren Buffett's quote on inheritance is often bandied about: "A very rich person should leave his kids enough to do anything but not enough to do nothing." This is a classic Buffett aphorism, but what does it really mean? We have had clients with children who have inherited a tremendous amount of money and barely noticed it, as well as children who waited for their parents to die so that they could begin living. It was not the amount of inheritance that caused issues, it was their feelings around money.

With that couple I was talking about in the beginning of the chapter, I said to them that ironically, if their children were running Fortune 500 companies, they may be better equipped to handle the money coming in because they would be used to dealing with money. That, in many ways, is the paradox. Those with the least amount of experience with money could financially use it the most, yet it would also likely be the most disruptive for them (in both good and bad ways).

So when you work on this part of the index, be prepared to have multiple meetings and ongoing conversations.

Subcategories for Have You a Philosophy on Wealth Transfer?

	Percent of Question	Percent of Category	Percent of Index
511 Determine the amount of after-tax inheritance and how it is to be received	40	28	5.6
512 Determine survivor liquidity needs outside of trustee control and to pay estate taxes	15	10.5	2.1
513 Direct proper ownership (including revocable trusts), beneficiary designations, and determine guardians and trustees	10	7	1.4
514 Determine where estate discounting techniques and wealth-transfer entities—FLP, QPRT, GRAT, defective trusts, ILITs, and others—are appropriate	10	7	1.4
515 Finalize documents and Crummey notices	10	7	1.4
516 Determine whether a family meeting should be facilitated and appropriate family governance prepared	15	10.5	2.1
Total	100	70	14

Determine the Amount of After-Tax Inheritance and How It Is to
Be Received—5.6 Percent

The first step in developing a philosophy around estate planning is by taking a hard look at the client's current situation through flow charting their existing estate plan (see Figure 13.1). Many clients want a visual representation of who is getting what as well as how they are getting it. The flowchart shows how the money moves after the first death in a couple as well as how much goes into trusts or beneficiaries, is given to charity, and is given to the federal and state government. When clients originally draft their estate plans, they often do it verbally. When they see the pictures of the results of those words, they sometimes have a conniption fit.

Once we have flow charted the estate plan, we can then open up the discussion around whether this plan meets their wealth-transfer wishes. It is important to distinguish between tactics and strategy. Saving estate taxes is a tactic. Insuring that the children are empowered by their wealth is a strategy. As professionals, we spend a lot of time understanding tactics, but to be effective, we must live in strategy.

As we go through the flow chart with the client, we discuss the whys behind the outcomes for which they are shooting. A client who says that they want to avoid estate taxes has not given you a why. Is it because they want their children to reap the maximum amount possible from the client's hard work? Is it because they feel like they can fulfill their philanthropic objectives through their estate

FIGURE 13.1 Basic Flowchart.

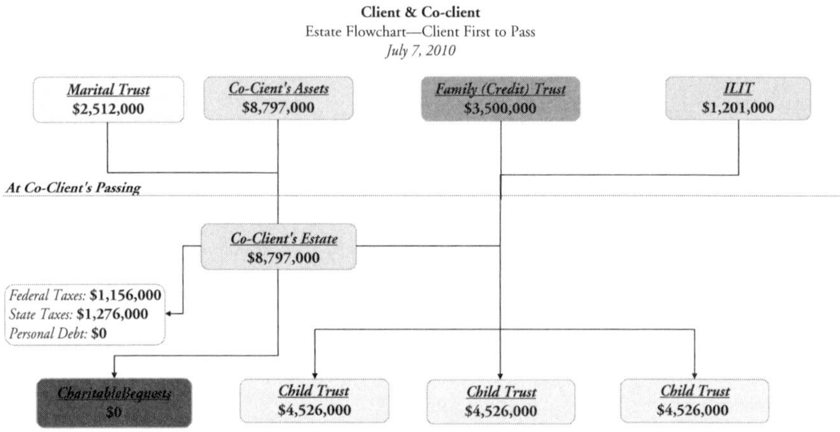

Note: Assumes the Separate Children's trust created under Co-clients will, and the Irrevocable Life Insurance Trust are assumed to be combined to one trust for each child.

plan? Is it simply because their disdain for paying taxes is their overwhelming motivator? Without really understanding the motivations behind the statements, it is blind luck if you get the results that match the client's values.

Appropriate questioning in this space also will result in an understanding of how the money is to be received. One of our clients had a friend who died and her husband spent their jointly earned assets on his new wife and her children. This observation is driving our client's desire to make sure that if she predeceases her husband, the money is tied up in such a way that her kids from a prior marriage are insured to inherit it. The husband cannot even fathom being in a situation where he would have to ask a trustee for money that he had earned throughout his lifetime. Both of these issues are around control and trust—a workable solution with these competing objectives can only happen through dialogue. We discovered these feelings as they saw the flowchart of how their assets were going to be distributed.

Some clients are very concerned about gifting money outright to their children because they are worried about what would happen if their child got divorced. Others are worried that their children would not handle the responsibility of the money very well. And other clients feel this way toward one, but not all of their children. The estate plan will not be meaningful if these areas are not fully vetted prior to its development.

There are some contrasting statements to which you can have clients react such as:

- I wish to be sure that anything my children inherit will stay with my children and grandchildren; or, I wish to give my children the freedom to do with their inheritance what they see fit.
- I wish to insure that if something happens to me, no one with whom my spouse may become involved will have a right to our money; or, I wish to give my spouse an unfettered right to our assets.
- I wish to experience the result of our charity while we are living; or, I wish to insure that after we both die, our charities are funded.
- I want each of our children to receive an equal amount of our estate; or, I recognize that not all of our children are in similar circumstances, so I would like an equitable, if not equal, distribution from our estate.
- I want our children to have free reign with their inheritance; or, I want to be sure that the inheritance is directed toward areas like education and experiences.

These are not all-or-nothing questions, nor are they intended to provide simple answers. They are asked so that a discussion can take place that will uncover some of the deeper issues related to how clients feel about passing the money on. These discussions will also help determine what tools and techniques would be most effective in meeting these objectives.

Another useful tool is a *Wealth Transition Checklist* developed by Roy Williams and Vic Preisser:[1]

- Our family has a mission statement that spells out the overall purpose of our wealth.
- The entire family participates in most important decisions, such as defining a mission for our wealth.
- All family heirs have the option of participating in the management of the family's assets.
- Heirs understand their future roles, have bought into these roles, and look forward to performing those roles.
- Heirs have actually reviewed the family's estate plans and documents.
- Our current wills, trusts, and other documents make most asset distributions based on heir readiness, not heir age.
- Our family mission includes creating incentives and opportunities for our heirs.
- Our younger children are encouraged to participate in our family's philanthropic grant-making decisions.
- Our family considers family unity to be just as important as family financial strength.
- We communicate well throughout our family and regularly meet as a family to discuss issues and changes.

This type of checklist was based on research, though, and presupposes answers to these questions that improve the likelihood of a successful wealth transition. The issue with this type of checklist is that some clients may not agree with all the statements above. Again, though, this is a good tool to uncover the hot areas that will allow you to develop an appropriate plan.

Our overwhelming preference for estate planning (as well as all other areas of planning) is to find the simplest solution that meets the client's objectives. While this seems obvious, I am amazed at how complicated estate plans can become.

For example, if a client feels comfortable with their children receiving assets outright, is not concerned about their own ability to meet their obligations, and has no stake in the outcome of what the children do with the assets, then ongoing gifting to the annual exclusion amount is the first option. If the client wants to begin to use up their unified credit, then they can make larger gifts. If the client is concerned that these larger gifts should have some restrictions or protection, then establishing a trust into which these gifts can go would be the next step, and so on. The estate plan begins to get more complicated for certain situations such as trying to move more dollars to the next generation but not wanting to permanently give up those assets. This is our client's estate plan, not ours.

Given that many state's estate tax laws do not match the federal government's', there are certain estate tax advantages that may cause a client to wish to accelerate strategies. For example, we had a client whose mother was quite ill. In this particular situation, we had already set up some vehicles with which to move money out of her estate, but some of those were dependent upon her surviving the term of the vehicle. Once her health became a larger concern, we increased giving levels dramatically because her state of residence did not impose gift taxes but did impose significant inheritance taxes. In this situation, the complicated, but reasonable, estate reduction strategies were less effective than the simple concept of very large gifts—in this case, beyond the unified credit amount, making this a gift tax, not inheritance tax, issue.

The book that should probably be in every wealth manager's arsenal regarding estate planning is the classic *Tools and Techniques of Estate Planning.*[2] This book has several checklists by which you can manage the estate plan and consider the various approaches, benefits, and drawbacks to each estate-planning vehicle.

Determine Survivor Liquidity Needs Outside of Trustee Control and to Pay Estate Taxes—2.1 Percent

We treat this area separately because there can be several areas with which liquidity may be needed including:

- Federal estate taxes
- Federal income taxes
- State estate taxes
- State income taxes
- Probate costs
- Income needs
- Debts or obligations due upon death
- Other taxes

Some wealthy clients have tremendous assets, but limited liquidity. This can cause huge problems for the beneficiaries. For example, one of our clients had significant art that was not liquid but had tremendous value. We needed to develop ways to create liquidity around this art so that if something happened prior to us getting an executed plan in place, we would not be at a disadvantage.

In another situation, a client in a second marriage wanted to be certain that the proceeds from the house in which they were living went to the children from the first marriage. The current spouse would not be able to afford this place on her own, so, without liquidity and timing provisions for her, would have had to move out and then try to sell the house. By providing a safety-net for liquidity and timing, there is a higher likelihood that more value will be created from the sale.

The other area that we like to insure is that there is a certain amount of money that does not automatically flow into trusts and is therefore subject to trustee control. Clients who are bereaved do not want to be dealing with a trustee to make sure that they have enough money to make it through the next few months. We had a client whose liquid assets were in a trust for his wife; the other assets were in his retirement plans. When his wife passed away, there was a timing issue before everything could get registered in such a way as to allow distributions from her trust to him. By maintaining some liquidity outside of the trust, we did not have to rush through the registration process or take extra distributions from his retirement plan.

While irrevocable life insurance trusts can often meet the estate tax liquidity needs, there are clients who may not have those vehicles and/or the cost of insurance is too great for the benefit. We need to develop lines of liquidity for these clients to be sure that there will be a timely disposition of needed assets to meet those needs. This may even come from securing credit in anticipation of those needs.

Direct Proper Ownership (Including Revocable Trusts), Beneficiary Designations, and Determine Guardians and Trustees—1.4 Percent

One of the easiest ways to insure proper distribution of the estate is by having appropriate beneficiary designations and placing appropriate assets in their required vehicles. How many clients do you know who have unfunded revocable trusts? While the estate planning may have been wonderful, it was also ineffective.

Every year during our estate-planning meeting with the client, we review all of their beneficiary designations on each asset that allows them. We also establish transfer-on-death accounts for those assets for which we have a direct beneficiary and want to avoid probate. Equally important, we provide an asset-ownership flow chart to be sure that clients see whether assets are appropriately titled and whether any changes need to take place.

The other area that we think is of critical importance is determining who the best people are to serve as agents, guardians, or trustees for the clients. This is especially significant for health care directives. We try to have a directive for each state in which a client is going to be spending time to insure that the directive is acceptable in the state in which the client becomes incapacitated.

These decisions need to be made very carefully. I have seen clients be very clear as to how they want their final wishes carried out should something happen to them and the person who was in charge of their health care directive not follow through with those wishes. Generally, the provider must follow the directive if the requests are reasonable; it tends to be the family member who doesn't follow through with where the person will receive care or what treatment should be withheld. At times, the client's wishes cannot be followed. One of our client's parents had hidden pills so that if his Alzheimer's advanced, he could take his own life. He didn't remember where he hid the pills, so he was unable to follow through with his wishes and his family could not help him.

When it comes to the appointment of trustees, we tend to discourage the appointment of corporate trustees even though they provide certain advantages such as independence and long-term capabilities. We have had to bust three trusts for clients where the trustee was not meeting the objectives as laid out by the decedent because they either misinterpreted the decedent's wishes or felt that it was not in the best interest of the survivor. Those battles are costly and unfulfilling. There are now smaller, private trust companies who serve primarily administrative functions that can serve in conjunction with other trustees. Depending on the relationship capabilities and fees of these trust companies, they may serve a useful role. Corporate trustees make good scapegoats when the beneficiaries are contentious, and corporate trustees generally do not succumb to whining.

Much care needs to be taken with the drafting of the will if a surviving spouse or family member is going to serve as trustee to be sure that their distribution power of the assets will not include them in their estate. If an individual trustee is named, it is imperative that successor trustees also be named in case of incapacity. We also believe that there should be clear rights of removal as well as a clear process by which successor trustees are appointed.

Our firm will not serve as a trustee. We have decided that this represents a conflict in which we don't wish to engage. We will happily be hired by the trustee to serve as a fiduciary manager of the client's assets.

Beneficiary designations are especially important when minors are involved. If a client has minor children, the cleanest way for them to inherit assets is through a trust. If the trust is not set up by the client through their will, the court will set one up for them.

When dealing with retirement plan assets:

- Clients who are not legally married or are beneficiaries of their parent's retirement plans generally should be setting up decedent Individual Retirement Accounts (IRAs). Since a non-spouse beneficiary cannot roll over an IRA, inheriting the IRA and not setting it up as a decedent would force the client to take a lump sum distribution. The decedent IRA allows the client to take out as much as they want at any time, as long as they meet the minimum withdrawals based on their life expectancy (or joint life if the deceased was taking required minimum distributions).
- The good news is that pension reform now allows non-spouse beneficiaries of 401(k) plans to transfer those assets into an inherited IRA, thereby allowing a stretch-out of the asset over the lifetime of the beneficiary, rather than paying it out in at most five years like before the Pension Protection Act of 2006 (and its subsequent 2008 clarification). The key aspect here is to understand all the rules regarding non-spouse beneficiaries. The stretch-out disappears if this is not done correctly from the very beginning.[3]
- Clients often like to leave their retirement plans to charities, thereby reducing their estate by the amount of the gift (on which no tax was ever paid) and circumventing the income in respect to a decedent rules. Clients should almost never leave their Roth IRAs to charity, though.

Asset titling is the easiest way to handle passing assets on. For clients who wish privacy and to avoid probate, many choose to set up revocable trusts. Since many of our clients are Minnesota residents and Minnesota has a simplified probate system, revocable trusts are not as necessary as they would be, for example, in California. On the other hand, we tend to like to put out-of-state property in revocable trusts so that we are not at risk of going through probate in multiple states. While revocable trusts are supposedly seamless, they add a layer of complexity that can at times be a pain. We most often find clients frustrated when they are retitling assets such as real estate to the revocable trusts and need to get lender and condominium-association approval.

Most clients either own assets in their own name (which goes through probate upon death) or through joint tenancy with rights of survivorship (which passes directly to the surviving spouse). These two types of titling are of greatest concern in a marriage separation, where one client can make unilateral choices with these assets (real estate is often excepted here). Tenants in common is where each owner owns their own specific percentage of the property. Upon death, their share passes to their beneficiaries. Community property exists only between husband and wife and state law determines specific ownership rights.

Determine Where Estate Discounting Techniques and Wealth-Transfer Entities—FLP, QPRT, GRAT, Defective Trusts, ILITs, and Others—Are Appropriate—1.4 Percent

As clients' estates become more complex, it is inevitable that their planning also gets more creative. You name the initials, and we have incorporated them into some clients' planning. Some of these strategies have been very effective, others not at all.

With interest rates low, we established Grantor Retained Annuity Trusts (GRATs) in 2007 and early 2008. Many of those were three-year trusts. None of them beat their hurdle rates. Yet the trusts we established in 2009 have allowed millions of dollars to pass to the beneficiaries free of gift tax. We usually set up the beneficiary of these trusts to be intentionally defective spousal trusts so that the spouse could retain income rights to the trust as long as they were alive. This was important because if too much of the gain passed to the next generation, there was a chance that the family setting up the trusts may not have enough assets.

Integrating this type of planning with any kind of distribution forecasting becomes very important. Think about it this way—when a client establishes a GRAT, they are basically accepting all the market downside while limiting their upside to the hurdle rate. This dramatically changes the numbers for spending policies. The way to handle this problem is by giving a spouse access to those returns. When that spouse dies, though, those returns go to the beneficiaries, thereby removing them from the estate. This kind of planning cannot occur in a vacuum. It must be coordinated with cash-flow planning.

Many of our clients have Irrevocable Life Insurance Trusts (ILIT) established to keep their life insurance proceeds out of their estate upon death. We have needed to monitor these regularly in a few ways:

1. We need to be sure that there is enough cash in the policies for them to stay in force, but not so much cash that there is no longer a significant death benefit. Establishing provisions where the grantor's spouse may have access to borrowing from the ILIT gives the grantor an indirect benefit. This needs to be watched carefully so as to not jeopardize the status of the vehicle.
2. We need to manage the Crummey powers (which are covered in a different part of the index).

3. We need to be sure that if there is a power to amend the trust (not given to the grantor but rather to a trust protector) that the trust is being reviewed regularly.
4. We need to monitor the trust to be sure that the trustees are still acting in accordance with the objectives of the trust.

We have had very mixed success with QPRTs. They have worked well in situations where the real estate is a family asset and all participants agree that it will stay in the family. They have not worked nearly as well when the asset is an asset where we had no ties and the purpose was to shift the growth of the asset out of the estate. In this situation, clients have disliked paying rent to their kids or asking them for permission to buy a new piece of real estate once they no longer were interested in living in one on which the QPRT was based. Couple this with little appreciation on real estate (granted, this came with hindsight) and a dramatic increase in the unified credit and we are left with a strategy that was often frustrating and ineffective.

We have used Family Limited Partnerships (FLPs) as a way to make gifts to family members, but we have been very cautious on the discounts which we use. These are complex instruments which are easy to mess up. We suggest hiring the best possible legal and tax help in establishing these. I also think that this is a last-resort idea rather than the first arrow in the quiver.

Finalize Documents and Crummey Notices—1.4 Percent

This is more the administrative piece for the estate plan that needs to be completed. While much of this is handled once, the Crummey notices require annual filing. Most important, this area needs to have all the Is dotted and Ts crossed.

For example, getting proper appraisals to back up values on estate and gift tax returns in case of an audit can alleviate significant issues down the road.

Once the documents have been completed, another flow chart is executed to describe the agreed-upon estate plan.

Determine Whether a Family Meeting Should Be Facilitated and Appropriate Family Governance Prepared—2.1 Percent

The most significant change as our practice has grown and our client situations have become more complicated has been the family-meeting area. Many of our clients are going to be passing significant wealth to the next generation and are still reticent to discuss things in a structured way.

One of our client's parents were extremely visible and successful. The father was a renowned CEO of a large company and was known both for his business acumen and philanthropy. Within the family, though, he never discussed his estate plan. The assumption was that the kids could work things out. But when he suddenly died, all hell broke loose.

One of his children was involved in a not-for-profit organization about which the others cared little. There were some private investments on which he had provided board leadership and now needed additional nurturing. The siblings had not dealt with each other in business and were ill-equipped to do so. The estate became embattled, with mounting legal costs and hard feelings. It may not be possible to completely avoid these things, but an appropriate family governance structure can help alleviate some of the problems or quash them before they start.

"From the point of view of cultural anthropology, families, as they extend into the third, fourth, fifth, and later generations, become clans and eventually tribes. These family tribes than recreate, as if new, the same basic governance structures that anthropologists have observed are common to all tribes. . . . Families recognize that as their numbers grow by birth and by marriage, they have a need for greater structure to successfully manage the family's business, whether it lies in the human, intellectual, financial, or social-capital dimensions of the family's activities."[4]

Managing families is difficult. If it is an area in which you are not comfortable, there are certainly wonderful resources to turn to for help. For example, the Family Wealth Alliance serves multi-family offices and can provide education and seminars on dealing with the ultra- and high-net-worth families. Russ Alan Prince has carved out a niche providing market research in this area. And there are psychologists, such as Jim Grubman, who counsel families of means on governance and relationship issues.

John Davis wrote for *Harvard Business Review* in November 2001 about the three components of family governance:[5]

1. Periodic (typically annual) assemblies of the family
2. Family council meetings for those families that benefit from a representative group of their members doing planning, creating policies, and strengthening business-family communication and bond.
3. A family constitution—the family's policies and guiding vision and values that regulate members' relationship with the business (family).

Creating a structure by which one can measure success in the ongoing family dynamics provides a way to help families keep their main goals on the forefront. This is hard work because families are hard work. You are help-ing families manage their human and intellectual capital as well as their finan-cial capital. The issues of love and meaning get wrapped up in the issues of money. If you can work with families in this area, though, it can be rewarding.

One of our clients organizes an annual retreat for his children where they go over all aspects of the estate plan and the objectives of the father (who has been divorced from their mother for decades) with regard to his money. The adult children (one of whom is in business with the father) can ask questions and pose their concerns. In this particular situation, these meetings don't need to be mediated or facilitated because of the relation-ship and openness that this family has with each other. We have generally found this to be the exception. Psychologist Jim Grubman notes that "all interactions with all financial clients actually exist along two dimensions: the Personal/Family Dimension and the Financial Dimension. Each of these dimensions can be categorized along an axis ranging from low complexity to high complexity."[6]

A governance model will develop protocol for many different aspects within the family, including conflict resolution, communication, building leadership, succession or transition planning, and stewardship development. Some of these areas are ones in which you will provide guidance, but the structure may come from an outside consultant.

Have You Articulated Your Charitable Philosophy or Mission Statement?

We break this question out to stand on its own because philanthropy is a sep-arate constituency from family. While not everyone has a charitable intent, we believe that this is an area that is worthy of discussion.

When a client dies, their money is going to go to one of three places: people whom they wish to directly benefit from their legacy, the charities that have causes consistent with the values of the client, and the government. Wealth managers usually spend their time trying to figure out how to get the most to the first beneficiary, the least to the third, and use the middle as an afterthought.

We have found that by directly talking to clients about their charitable intent, it allows them to focus better on what they want their friends and family to receive and why they should receive it. If clients think their options are the government or the kids, their decision is easy; if it gets truncated with charity, they are more thoughtful.

Subcategories for have you articulated your charitable philosophy or mission statement?

	Percent of Question	Percent of Category	Percent of Index
531 Develop and share your charitable mission statement and money values	50	5	1
532 Evaluate lifetime giving and/or giving at death	25	2.5	0.5
533 Evaluate charitable lead trusts, remainder trusts, gift annuities, donor-advised funds, and private foundations	25	2.5	0.5
Total	100	10	2

Develop and Share Your Charitable Mission Statement and Money Values—1 Percent

The purpose of a charitable mission statement is to create a way to evaluate requests for donations and determine whether the gifts have had the impact that the client wishes for them to have. This mission statement provides a reference point for the client to sit down and annually discuss whether philanthropy has played the role in their lives that they had hoped.

We like to break down broad areas of charity—things like education, the environment, social services, the arts, religious organizations, and so on—as well as geographic preferences—is the client most interested in serving the local, regional, national, or worldwide community.

We also think it makes sense to include within the mission statement the targeted amount that the client wishes to give annually or at death to charity. I know that personally, when my wife and I committed several years ago to giving 10 percent of our income to charity it provided a focus that we had been lacking.

Each year, the client should be sitting down and evaluating their gifting to see whether their gifts had the impact that they intended. One of our clients, after doing this, decided that they were best served by providing matching gifts to the charities in which they were interested as a way to insure that the charities also had skin in the game.

Evaluate Lifetime Giving and/or Giving at Death—0.5 Percent

I would venture to say that any client who was philanthropically inclined and knew that they would not run out of money would make lifetime gifts rather than bequests upon death. Given current estate tax laws (a $10,000,000 lifetime gift exclusion for couples), most clients are no longer in a situation where giving to charity upon death will save them estate taxes. If this was their sole or primary reason for giving, then not only has the game changed for them, but for their charities as well. But we have found this to not be the case for most of our clients.

Generally speaking, we try to prove to clients that they have enough resources to give today as well as tomorrow. We believe that this philosophy is regenerative for them; the benefits that most clients get from giving exceed their costs.

Some clients have a propensity to give too much, thereby jeopardizing their objectives as described to us. For these clients, we are more inclined to encourage bequests at death.

Evaluate Charitable Lead Trusts, Remainder Trusts, Gift Annuities, Donor-Advised Funds, and Private Foundations—0.5 Percent

Each of the above-mentioned techniques has served purposes for clients. Each of these techniques also has a cost greater than their charitable value. This means that anyone who is suggesting a client set up one of these vehicles to enhance their financial wealth is missing something. There is always a net financial cost in giving to charity while living.

We establish donor-advised funds for a very high percentage of our clients. We either set them up through their custodian, or use a community foundation if they would rather have profits distributed within their communities. The community foundations tend to be a bit more expensive and often don't allow for the same small gifts to be made, but they also provide community events that the donors like to attend as well as serve as a resource on background for local charities. We love these donor-advised funds because it is easy to transfer low-basis stock or mutual funds into them and avoid capital gains. Most of them now allow online grant making; clients love that convenience.

While we manage and have started some private foundations, we tend to discourage them unless a client is going to fund it with a few million dollars and really wants the panache of the foundation, has enough assets so that managing the foundation may provide an income stream to someone in the family, or wants it to last several generations.

Other options are more flexible and less costly. For example, the local community foundation in Minnesota will create a donor-advised fund that doesn't mention the Minneapolis Foundation and, to the recipient of the gifts, looks like a private foundation. They allow beneficiaries to be named so that the fund can continue to be managed after the death of the grantor. The client does not have to adhere to the 5 percent rule for annual gifts, so money can accumulate.

Several clients have set up charitable remainder trusts, many with net-income make-up provisions. These have worked especially well for clients who wish to be recognized for a gift during their lifetime, clients who wish to have a different beneficiary receive income, and for clients who want an income stream for a set period of time but have confidence that they won't need the assets on which to live. While some clients choose to receive income for life, most elect a term-certain option. Since we do not fund these using annuities or other tax-free vehicles, generally speaking, clients take the greater of net income or the payout amount. If the net income is less than the payout, then the client's deficit account builds and they are only required to take a make-up amount in subsequent years to the extent that the trust gains are larger than the payout amount. We also tend to use Charitable Remainder Unitrusts (CRUT) (with a variable payout based on fund value) over Charitable Remainder Annuity Trusts (CRAT) (fixed payout) because we feel we can create greater distributions over the time horizon (given a reasonable payout rate).

We are careful with charitable gift annuities because they are subject to the credit worthiness of the particular charity that issued it. This can create a level of risk that a client may not wish to take. Also, a calculation needs to be performed as to whether the payout rate and tax advantages for the charitable gift annuity are the most viable option as opposed to an outright gift and managing the portfolio (or buying a taxable annuity). We used a charitable gift annuity for one client who was making annual gifts to her twin sister (see Figure 13.2). This client had been a board member for a large non-profit organization to whom she wanted to make a significant gift. We established the gift annuity with the sister as the beneficiary but with a provision indicating that the beneficiary could be changed (so it was not a completed gift).

While interest rates are low, some clients have expressed an interest in charitable lead trusts. The charity receives the income stream for a specific period of time and then the corpus typically goes back to the owner or to the next generation. One of our clients and her sister had inherited wealth. The sister became gravely ill. She had a daughter, who was of the age of majority, but not financially competent. Upon her death, a lead trust was set up for a charity with the daughter as the remainder beneficiary in 20 years—hopefully after she has matured.

FIGURE 13.2   Charitable Strategies Illustration.

Client
Charitable Strategy Options
Date

Goal	Vehicle	Timing (When It Is Most Advantageous)
Charity to receive dollars today; Move assets out of your estate; Transfer remaining assets to kids	Charitable Lead Trust (CLT)	Low interest rate environment
Receive income tax deduction today; Utilize most flexible vehicle	Donor Advised Fund	When you anticipate high years of income (can match large gift in year of higher income)
Receive income tax deduction today; Utilize organization resources	Donor Advised Fund through a Community Foundation	When you would like assistance with grants and developing philanthropy goals
Obtain an income stream for a period of years; Remaining assests transfer to a selected charity	Charitable Remainder Trust (CRT)	High interest rate environment
Similar to CRT; Charity administers the annuity	Charitable Gift Annuity	Later stage of life (provides a more advantageous mortality calculation)
Pass on large amount to charities; retain as much control as possible; involve future generations	Private Family Foundation	Significant assets for charitable giving

Have You Planned for Incapacitation, Elder Care Issues, and Final Planning Needs?

The last few months of a client's life, for those who don't die suddenly, are obviously often quite turbulent. Family members reappear after possible years of absence, the client is possibly dealing with the fear or anger of their situation, the client's partner is trying to work on *what's now* while being concerned about *what's next*. No one can adequately prepare in advance for this because none of us experience it more than once.

Working through how clients want to be remembered and how they wish to be treated is useful not only for when their time comes, but in anticipation of its arrival. Memorializing one's life through an ethical will or by using a personal historian makes a client think about what they are doing and how they are living their lives.

Walking with clients through the preparation for this stage deepens a relationship more than almost anything else that we do. While we may not be immortal, our memories live on. How do you want to be remembered?

Subcategories for Have You Planned for Incapacitation, Elder Care Issues, and Final Planning Needs?

	Percent of Question	Percent of Category	Percent of Index
541 Discuss writing an ethical will as well as creating a DVD through a personal historian to communicate your values	30	6	1.2
542 Implement power of attorney documents for financial and health care purposes	40	8	1.6
543 Establish pre-need written procedures for family to execute final wishes	30	6	1.2
Total	100	20	4

Discuss Writing an Ethical Will as Well as Creating a DVD through a Personal Historian to Communicate Your Values—1.2 Percent

While a regular will passes on a client's valuables, an ethical will passes on their values. Personal historians can help clients save their story for future generations.[7]

Clients have wishes for the next generation. They have messages that they wish to impart, values they wish to share, and stories they wish to tell. When prospects come to us, we talk about their money messages growing up; but those are narratives that the prospect creates. Ethical wills or life-story videos are narratives that the client creates for the people close to them.

Ethical wills are life legacies that get communicated in written form which were originally intended to pass on ethical values from one generation to the next. When we work with clients in drafting them, we encourage them to share their beliefs and their good wishes for the people who have mattered most to them. The web site www.ethicalwill.com provides examples as well as background on this approach.

Beyond the ethical will, though, some clients have wished to create a DVD or a picture book that describes their story and discusses the things in their lives that had the greatest influence on them. While this can certainly be done by a family member interviewing the patriarch or matriarch, professional personal historians are far more experienced at probing and uncovering valuable information. They then package this in a DVD or book that can be shown to the family and passed down to each successive generation.

Implement Power of Attorney Documents for Financial and Health Care Purposes—1.6 Percent

The wife of one of our clients lived through 10 years of Alzheimer's. He is now in the early stages of this tragic disease. His daughter has taken over his finances and is writing his checks. The degree of control that she exerts is determined by the power of attorney that he signed. A general power of attorney would give her authority over all his affairs; the limited power gives her control over only specific acts. Since the power of attorney will remain valid even if the client becomes incompetent or disabled, it is durable.

This is an area in which great caution needs to be exercised. One of our clients had a child who was handling their financial power of attorney. We felt uncomfortable with some of the decisions that he was making, so, after notifying the client of our discomfort, we excused ourselves from the relationship.

These powers are necessary, though, in case a client can't or doesn't want to take care of their own affairs. If the client is incompetent, the power of attorney avoids having to go through a court-appointed conservatorship.

We also encourage our clients to create health care directives for each state in which they own property. This is especially important for those couples who are unmarried. Since the directive spells out the client's goals with regard to medical treatment, artificial nutrition and hydration, and organ donation, the person to whom this power is granted needs to be on the same page as the client.

In Minnesota, funeral wishes can also be included in the health care directive. There are a number of decisions that must be made after someone dies; to the extent that these are spelled out through these powers, a client's beneficiaries know that they are doing what the person wanted.

Establish Pre-Need Written Procedures for Family to Execute Final Wishes—1.2 Percent

While some of a client's wishes can be expressed in the health care directive, taking the time in advance to plan final arrangements can be an important exercise. As I mentioned, the fewer decisions that family members have to make, the more smoothly things will go and the less expensive things will end up being. From identifying and purchasing a grave site or cremation urn to determining whether there will be limousines for the mourners will insure that the client's passing will be played out through his or her wishes rather than the emotions of grief or guilt that the family often experiences.

Some clients choose in advance who they would like to speak at their memorial, what music they wish to have played, and which poems they want read. Some clients write their obituaries in advance. By the way, that exercise is quite instructive whether you intend to use the obituary or not.

Conclusion

No one simply passes on their estate. They also pass on the years of experiences and teachings and memories that were the sum total of their lives. While focusing on what gets distributed to whom is central to estate planning, it may be equally important to also focus on the effect that the client has had beyond their money.

Estate tax laws are constantly changing. This area should be reviewed annually. There also should be enough flexibility with strategy that the client's situation can evolve as the laws do. While there are areas where flexibility may be less of an option, there are many ways with which an estate plan can keep breathing as long as the client keeps breathing.

Notes

1. Williams, Roy, and Vic Preisser. *Preparing Heirs*. San Francisco: Robert D. Reed Publishers. 2003.
2. Leimberg, Kandell, Miller, Polacek, Rosenbloom, Levy, Kasner. *Tools and Techniques of Estate Planning*. Cincinnati: The National Underwriter. 2006. (This is the 14th edition, but a new one comes out very regularly).
3. We have been long-time subscribers to Ed Slott's IRA newsletters, which are terrific for providing expertise in this area.
4. Hughes, Jr., James E. *Family Wealth*. New York: Bloomberg. 2004.
5. While this was written about family businesses, it applies to the business of the family as well.
6. Grubman, James, PhD. *A Two Axis Model of Financial Advising*. Turners Falls, Massachusetts. 2007.
7. http://www.personalhistorians.org/.

Epilogue

If you go flying back through time and you see somebody
else flying forward into the future, it's probably best to avoid
eye contact.

Jack Handey

When I look back over the last several years and think forward to the
next several years, I can say that I didn't expect what has happened to
me and can't imagine what's ahead of me. And I suspect many of you feel
the same way. So why do any of us think that we can create a plan and
that it is a sacred script never to be altered? Not only do tax laws change,
but so do clients, and so do we. The Wealth Management Index™, too,
has changed.

I ended my book 15 years ago this way:

The Wealth Management Index™ is many things. It is a client expectation management tool. It can be a performance appraisal device. It can
be the radar to help the client find his or her way to financial success.
But in my mind, the most important thing that the Wealth Management
Index™ represents is sensibility. If used properly, your clients can rest
assured that you have together looked at their situation, developed appropriate goals and strategies, and regularly reviewed their progress toward
their objectives.

Markets have boomed and busted, taxes have shifted, laws have been
written and removed, and our clients have continuously experienced the
unexpected, but the purpose of the index has not changed.

What has changed is our practice. The index has grown with us.
We have had clients die, become disabled, get divorced, have special needs,
start businesses, sell businesses, file bankruptcy, and experience most

imaginable life events. The index has been enduring. When I first wrote the book, our practice wasn't seasoned enough to go through all of these things with clients. Now, in some ways unfortunately and in others gratefully, it is. But throughout the years, clients have wanted to know how they were doing. And for the moment in time when they ask and for each future moment they ask, the index is a way of letting them know.

About the Author

Ross Levin, CFP®, is the Founding Principal and President of Accredited Investors Inc., a 25-year-old fee-only wealth-management firm based in Edina, Minnesota. He is a regular columnist for the *Journal of Financial Planning* and the *Star Tribune*. He has a compilation of some favorite columns in the book, *Spend Your Life Wisely*™: *The Deeper Meaning Of Money*. He was named by *Financial Planning* magazine as one of the five most influential people in financial planning and received their first lifetime achievement award. *Investment Advisor* magazine named him one of the 30 most influential individuals in and around the advisory profession over the last 30 years. He was the first recipient of the Financial Planning Association's Heart of Financial Planning Award.

Index

10b5-1 plans, 174

accounts, decisions about, 222–224
Accredited Investors, Inc.
    client commitment to, 20
    commitment to community, 20–21
    wealth-management programs, 48
    wealth-management services at, 47
active management, 221
adjustable rate mortgage (ARM),
    196–198
Advisor Products, 75
after-tax inheritance, 234–237
agenda, 92
agenda meeting, 85–86
alarm, 214
Allen, Woody, 99–100
allocating investments, 220–222
allocation, 213–214
    goals-based, 215
Alpha Group, 3
alternative asset class, 218–219
alternative minimum tax (AMT),
    187–188
AMT. *See* alternative minimum tax
Anthony, Mitch, 149
AP. *See* asset protection
appraisals, 242
ARM. *See* adjustable rate mortgage
Arrow, Kenneth, 15

Arthur, Brian, 15
asset allocation, determining, 217–222
asset location, determining, 224–225
Asset Protection, 137
asset protection (AP), 67, 95–98,
    117–119
    costs, 137–138
    strategies, 137–138
asset titling, 240–241
asset transference, 137–138
asset-class investing, 218–219
Authentic Happiness, 109

Be Our Guest, 2
Beebower, Gilbert L., 218
behavioral finance, 207–208
benchmarks, utilizing, 225–228
beneficiary designations, 238–241
benefits, utilizing, 101–102, 168–176
Bennett, Walter, 38
Bollerud-Holland Associates, 89
Bollerud, Kathy, 51, 89
bonds, 219
Boone, Norm, 218
Briggs, Katherine, 22
Brinson, Gary P., 218
Bruckenstein, Joel, 30, 75
Buber, Martin, 42
Buckingham, Marcus, 14
budget, 146

budget needs, 150–152
Buettner, Dan, 157
Buffett, Warren, 233
business acumen, 61–62
business continuation agreements,
    140–141
business interests, 97–98, 138–142
business model, integrating, 14
business plan, 17–18
business structures, 139
business valuation, determining,
    139–140
buy-out funding, 141–142
buy/sell agreement, 22, 140–141

cafeteria plans, reviewing, 170–171
Callan Periodic Table of Investment
    Returns, 230
cash, 219
cash flow, 98, 145–146
    current, 150–152
    illustration, 158
    needs, 198
    projection, 152
Center for Retirement Research, 131
Charan, Ram, 51
charitable giving objectives, 157–159
charitable lead trusts, evaluating,
    246–248
charitable mission statement, 245
charitable philosophy, 109, 244–248
Charitable Remainder Annuity Trusts
    (CRAT), 247
Charitable Remainder Unitrusts
    (CRUT), 247
charitable strategies, 248
circumstances, affect on portfolio,
    217
client, 17
    behavioral types of, 35–39

commitment to, 19
curious, 38–39
documents needed from, 40–41
fear-based, 37–38
greedy, 39
letters to children, 110–111
personality, 198–199
prospective, 39–46
relationship, 36–37
client deliverables, 76–81
client feedback, 89–90
client meeting, 80–81
    after, 87–92
    agenda, 92
    before, 85–87
Clifton, Donald O., 14
co-pays, 129–131
COBRA, 129–131
Collins, Jim, 17
communication, 57–60
    methods, 57–58
company retirement plans, 171–172
components, of Wealth Management
    Index, 119
comprehensive wealth management, 28
conflict resolution, 58–59
continuity of staff, 64
Cordaro, Chris, 224
cost basis, life insurance, 125
cost, life insurance, 124–125
CRAT. *See* Charitable Remainder
    Annuity Trusts
Creating an Investment Policy Statement,
    218
credit, 103–104
    philosophy about, 192–196
credit cards, evaluating, 194–195
credit lines, desired level of, 193–194
credit rating, 200
Crummey notices, 241, 242

CRUT. *See* Charitable Remainder
    Unitrusts
culture, 53–54
curious clients, 38–39
current income, needs, 163–164
current ratio, 200

Dahl, Owen, 27–28
Daily, Glenn S., 125
Daryanani, Gobind, 224
database scavenger hung, 76
Davis, John, 243
death
    giving at versus lifetime giving,
        245–246
    income needs for survivors, 164
debriefing, 87–89
debt, 104–105
    appropriate types, 196–200
debt free, strategy for, 195–196
debt management (DM), 67, 103–105,
    191–192
decisions
    making in partnerships, 21–22
    making right, 13–14
deductibility terms, reviewing,
    199–200
deductibility, of interest, 196–199
deductibles, property and casualty,
    133–134
*Deena Katz's Complete Guide to Practice
    Management*, 168
deficit account, 215
deliverables, client, 76–81
dependents, liquidity needs of,
    121–123
DI. *See* disability and income
    protection
The Diary of Anais Nin, 193
Diliberto, Roy, 2, 149

disability, 141–142, 152–154
disability and income protection (DI),
    67, 98–103
disability coverage, 152–154
disability insurance analysis, 153
DM. *See* debt management
documents needed from clients,
    40–41
Dodson, Bert, 145
donor-advised funds, evaluating,
    246–248
drag, 208
*Drive—The Surprising Truth About
    What Motivates Us*, 30
Drotter, Stephen, 51
Drucker, David, 30, 75

E&O. *See* errors and omissions
    insurance
earned income, understanding,
    160–161
earnings streams, inconsistent,
    193–194
education, 62–63
    paying for, 154–155
elder-care issues, 110–112, 248–251
Ellis, Charles, 206
emergency fund, desired level of,
    193–194
emotional decision making,
    207–208
Employee Retirement Income Security
    Act (ERISA), 172
The Energy of Money, 147–149
EP. *See* estate planning
ERISA. *See* Employee Retirement
    Income Security Act
errors and omissions insurance (E&O),
    137
estate discounting techniques, 241–242

estate plan, flow chart of, 234–237
estate planning (EP), 68, 107–112, 231–232, 234–237
estate tax wealth replacement, 127
estate tax, paying, 237–238
estimated tax payments, 179–184
ethical will, 110, 249–250
Evensky, Harold, 100–101
expense reconciliation, 151

FA, 2
The Family Caregiver Alliance, 129
family governance, 242–244
family limited partnership (FLP), 242
family meeting, 242–244
family members, assisting financially, 156
fear-based clients, 37–38
federal tax liability, 180–181
feedback, 22, 58–59
  client, 89–90
  immediate, 91
filings, stocks, 172–176
final planning needs, 110–112, 248–251
final wishes, instructions for, 250–251
financial independence goals, 157
Financial Planning, 2
Financial Planning—The Next Step, 149
financial power of attorney, 250
financing terms, 196–199
  reviewing, 199–200
finding balance exercise, 149
Fitzgerald, F. Scott, 118
floor, 214
FLP. *See* family limited partnership
forgiveness, 16
fortune, good, 15

foundations, private, 246–248
Fox, Justin, 114
friends, assisting financially, 156
Fundamental Interpersonal Relations Orientation-Behavior™, 22

Gardner, Daniel, 105
gift annuities, evaluating, 246–248
gifts
  expected, 168
  giving, 186–187
Gilbertson, Steve, 213
Gingold, Judith, 114
Gitman, Lawrence J., 124
Gluck, Andrew, 30, 75
goals-based allocation, 215
Good to Great, 17
grantor-retained annuity trust (GRAT), 186–187, 241
graphics, 225
grasp, exceeding, 14
GRAT. *See* grantor-retained annuity trust
greedy clients, 39
Group 2020, 3
growth, incremental, 14
Grubman, James, 51, 89
guardians, determining, 238–241
guiding principles of Accredited Investors, Inc, 18–19

Handey, Jack, 253
HAS. *See* Health Savings Accounts
health, 165
health care power of attorney, 250
Health Savings Accounts (HSAs), 129
Heibuhr, Reinhold, 15
Heupel, Wil, 3, 16–17, 21–22, 25–28, 31, 193

historian, utilizing, 249–250
Hoagland, Mahlon, 145
Hollis, James, 37
Hudson, Richard L., 214
Hughes, Everest, 114
human capital, value of, 26–27
Hurley, Mark, 24
Hurqitz, Josh, 131

I and Thou, 42
I-Rebal, 86
Ibbotson, 209
ILIT. *See* irrevocable life insurance trust
incapacitation, 110–112, 248–251
income needs, 147–159
income
    deferring versus accelerating, 187–188
    evaluating, 100–101
    replacing, 123, 152–154
    sources of, 159–168
    spending versus, 152–153
incremental growth, 14
Individual Retirement Account (IRA), 137, 176
    conversions, 188–189
    decedent, 240
    rollover, 176
    Roth, 188–189
inheritance, expected, 164–165, 168
Inside Information, 2, 76
insurance, professional liability, 134, 137
interest rates, 196–199
internal rate of return, 124
intra-family loans, 199
Investment Beliefs, 205
Investment Advisor, 2, 14–15
Investment News, 2

investment philosophy, 105–106
    developing, 205–222
investment planning (IP), 67–68, 105–107, 203–205
investment policy statement, 218
    sample, 219–220
Investment Policy—How to Win the Loser's Game, 206
investment restrictions, on portfolio, 217
investment risk, attitude toward, 207–208
investments, allocating, 220–222
IP. *See* investment planning
IRA. *See* Individual Retirement Account
irrevocable life insurance trust (ILIT), 241

J.K. Lasser Your Income Tax 2011, 165
Joenhk, Michael D., 124
Joiner, Bill, 55
Josephs, Stephen, 55

Kandell, Stephen, 142
Kasner
Katz, Deena, 17, 168
Kinder, George, 46
Kitces, Michael, 119
Koedijik, Kees, 205
Kolbe Index, 28, 82–83

Lasser, J.K., 165
leadership, 54–55
leadership agility, 55
leadership pipeline, 52–63
    developing, 31–32
The Leadership Pipeline, 51

legal restrictions, on portfolio, 217
Legend Financial Advisor, 25
Leimbert, Stephen, 142
letter, after meeting, 91–92
leverage, 192
liability, 96–97, 128–138
　limits, 129–131
life expectancy, 213
life insurance, 95–96
　client feelings about, 120
　cost basis, 125
　cost of, 124–125
　income replacement, 123
　secondary market, 125
　types of, 124
life insurance philosophy, articulating,
　119–128
life needs analysis, spending, 122
lifestyle needs, 147–159
lifetime giving versus giving at death,
　245–246
limited liability corporations (LLCs),
　161–162
limits, property and casualty, 133–134
liquidity, 121–123
liquidity needs, of survivors, 237–238
The Little Book of Behavioral Investing,
　207
living benefits, 123–126
　features of, 125–126
LLC. See limited liability corporation
loans, intra-family, 199
long-term care, 131–133, 137–138
　analysis, 132
　cost of, 128–138
Longo, Kathy, 22, 31
loss aversion, 208
The Lost Art of Listening, 43
Lubitz, Linda, 218

MacBean, Chris, 213
management, styles, 221
Mandelbroit, Benoit, 214
Martin, Brian, 70–74
maverick risk, 208
mean reversion, 210
medical costs, 128–138
medical insurance, 129–131
Medicare, 129–131
Medicare and Other Health Benefits:
　Your Guide to Who Pays First, 130
Medicare Premiums: Rules for Higher-
　Income Beneficiaries, 130
meeting
　after, 87–92
　before, 85–87
Miller, Ralph, 142
Mintz, Robert, 137
The (Mis)behavior of Markets, 214
mission statement, 109
　articulating, 244–248
mistakes, avoiding, 13–14
money autobiography, 147–149
money values, 245
Montier, James, 207
mortgage debt, 195
mortgage refinance analysis, 197
Munnell, Alicia H., 131
Myers-Briggs Type Indicator®, 22
Myers, Isabel Briggs, 22
The Myth of the Rational Market, 114

National Association of Insurance
　Commissioners, 124
needs, 98–100, 206
Nemeth, Maria, 147–149
new hires, 27
　process, 65–83
　schedule, 66

The New Retirementality, 149
Nichols, Michael, 43
Nin, Anais, 193
Noel, James, 51
non-qualified retirement plans, 171–172
Now Discover Your Strength, 14
Nudge, 95
nursing home costs, 131

objectives, 95
Oliver-King, Lorenz, 4
One Percent Club, 159
options, expiring, 173
organization
    work of, 28–30
    work on, 30–32
organizational chart, 28–32
others, 15–16
ownership, 238–241
    broader, 23–28

P&C. *See* property and casualty
partner, wanting, 23
partners, 21–23
    age differences, 165
partnership, 161–162
    decision-making in, 21–22
    sharing in, 22
pass-through income, 161–162
passive management, 221
pension income, maximizing, 126–127
pension, pay-out options, 162–163
performance handout, sample, 117
personality, of client, 198
Pink, Daniel, 30
Polacek, Timothy, 142
portfolio objectives, 219–220

portfolio performance, reviewing, 225–228
portfolio return objectives, 209–212
portfolio withdrawals, 168
portfolio
    managing, 106–107
    mechanics of managing, 222–228
The Power of a Positive No, 44
power of attorney, 250
pre-tax reimbursement plans, reviewing, 170–171
Preisser, Vic, 236
price paid, 99–100
private foundations, 246–248
procedures
    modifying, 74
    staff, 70–73
professional liability insurance, 134, 137
professionalism, 59–60
property and casualty, 133–134, 136
    deductible comparison, 135
    losses, 128–138
prospect meeting, 39–42
prospect metrics, quantitative, 33–35
prospective clients, questions for, 42–46
prospects, behavioral types of, 35–39
purchasing power risk, 207

QPRT. *See* qualified personal residence trust
qualified personal residence trust (QPRT), 232, 242
qualified retirement plans, 171–172
questions for prospective clients, 42–46

regulatory restrictions, on portfolio, 217
relationship clients, 36–37
relationships, 55–57
remainder trusts, evaluating, 246–248
required minimum distributions (RMD), 165–168
resilience, 16
restricted stock, 172
restrictions, on portfolio, 217
retirement age, full, 164
retirement plans
    company, 171–172
    required minimum distributions, 165–168
retitling, 137–138
return objectives, 220
returns, volatility versus, 210
revocable trusts, 238–241
risk, 205–206
    investment, 207–208
    maverick, 208
    objectives, 220
    versus return, 211
risk-tolerance number, 208
RMD. *See* required minimum distributions
Rosenbloom, Morey, 142
Roth Individual Retirement Accounts, 188–189

S-corporations, 161–162
safe harbor calculator, 184
savings, 103–104
    philosophy about, 192–196
scavenger hunt, 76
Schwab Charitable™ Donor-Advised Fund, 158
The Science of Fear, 105
secondary market, life insurance, 125

Seligman, Martin E.P., 109
separately managed account (SMA), 220
Serenity Prayer, 15
SERP. *See* Supplemental Executive Retirement Plans
Seven Signs of Money Maturity, 46
SharePoint, 65–66
sharing, in partnership, 22
silos, 29–30
Singer, Brian D., 218
skills, 22
Slager, Alfred, 205
Slott, Ed, 240
SMA. *See* separately managed account
Smart, Bradford D., 26
social security
    analysis, 166
    income options, 163–165
solutions, 95
SPA. *See* strategic planning area
spending number, 214
spending policy, 213–216
    deliverables, 216
spending power, 208
spending, income versus, 152–153
spread, 198
staff procedures, example, 70–73
staff
    building, 25–28
    continuity, 64
Stafford, William, 147
Stanasolovich, Lou, 25
state tax liability, 180–181
Steinem, Gloria, 146
stock option plans, 172–176
stock-purchase plans, 172–176
The Strategic Coach, 87
strategic planning area (SPA), 82

Stumbling on Happiness, 100
success, 106–107
  evaluating, 222–228
succession plan, determining,
    139–140
successor trustees, 239
Sullivan, Dan, 87
Sunstein, Cass, 95
Supplemental Executive Retirement
    Plans (SERP), 172
supplemental retirement plans, 176
surplus account, 215
survivors
  income needs for, 164
  liquidity needs, 121–123,
    237–238

table of contents, Wealth Management
    Index, 68–69, 74–75
tail insurance, 134, 137
task assignments, 91–92
tax bracket, income and, 187–188
tax planning, 176–189
  proactive, 102–103
tax projection assumptions, 180–184
tax rates, stock and, 174
tax withholding
tax-free exchange, 125
tax-loss harvesting, 184–186
testing, pre-employment, 22
Thaler, Richard, 95
Thoreau, Henry David, 99
Thrive, 157
Tibergien, Mark, 14–15, 27–28
time horizon, 196–199
  defining for goals, 212–216
titling, assets, 240–241
Tools and Techniques of Estate Planning,
    142, 237
Topgrading, 26

tracking progress, 9–11
trust companies, 239
trustees, determining, 238–241
Tufte, Edward, 225

Uniform Limited Partnership
    Act, 137
universal life, 124
Ury, William, 44

vacation homes, 155–156
valuation, business, 139–140
values
  communicating, 249–250
  money, 245
Veres, Bob, 2, 30, 76
viatical settlement, 125
volatility risk, 207
volatility, returns versus, 210

Wagner, Richard (Dick), 45
Walden, 99
The Way It Is, 147
*The Way Life Works: The Science
    Lover's Guide to How Life Grows,
    Develops, Reproduces and Gets
    Along*, 145
Wealth Management Index (WMI),
    2–3
  components of, 119
  fundamentals, 67–76
  introduction to, 67–69
  scoring, 114–115
wealth replacement, 127
wealth transfer, 107–109
  philosophy on, 232–244
wealth-management programs,
    at Accredited Investors,
      Inc., 48

wealth-management services, at
    Accredited Investors, Inc., 47
wealth-transfer entities, 241–242
Wealth Transition Checklist, 236
Webb, G. Randolph, 104–105
What Is 'Class'? And Will It Work?, 131
What Matters Most, 37

Whitacre, Kirstin, 70–74
whole life, 124
will, ethical, 249–250
Williams, Roy, 236
withholding, levels of, 179–184
WMI. *See* Wealth Management
    Index